Claiming Your Creative Self

True Stories from the
Everyday Lives of Women

Eileen M. Clegg

With Margaret McConahey,
Susan Swartz, and Deborah L. S. Sweitzer

New Harbinger Publications, Inc.

Publisher's Note

This publication is designed to provide accurate and authoritative information in regard to the subject matter covered. It is sold with the understanding that the publisher is not engaged in rendering psychological, financial, legal, or other professional services. If expert assistance or counseling is needed, the services of a competent professional should be sought.

Distributed in the U.S.A. by Publisher's Group West; in Canada by Raincoast Books; in Great Britain by Airlift Book Company, Ltd.; in South Africa by Real Books, Ltd.; in Australia by Boobook; and in New Zealand by Tandem Press.

Copyright © 1998 by Eileen M. Clegg
New Harbinger Publications, Inc.
5674 Shattuck Avenue
Oakland, CA 94609

Cover design by Blue Design
Cover illustration by Donna Ingemanson
Edited by Angela Watrous
Text design by Tracy Marie Powell

Library of Congress Catalog Card Number: 98-67407

ISBN 1-57224-117-9 Paperback

New Harbinger Publications' Website address www.newharbinger.com

First printing

To our mothers, Iris Ridgway, Maxine McConahay, Helen Frey, and Peg Sweitzer, who showed us love and wonder; and to the memory of Malee Namsirchai Humphrey, who lived her beauty and taught her friends the way.

We also wish to acknowledge, with warm appreciation, our editor, Angela Watrous, whose creativity and care helped shape this book throughout.

Contents

Introduction

Each of us possesses a creative self. Claiming that is a transformational act. When you begin to act on your creativity, what you find inside may be more valuable than what you produce for the external world. The ultimate creative act is to express what is most authentic and individual about you.

Awareness came to me in one of those blessed hit-you-over-the-head messages that sneaks up from behind when most needed and least expected. For years I had been writing—journalism, fiction, and essays—in a tidy, conventional way. Occasionally I'd catch a glimpse of the refractory muse, stopping by momentarily with inspiration for a sprightly phrase or perhaps even a nudge toward a wiser perspective. Mostly, though, I was trying to follow the same set of rules, defined early in my career by the expectations of others. A glib definition of creativity lingered from something I'd read during my college days: "Creativity is making order out of chaos." But in truth, what I was most interested in making was deadlines. That all changed after one bizarre evening.

I was visiting a friend and saw one of her new paintings hanging on the wall. The woman in the painting wore this odd half-smile, half-grimace, and her eyes seemed to emit simultaneous fury and compassion. I sat on the couch and stared at her, feeling that furtive sense of mild invasion I get while people-watching at airports, conjuring up fantasies about strangers' lives. Still captivated by the image when I got home later that night, I sat down and wrote a short story about the woman in the painting, from beginning to end, with no idea how her curious expression had inspired my tale of a woman coming into her strength. A few days later, I showed the story to my artist friend, who read it with incredulity. My character's actions reflected the character she had envisioned when she painted the picture. Her character didn't exist in real life any more than mine did, but they were the same in our imagination. I'd been visited by something well beyond my comprehension. Understanding the source seemed secondary to recognizing the effect. It was dizzying. It made no sense. It felt like magic.

The literary caliber of the work seemed oddly off the point. What mattered most was not the response from others, but instead what this story offered to me: access to an intuitive part of myself and connection with some artistic spirit that somehow moved back and forth between my friend's painting and my writing. I was part of something much larger than myself, something that made me feel more at home in the world. Coveting more such experiences, I began reading book after book about artists and the creative process, getting tips for bringing more creative flow to my life. And I began talking to others who were trying to do the same.

One unexpected and glorious result has been the discovery of a creative community. Right in front of me every day there are so many women—women I encounter through work, at my son's school, doing errands—who are involved in similar journeys. They've managed to veer away from the expectations of others and have chosen pursuits that resonate with something deep inside them.

If you look around your own life, you'll likely recognize that creative women surround you as well. There is something transcendent about them, a brightness of spirit, because they found a way to externally express their internal essence. Actively creative women may possess obvious confidence, a flair in dress or decor, a quick wit, or a particular way of being that makes others say, "That is so *you*." They may be anything from lawyers and clerks to artists, moms, cooks, or volunteers, and usually they will have some combination of roles. The point is not what creative women are doing with their lives, but how they're doing it. Someone can shine just as brightly in a waitress job as on stage at the Met, feel as much satisfaction by producing a garden as producing a film.

Sharing Wisdom

This was a revelation: Ordinary women become extraordinary when they find a way to tap into the wellspring of creativity. Joy comes from figuring out how to keep the flow going despite everything that tries to block it off. It began to dawn on me that there is no creative "club" that requires certain credentials. You don't need a MacArthur Foundation grant, an invitation from someone with a gallery resume, an art school degree, or even a reputation as "the creative one in the family." You only need to be attentive enough to recognize the right tool when it comes along. Then you just need to dig in and keep going.

As I observed and began talking more to creative women, a formula for success emerged: a leap of faith and then perseverance. It looked like a simple formula, so I wondered why I and so many women I knew felt stifled in our creative expression. I could see the shiny glow in the lives of creative women, but I knew they had to work through a lot of grit to get there.

I wanted to get down to the practical mechanics. How do women know when it's time to take the leap? And after finding a creative calling, how do they cope with all the subtle pressures that can get in the way? How do women take time and energy for creative work when they have the responsibilities of home and family and a nine-to-five job to pay the bills? What happens when others discourage you? How do you know when you've found the "right" creative outlet? How do you find physical and emotional space to work on it? How do you renew your wellspring? How do you talk back to external and internal critics? Are there magical moments when everything "comes together," and how do you know when you're experiencing one of those moments?

It wasn't easy to find high-profile role models to reveal their tricks for maintaining inspiration and breaking through the barriers. The biography section of the library offered books about artists, a small minority of whom are women. But the library also held some shocking reminders that it wasn't so long ago in history that the creative world was mostly reserved for men. One book, called the *Creative Experience,* published in 1970, told stories of twenty-three creative people in various endeavors from science to the arts. Only one of the twenty-three was a woman. It just hasn't been that long that women have had "equal access" to the art world. Nor has it been long since fabric work and cooking—once "domestic duties"—have been recognized as art forms.

Many people now see that activities once cast aside as "women's work" are creative endeavors, affirming the girlhood satisfaction many of us experienced cooking alongside grandma or making a doll's dress by ourselves. At the same time, more and more women are achieving access to the world of fine art and redefining the historically male perspective about what belongs in galleries. Some women are choosing to tend full time to hearth and muse, others are finding ways to claim their creativity in the context of their careers. The choices are liberating, though one potential side effect is translating "you can have it all" into "you must do everything." The women most at ease with their creative selves seemed to be those who are passionate about a particular activity, who recognize their priorities, and who have the confidence to pursue their passion and whittle down the long list of "shoulds" to make time for what's really important.

I started spending more time with women who had made it through the morass of life's expectations and had found something purely their own that they could express in the world. Slowly I began trading confidences about the day-to-day realities of trying to lead a creative life. I found that many women had experienced some epiphany moment, often following a personal life drama, that ignited their passion for a creative pursuit. The lines between life and work often were blurred, and there was an interplay between personal growth and creative development: Self-awareness helped creativity, creativity led to positive life changes. Almost everyone had struggled with feelings of inadequacy and had to find some source of strength to persevere.

I was pleased to find that these women I wanted to be like turned out to be so much like me, and you will likely discover the same. There are similar themes to the challenges most women face while carving out new definitions of work and creativity. While it's up to each of us to figure out what works individually, it helps immeasurably to hear other women's stories and look to them for guidance.

Learning seems to happen in layers. For example, I've heard Virginia Woolf's assertion that "every woman needs a room of her own," over and over again. Yet it wasn't until I saw how other women had made studios in their garages or found cubbyholes to rent and then tried it for myself that I fully understood the potential impact of the idea. Sometimes I have to read an idea many different ways and see several other women implement it successfully before I can figure out how to use it in my own life.

Ideas that may seem mundane turn out to be vital: A lot of creativity seems to revolve around practicalities. Habits are hard to change, especially for women schooled in looking after everyone else first. Laughing and lamenting together, women seem to be able to help each other make shifts in their lives. It became clear to me that a collection of real life stories could help women everywhere who are ready to explore their creative urges.

When I proposed a book on creativity to New Harbinger editor Kristin Beck, we immediately drifted into storytelling about ordinary women we know and how their lives had been transformed through creativity. Instead of talking about the process abstractly, I wanted to show it through the lives of women. Stories are truth in action and, for many women, one of the best ways to learn. In between the lines of the stories in this book is an emerging new definition of creativity that comes from the inside out. Process is more important than product. There's more to it than ending up with a painting or a song. Through creativity, women can discover themselves, embrace their history, and make deeper connections with others. You dazzle yourself first, others second.

Finding stories and reflections to illustrate this new perspective called for collaboration, so I gathered together three friends and colleagues, women who are very different from each other and all just adventuresome enough to go on a treasure hunt. Meg McConahey is a longtime newspaper reporter, Susan Swartz a newspaper columnist, and Deborah Sweitzer an architect and college instructor. We decided to look close to home for stories and examine our own experiences for interpretation.

We set out as professional observers on an intensely personal task: to look closely at women who had touched our lives with their creativity. The women whose stories we chose were right in front of us in our daily lives. Some we encountered in our meanderings around the community. Some are close friends. One is Deborah's sister. They came to be in these pages because—usually unbeknownst to themselves—their lives illustrate something about creativity that can teach and inspire others.

Finding the Creative Self

One quality shared by the women in this book is self-awareness. They've made friends with their nightmares as well as their dreams. Claiming your creative self leads to a certain ease with yourself. It is a way toward authenticity.

Appropriately, this book on creativity follows the book that Susan Swartz and I wrote about women who are moving away from all of the "shoulds" and guilt they experience in their lives. In *Goodbye Good Girl: Letting Go of the Rules and Taking Back Yourself*, we explored the "good girl" syndrome, whereby women look outside themselves for cues about the "right" way to behave, responding to others' expectations. Women come to our readings hungry to talk about the frustration of trying to meet so many competing expectations in their lives. They are working to clarify their values, to organize their lives around something of meaning rather than merely doing whatever it takes to please others.

Free from the old notion that self-expression is self-indulgent, many are channeling their newfound energy into creative pursuits. Women are dusting off their old paintbrushes, sitting down to the piano, enrolling in classes, and finding all manner of ways to tune in to old passions. Ironically, they are finding that instead of being "selfish," following these pursuits actually gives them more energy and desire for involvement in other aspects of life.

When the four collaborators for this book sat down to talk about this project, we recognized how much our own experience would come into play as we selected and interviewed women to be in our book. Unlike many of our journalistic experiences, this was not an exercise in striving for detachment from our subjects, but instead an invitation to make deeper connections with women we already knew well or hoped to know better. In many ways, the process of writing this book demonstrated the themes that so many women shared: trust yourself, follow your intuition, allow mistakes, persist, claim your time and space, be in the moment, don't be afraid to be yourself, expect bumps, and—above all—enjoy. Wisdom emerged from the stories and our discussions about them. This book started out with curiosity.

Meg was intrigued by the chance to climb into other women's stories, in part to help get past the mystery of her own creativity. Asked once by a University of California, Berkeley, researcher to dissect her strategy for researching and writing, she recoiled at the prospect of analyzing how she works: "I think I operate something like a Rube Goldberg contraption: impossible to disassemble to figure out how it operates, but throw in a bunch of information, and after many fits and starts and cranks and groans, something miraculously spits out. Collaborating on this book and examining creativity in the lives of everyday women inspired me to look at my own peculiar processes, which in their odd way seem to work." Meg was particularly interested in how women find confidence and new opportunities as they begin to reflect upon their methods.

Susan loves looking for the common experiences that women share, finding new strategies and sources of inspiration for balancing the creative life with everything else. Susan says, "The thing about women and creativity is that we're so used to juggling households and jobs and kids and parents that we're pretty adept at finding time to fit in our projects. When you read about the great male composers and painters they seemed to always have someone there to make sure they had lunch and their clothes were clean in order to be free to be a genius. Most women get their own lunch, along with everyone's else's, and then go back to being a genius. I'm always fascinated to learn how other women squeeze it all in. What tricks can we learn from each other?"

Deborah has studied the creative process for years and, in the male-dominated profession of architecture, has come to understand the difference between men's and women's approaches. She was interested in exploring some of the unexamined aspects of creating in daily life. "Typically men will design from the outside of the building inward, while women tend to design the building from the inside outward. The men tend to place more emphasis on the sculptural aspect of building—the form. Women tend to care more about how the building will actually be used and about the relationships among spaces and activities accommodated in the building and the surrounding environment—the context. I believe that this wish to create community in the creative process is typically female." As she worked on this book, Deborah sought to expand the definition of creativity that honors women's more holistic approach to their creative endeavors.

Meg, Susan, Deborah, and I will be your guides as you enter the lives of the remarkable women whose stories will be told in the coming pages. Along with the tales, in each chapter I will share some of the conversations and reflections that came up for my collaborators and me and how the stories connect to personal life lessons and some of the latest research from experts on creativity. As you read, you may want to take notes or draw pictures or talk with friends about what the stories stir in you. From this process, I hope that you will be able to move past any barriers that may be preventing you from fully exercising your creativity.

The Women

You will meet:

- Annie Wells, a photographer
- Sherry Jean O'Malley, a waitress
- Sarah Andrews, a mystery novelist
- Birgitta Schofield, a baker
- Linda Kammer, a hairdresser and artist/poet
- Nancy Jenkins, a mom who volunteers in the schools
- Vera Aubin, a teacher
- Sara Pond Poyadue, a musician and singer
- Donna Freeman, a gardener
- Helen Lordsmith, a free-spirited psychic
- Pauline Pfandler, an actor
- Carole Rae Watanabe, an entrepreneurial-minded painter
- Dyan Foster, a social activist

Some of these women are at the beginning of their creative paths, while others are way down the road. They show the various phases of creativity—from the "aha" moment of recognizing what you want to do, through the phases of hard work, and ultimately to the magical moment when it all comes together. They demonstrate that the products of creativity are secondary to the process and that creativity can manifest itself anywhere doing anything. Baking love into bread. Putting life's experiences into a novel. Singing in harmony. Going on stage. Growing a garden. Working with children. Painting dreams on canvas. These women share their secrets for perseverance and satisfaction. And, even more generously, they tell about the life experiences that contributed to their work. As soft-spoken Linda said in a knowing whisper, "You have to go deep enough to find the blood."

Most of them started out with the all-too-familiar family complexities, self-esteem issues, and abundance of roadblocks standing in the way of reaching their dreams. Some are struggling economically, some have financial resources. Some grew up knowing they had a creative gift, others first discovered it in midlife. From each of them comes a different face of creativity and a different process. Yet there are great similarities. Many of the women in this book once thought their creative process was quirky and odd, but they came to see that their self-criticism stemmed from comparing themselves to a stereotypically male model. It has been so freeing for me to hear these stories, feel a kinship, and participate in fostering an emerging definition of creativity that includes each of us and all of our different ways.

Creativity may start as an individual's private expression of something glimpsed inside—the literal vision that gave rise to Donna's garden, the memory from childhood that inspired Birgitta's baking. It may start with a key that unlocks the inner door, as did Annie's camera, Sarah's writing, and Pauline's theater work. Creativity may begin as a private source of fulfillment—Sherry Jean's apron collection and Helen's unique touches—until others see it and ask for more. Linda's painting and poetry and Vera's folkdancing were personal pleasures that ended up bringing joy to others. Sometimes creativity blossoms amid imagining and organizing so that others can shine, as Dyan shows in her work with teens, or the transformation of a simple project into something grand, like Nancy's project at her children's school. The challenge for some is taking a latent talent and putting all of one's self confidently behind it—feeling entitled to take credit and earn money for it—as Sara learned in her singing career and Carole discovered through her art.

All of the women in this book had a lot to overcome before they could claim their creative selves. They've come to tell the rest of us: "If I can do it, so can you."

1

Covering the News, Uncovering the Self

*I didn't think I had a creative bone in my body before
I started to photograph.*

—Annie Wells, Pulitzer prize–
winning photographer

Meet Annie in the Newsroom

Laughter peals out from the photo lab and fills the newsroom. It's Annie, having fun again. Her antics make for workplace legends. After an office fundraiser, she buys bicycle parts with the money and brings them into the newsroom for assembly—gifts for economically disadvantaged children. On "Take Your Daughter to Work Day," she takes the kids into the darkroom to show them how pictures are made. In her spare time, she and her camera document the lives of local migrant farmworkers; she shares her photos with her subjects—an effort in community building. In the spring, she gathers up her buddies for a day's walk in a butterfly habitat owned by a charming, eccentric naturalist who keeps cocoons in her bathroom. Annie is drawn to the unusual, unabashed in her enthusiasm, and she lets her feelings show.

She has short, blonde, baby-fine hair and blue eyes that focus intently on whatever's in front of her. On assignments, she often sets her camera down and asks her own questions along with the reporters'. People have called her puppy-like because of her guileless ways, curious nature, and boundless energy. She's usually nowhere else but in the moment. That extraordinary focus on an ordinary assignment catapulted her to the top of her profession. One day, on a normally quiet Sunday shift, Annie captured an image in her camera that turned out to be the big kahuna of news photographs. A few months later, she reeled in the most prestigious award in journalism: the Pulitzer.

Whoops of pride and pleasure from friends and colleagues continued for weeks as she unabashedly made the talk show and lecture circuit with her newfound fame. She made it look easy, though it was actually exhausting for her. Annie's specialty is making things look easy. But her creative skills have grown from struggle—personal and professional. While building her career, her marriage was shaky, her sister was ill, and she had been coming to grips with unprocessed grief from her childhood. A disciplined effort to understand her own emotions has enabled her to recognize and capture the emotions of others in her camera.

Annie has an introverted nature, though it didn't show in the Pulitzer limelight as she said, exuding delight, on TV, "Of course, I'm thrilled beyond belief." She projected the same quality of enthusiasm those kids probably felt when they found the bicycles she'd helped make under their trees at Christmas. Major newspapers competed to grab her up. She had a portfolio to back her prize. She chose the *Los Angeles Times,* the second largest newspaper in the country.

As these changes came in her professional life, she also experienced significant changes in her personal life; Annie has learned how to handle upheaval with confidence and introspection. She's proud of her worldly accomplishments but continues her inner work, always asking herself: "What am I supposed to be learning now?"

Learning to Trust Inner Knowledge

On the surface, Annie's story sounds like a modern fable: Sunny person known for her generosity wins big prize and the world opens up. At a time when many people are skeptical of the media, here's a woman who obviously brings soul to her work. The fates come into play and deliver a lucky break to a deserving woman. But there's a deeper level at which Annie's story is allegorical, carrying a significant message about the creative process: Getting to know yourself is a necessary step toward seeing what vision you might share with the world.

Annie shows how the creative life involves an interplay between her interior and exterior worlds, with sometimes joyful and sometimes painful results. The ability to look inward has sharpened her ability to perceive what is happening around her and vice versa. Success has been delivered to her on both fronts: She has developed a depth in her personal life and won accolades in her professional life. Her stellar award catapulted her out of her status as a local photographer "just doing her job," but her success bubbled up from self-awareness in the routine course of her work.

Annie's is a hopeful story for anyone who worries that you need to grow up with a certain kind of education or environment or level of confidence to develop creativity. Annie grew up like the majority of people, flailing around to find meaning in her own experiences and confused about the workings of the world. Growing up, no one talked to Annie about looking inward for guidance and confidence. She struggled with feelings of low self-worth. She didn't recognize the tool of her trade until her late twenties—proof that the creative urge doesn't operate on any particular clock.

How could a twenty-something Annie—with a fragile sense of self, no artistic training, and only an inkling of self-understanding—become such a successful vessel for the creative spirit? Annie's story demonstrates the power of tuning into the signals from within, having the drive to act on them, and being willing to learn as you go along—even when it's painful.

Opportunities for creative growth are everywhere, as Annie discovered. The trick is to recognize them, stripping away what's extraneous to get to the meaning of the moment. For Annie, the knowledge came visually. Images have appeared to help her through the darkest of times, often making no sense until much later. She has allowed herself to "see" things that to others may seem nonsensical or impossible. She is open. Intuition is what guides her. That's why she first picked up a camera, moved toward subjects who touched something inside her, and found herself doing the right thing in the right place at the right time to make journalistic history.

Annie's story helps to dispel many paralyzing fears that can threaten the tentative beginnings of creative exploration: Is it too late to try something new? What if someone resents me? The answers are different for everyone, and Annie is a role model for looking inside to find your own answers. Her intuition led her on a strangely circuitous route that somehow landed her at a particular scene at that singular moment in time when an opportunity arose to touch millions with her vision. Yet when asked how she got there, she shrugs and says, "It's like playing 'connect the dots' . . . I really had no coherent plan."

Annie's Path

Of Beginnings and Diversions

Annie grew up in a middle-class southern family. "Creativity was neither encouraged or discouraged. It wasn't discussed. My family valued education, but I grew up with the expectation that one day I'd find a man to take care of me." She was an athlete and a horsewoman who enjoyed the kinesthetic pleasure of a good physical challenge. Looking back now, she realizes that sports were the constant in her life, a source of personal power through difficult years.

Annie's mother died the summer after she graduated from high school. Her family didn't talk about grief. She left for college at a low emotional point in her life, not having dealt with her mother's death in any meaningful way. She sought distraction and quickly became involved in a romantic relationship. "I had no sense of who I was." During her junior year, she changed boyfriends and coasts in a single semester, taking off for California, where she enrolled at the University of California, Santa Cruz. English interested her, but her confidence was low and she didn't declare a major. She worked different jobs, waiting tables and working as an assistant to a veterinarian, while drifting in and out of school. "I was really lost in my early twenties.

Looking back, I probably was depressed." Athletics gave her a boost. She got into women's soccer, then a fledgling sport in the U.S., and made the Olympic development team for northern California.

She had the physical confidence of an athlete, but her self-image suffered because of her academic shortcomings—math in particular. "I could not remember numbers, I could not remember a formula." Her memories of going cross-eyed over multiplication tables as a child became a symbol of her low self-esteem.

She had a sense of outrage, though, when others treated her disrespectfully. In her twenties, when she worked in an animal clinic, she felt that the veterinarians were treating her as someone of lesser intelligence. "I knew I was as smart as they were. I felt like they were dissing me." The put-downs galvanized her: "I decided, 'I don't care if it takes me five years, I'm going to pass calculus.'" So she enrolled in mathematics courses and studied with a vengeance. It worked. She excelled and began feeling more competent.

She found ways to make math more visual, and her sense of confidence moved to physics. She realized she could remember what pages looked like, and she could learn from studying the pictures. Science fascinated her, and she chose that as her major, a realistic one with her newfound math acumen. She decided to become a science writer, and that meant taking journalism courses.

Rapture

A serendipitous turn of fate landed Annie in a photojournalism class. It was one of the requirements for her program that happened to have class space available. Photography had long been a source of curiosity. She owned a tattered copy of the great photojournalism collection *The Family of Man* and pored over *Life* magazines, but never imagined photography as a career possibility. She didn't even have a camera. For the photojournalism class, she borrowed an old Canon camera from her boyfriend, completely unprepared for what she would find in her grip: "Once I got it in my hands, I could not put it down. Every spare moment, I was taking pictures or in the darkroom. I was compelled to take photographs. It was like an epiphany . . . I didn't think I had a creative bone in my body before I started to photograph."

She didn't dare to think that she could make a living from her passion. Photography was an avocation, an exciting hobby. She expected to get a job in science or technology fields, doing technical writing for one of the firms in nearby Silicon Valley. Then another happenstance led to a deeper awareness of her creative self. She contracted a bacteriological infection that left her feeling ill and without energy. "I saw a nurse practitioner. She treated my ailment and then asked me a strange question. 'Why do you think you got sick?' She wasn't asking me about the organic reason. She wasn't talking about physical cause and effect. She was asking about my whole life, what it was about my life that was making me sick. I'd never considered anything like that before, that how you were living could make you ill."

The nurse practitioner gave her a book called *The Power of Your Subconscious Mind*. Thinking back, Annie says, "It was a little 'woo-woo' for me," but it gave her a glimpse at a new way of thinking. She realized that she didn't want to be a technical writer at all. Photography was what made her feel alive, fully herself, and healthy. She scuttled her plans for technical writing in Silicon Valley and started wracking her brain for ways to make a living with photography. Sleepless one night, she thought of a friend with connections in the field of photography: "I literally got up out of bed and made a telephone call. I got a job photographing for the government. Looking back, I realize I was following my bliss. But at the time I didn't see it that way. I was just following my intuition."

Working for a military research institute, she bopped around on command, photographing everything from ceremonies to new equipment. Meanwhile, she enrolled in art classes and photography classes at various schools. By now she was married, and her husband was supportive of her enthusiasm about the work. "No one ever stood in my way and said 'you can't do this' or 'you suck.' I was like an overzealous child with something new. It was years before I knew I had any talent at all. Photography was something I did because I couldn't help it."

Claiming It

Annie enjoyed the government photography job, but it seemed to be a dead end. It was a temporary position and every six months or so her boss would have to fight to keep it funded. So she decided to drop it, continue her photographic schooling, and work for a more substantial paycheck as a legal assistant in a law firm. The money was good and she performed competently, but the high heels—part of the obligatory costume—squeezed her feet. She felt as if she couldn't breathe, being indoors all day. She decided that news photography was what she wanted to do—it would allow her to be outdoors, in the center of action, with a camera in her hand.

A supportive photojournalism instructor helped Annie find opportunities to fill her portfolio. One day, a chance came for a real news photograph. She dropped everything else, picked up her camera, and ran to the scene of an animal rights demonstration on San

Francisco's Presidio army base, where Annie lived with her husband. She caught the action on camera and ran her film down to the Associated Press. It felt like a breakthrough to Annie to walk into a professional news organization with her film, regardless of whether they used it or not.

Thrilled and exhausted, she arrived home and realized she was late for dinner. Her husband was clearly angry. "I'd had this huge victory, but I knew from the moment I walked into the house that he was pissed off, and there I was feeling all contrite that I'd upset my husband. Then he complained about how disheveled I looked. That's when I thought, 'No, I don't have to look a certain way and be a certain way.' That was a fairly defining moment in terms of how I was going to live my life."

Annie grew up with no training in assertiveness nor with the concept of staying in touch with her feelings. She was self-taught. In an earlier relationship, she had been dishonest with a boyfriend, causing a complicated mess. After that, she resolved to let her feelings out instead of stuffing them. "If you don't express them, you end up acting out." Thus, on the day when anger started to boil at her husband's expectations of her, she let him know what she was feeling: fury.

"I wasn't going to have someone else telling me how I was going to live my life. He understood and accepted that." Once he understood how she felt, they settled into a companionable mutual understanding about the importance of her work. Although Annie's affectionate ways are a source of warmth to her friends and colleagues, she's also quick to bristle when someone crosses her boundaries. In professional settings, Annie has learned to moderate her emotions, noting them without necessarily needing to give them voice. With time has come more diplomacy, but, vocalized or not, she always pays attention to the feelings. "What's inside me tells me when and where I am going. My emotional response is what tells me, 'There is something here.'"

Moving Out, Seeing In

The protest photograph didn't make any newspapers, but to Annie it signaled the possibility of a career. With encouragement from her professor at San Francisco State, she began sending her portfolio to potential employers. The collection was good enough to land her a job with a news wire service, and she delved into the business of covering spot news events.

She had no problem with the "go here, quick, go there" nature of the business—fast movements, immediate deadlines, never knowing what would come up next. She found it energizing. She would dash to the scene on a moment's notice. Her enthusiasm and skill led to a job on a daily newspaper, where some assignments were conducive to a more meditative pace. Inexplicably, she gravitated toward stories that involved death, including one that involved documenting the work of hospice workers. She found herself feeling connected to her subjects. She was the recorder of events, but she also felt the significance of being a witness to the suffering of others.

In her personal life, Annie sought fun and a sense of balance— playing soccer on a recreational women's team, learning to swim to overcome a lifelong fear of the water, and practicing yoga. At home, she and her husband mostly spent quiet time together, reading, walking, and writing. The yoga added a new depth to what it meant to Annie to be quiet inside: "Yoga was no small influence. It's subtle but not small. I learned to be kind to myself and not judge myself harshly." She began to see her work in more philosophical terms.

Making Space for Creativity

Looking back, Annie sees subtle ways in which her place in the family prepared her for her career: "As the youngest child, I learned a lot by listening and not talking." She grew up hanging back from the action, watching: "I learned to learn by observation, so I wouldn't get yelled at for doing something wrong. My mother was an alcoholic and could be very demanding. This was the source of many of my insecurities and low self-esteem as a young adult." In retrospect, Annie sees that her childhood fear of criticism probably kept her from expressing herself verbally.

Over the years, though, she became more gregarious. While covering stories, she liked that people wanted to talk and interact with her. At the same time, she needed to create a quiet space around herself while photographing. She learned to let people know when she needed to concentrate. To do her best work, all of her attention needed to be on what she is feeling and seeing through the lens: "I absolutely and truly believe that when I'm behind the camera I'm invisible. As extroverted and 'out there' and loud as I am, there's part of me that is an introvert, sitting back. There's definitely a repose when I am shooting. I disengage from all the social aspects. There's a certain concentration. I'm in the visual response mode, aware of what's already inside of me and what I am witnessing when I take a photograph." It's a meditative process for Annie—being able to concentrate while remaining connected, tuning in emotionally and being prepared for what she describes as "the signal to release the camera shutter." She recognized that her creative space was portable, a place she could go whenever she needed to focus.

Life and Death in Pictures

One story would show Annie the permeability of her creative space, and she learned how the emotional exchange of her work went both ways. Annie was working with a reporter on a series of stories and photographs about a teenage boy who had cancer, hoping it would be a story of a young man's courageous triumph over disease. Andy Azevedo was an exceptional young man, an athlete popular with friends, part of a big farming family, and he was determined to beat the disease. Annie would visit him over the months, photographing him soon after the diagnosis, documenting his remission, and going back when he got worse again, recording the valiant comebacks he made time after time.

Annie became friends with the whole family, and she was especially close to Andy and his mother, Marilyn. The family came to see Annie and reporter Ronnie Cohen as part of the community of people supporting them through the most difficult time of their lives. For Annie, the intimate connection she had initially made through a camera lens now was touching something raw inside herself: unfinished grief over her own mother's death.

"Sometime in the spring before Andy died, I started having these visions in the morning. I knew I wasn't asleep, but I wasn't awake either. I could see two of me. One standing outside the scene watching, and the other in the scene. A bunch of people dressed in white muslin were carrying my mother away. There was me up there watching, and me on the ground nearby. They were carrying her alive. They were taking her into a river. She turned into some kind of wood."

Annie decided to see a therapist to work through feelings about her mother's death. She talked about the night her mother died: "I stood at the door and I looked and almost went to say 'I love you,' but I thought I'd do it when she was awake." Her mother didn't awaken but died that night. Annie began see her connection with the Azevedo family as more than her job—it was part of her life's work.

Then the long-dreaded phone call came. Andy was dying. Annie drove to the countryside, walked into the house, and found the family gathered in the living room. Andy was in a bed in the middle of the room, drifting in and out of consciousness. He sat up suddenly, then lay down again. Andy's brother, not ready to say good-bye, went to Andy, lay next to him, and embraced him. Andy began to turn blue. He was leaving them.

Annie's invisibility had disintegrated. She was not here as a photographer, but as a friend. Tears blurred her vision. She could hardly bear the grief of this good and loving family. Or her own. She was too close. "I felt almost a sense of guilt. This wasn't my family.

Andy wasn't my brother. I felt awkward and confused. I shut my eyes and I could feel a white light. I felt my mother's presence. I saw a light coming through an open door. Andy sat up in bed. He said, 'Shut the door!' I felt I was seeing what Andy was seeing and that my mom was present. Then Andy came back."

Annie told Marilyn about sensing the presence of her mother in the room. Marilyn talked to Andy later and asked him about the light. Andy talked about who he had seen, including an older woman he didn't recognize. Annie and Marilyn talked about their feelings that the spirit of Annie's mother had appeared to take care of Andy, who was slipping away from life and seemed to be making some peace with his death.

Andy died within a few days. There was so much grief, even though Andy's death was expected. "I saw the door as the door Andy would have walked through had he chosen to die at that moment, and the light as the light that people travel through in near-death experiences. He said, 'Shut the door.' He wasn't ready to go." Annie believes the love that was in the room with Andy that day allowed her own healing, even though the scenario defies rational laws. She's not on a crusade to prove or disprove what happened. She saw those images, they were real to her, and they helped her with the delayed grief over her mother's death.

"I spoke to my therapist about sensing my mother's presence at Andy's death bed. I thought I was overreacting, but my therapist thought it made sense. I was eighteen when my mother died. Andy was eighteen. Mothers help other mothers, especially with their children. She saw a certain balance that my mother would help my good friend's son while he was dying. She reassured me that uncommon things happen when people die and that my experience was not something that I should deny. It was this out-of-the-normal thing that happened. I've got to pinch myself when I think about it."

Resolving the Images

Opening herself to painful experiences turned out to have a liberating effect on Annie's spirit. She was more self-aware and self-assured. She had always enjoyed life and taken on challenge and done things that she thought were impossible, but something had been clouding her experience and now the fog lifted: "I think I got over a certain depression that I carried with me because of ungrieved grief."

She had even more energy inside and outside of work. She started organizing field trips for friends to see places she'd discovered through her work, visiting schools to talk about journalism, and mentoring several young people who aspired to photojournalism. At Christmas, she raised money for the newspaper's Giving Tree: "It was very self-serving. I don't have a family out here, and it was very fun to see how much money I could get from people. And I love the hearts. I loved walking through the mall with those hearts and buying things that people asked for. I shamelessly begged and used other people's money for my own fun."

She polished her Spanish and went to Mexico, on a vacation with a friend, who introduced Annie to her friends and family while there. She found ways to go deeper with her work, challenging herself to push the limits. She collaborated with Susan Swartz to document the last months of the life of a woman who had choreographed her own death process and funeral. She worked with another reporter on a series of stories in Central America. Both of those series won awards for the writers. Still, there were those spot news assignments, weather photos, ribbon-cuttings, mug shots, and floods. She had fun with those, too. There's one photo that Annie's fans especially remember of an extreme close-up big-eyed ostrich looking right in your face: "He came over to check me out and I let him look." Click.

It All Comes Together

All of Annie's inner and outer work paid off on an assignment where glory was the least expected. It was one of those drenching winter Sundays when the city editor, Janielle Jobe, was listening to the predictable police radio bulletins. Flooded roads, fallen trees, traffic jams, wet basements, and overflowing creeks—nasty, but more annoying than dangerous. Moment-to-moment decisions were required— where to send the reporters, where to send the photographers. "Girl stranded in creek," came one call. There was a rescue in progress. The sheriff's helicopter was on its way. Janielle, herself the mother of two young girls, sent Annie and a reporter to cover the story.

Annie arrived at the scene and saw a girl clinging to a scrawny tree trunk protruding from the middle of a rain-swollen creek. Emergency crews were assembling. The water was too strong for the firefighter to wade out, so he jumped in upstream and the current yanked him down to her. Family members were there. Rescuers were on scene. Annie's job was to record it. She went into her "zone."

The rescue was a delicate matter. Ropes were needed to secure the firefighter to prevent him from getting caught in the swirling whirlpool along with the girl. Fellow firefighters held him in the balance as he maneuvered himself to the tree where the girl was clinging. Annie could hear her pleas over the roar of the water, a young teenager's scream that she couldn't hold on much longer.

Off to Annie's side, on the same bank where she was standing, stood a pale woman making agonizing cries. Later, Annie would learn this was the girl's mother, watching in horror as the firefighter held on to her daughter. His muscled arms, strong hands, and unblinking eyes showed concentration and competence. He was risking his life to do his job. The girl's dark-haired head and neck were above water, but she obviously was caught on something. The firefighter's job was to keep the girl calm, keep her head above the water, and help her work her way free.

The image in Annie's lens was a powerful one. Time disappeared as she captured each small change in the situation. She was aware only of what she saw suspended in the moment, her proximity to the precariousness of life, and the hope that surged through her body that the girl would be saved and the mother delivered from her anguish. "I was so intent, so focused. I knew that she either would be saved or lost. My concern was to stay out of everyone's way, and that I had enough film."

Later, however, she would rewind the scene and recognize the familiarity of the images from that day, as they mirrored those from the dream about her mother that she'd had during Andy's illness: the dream images of her mother, the river, and the log were inside her as she focused on the girl, the creek, and the spindly tree trunk. The firefighter was struggling to get his grip as the current pulled at him. The girl wore a look fusing a child's trust with an adult fear, while the firefighter's eyes were telling her that he would not let her go. When Annie saw that moment and shot it, she knew instantly it was the best news photograph she'd taken in her life.

When the girl worked her foot free from the tangles and the firefighter guided her to safety, it was one of the most triumphant moments that Annie had witnessed in her career. As the girl was carried out of the water, she whimpered to the woman on the bank, "Mom, I love you."

The photograph was picked up by wire services and reprinted in newspapers and magazines around the world. The photograph seemed to take on a life of its own, being reprinted time and again and creating a small celebrity for the firefighter who had, fortuitously, just completed a course in swift water rescue techniques weeks before the near-fatal incident in the creek. Annie saw the layers of meaning in the image.

"That picture was obviously a good news picture, but it's also symbolic as well. It was all right there—the damsel in distress in life's torrent—and she gets to live."

In Life's Swirl

Annie had been interested in the subject of creativity for a couple of years, reading, among other books, *The Artist's Way* by Julia

Cameron. One of Cameron's exercises was to imagine a perfect day. Annie envisioned herself in a cottage, living alone. She felt that something was holding her back in her life. "I wanted to jump into the swirl."

Then came the unbelievable news that Janielle, the editor with whom she'd worked closely for years, was diagnosed with ovarian cancer. She died within three months, leaving behind a husband and two young daughters. Annie and her co-workers were bereft over Janielle's death. At the same time, Annie was caught in her own life's eddy, feeling stifled by the lack of communication in her fifteen-year marriage. After unsuccessful efforts to work through their differences, Annie separated from her husband, found the tiny country place she'd envisioned, and began building a life alone.

An editor called her into work on a Monday in April. It was her day off and the excuse they gave her was lame enough to raise her suspicions. She knew her photo had been nominated for a Pulitzer and that it was about the time when the winners would be announced. She went into work and at some point everyone gathered around the wire desk to watch the names of the Pulitzer winners come up on the computer screen. Names were announced one by one, and about twelve passed before it came up: "Annie Wells—Spot News Photography." There it was, the highest honor in her profession. Laughter and cheers and champagne flowed through the newsroom. Then came the memory of who sent her on that fateful assignment, and the joyful tears turned to sad ones as Annie dedicated the prize to Janielle.

The coming days and months were exciting but stress-producing and draining: "I have a very introverted element of my personality that wanted to crawl under a rock for the entire year. I was completely stressed for several weeks after the announcement, and I needed to go to my doctor and get sleeping pills, which I used the night before every speaking engagement I had."

Her refuge was the little house in the country that had come to be home, and she was growing more and more attached to the friends with whom she'd grown close since the breakup of her marriage. But now it was time to move on. Job offers came her way from several big papers, and she chose the biggest, the *Los Angeles Times,* exchanging life in a cool, green, northern California valley for the bright southern California life. And she began to live the challenge of being a Pulitzer Prize winner, to whom people inevitably ask, "But what have you done lately?"

Annie's Life These Days

Annie has begun studying mythology and art, gaining a deeper understanding of how visual images have become metaphors in her life. At the same time, in urban L.A., just as in rural northern California, she photographs children and animals and Christmas tree farms, as well as floods and crime scenes and celebrities. She's practicing her Spanish and finding herself drawn to Mexican and Central American cultures. She's content for the moment and not sure where it all will ultimately lead. On the one hand, she loves journalism. On the other, she's not sure it will be entirely dignified to still be shuffling through locker rooms shooting photos of jocks as she ages.

These days, Annie trusts the seemingly random events that somehow have come together in her life. To remind her to continue paying attention to her inner cues, she has a quote from Martha Graham on her desk at home:

> There is a vitality, a life force, a quickening that is translated through you into action, and because there is only one of you in all time, this expression is unique. And if you block it, it will never exist through any other medium and be lost. The world will not have it. It is not your business to determine how good it is, nor how valuable it is, nor how it compares with other expressions. It is your business to keep it yours clearly and directly, to keep the channel open. You do not even have to believe in yourself or your work. You only have to keep yourself open and aware directly to the urges that motivate you. Keep the channel open. . . .

Conversations and Reflections: Investing in Your Creative Self

Up close

A lot of preparation led to two of the notable epiphanies in Annie's work: becoming a photographer in the first place and taking a Pulitzer prize–winning photograph. Both happened because she has worked hard to understand herself and to connect with people through the lens of her camera. She's brave physically and emotionally, not afraid to take risks, not afraid to cry—unless it blurs her vision for a picture.

The most salient lessons from Annie's story seem to be facing, rather than turning away from, what you see and acknowledging the power of the subconscious. She found her creative tool and learned how to use it by paying attention to her feelings and honoring them.

Romancing the Muse

You may have already had epiphanies in your life when you picked up a creative tool and felt like it always belonged in your hand, whether it was a paintbrush or a camera or a pen. Or maybe you've experienced a feeling when you moved your body to music or used your voice in a way that felt just right. Instinctively, you recognize the kindling of a passion.

During conversations we had about the stories in this book, my collaborators and I talked about how certain activities just seem to "fit." I get physical sensations of delight when I paw through fabrics, imagining what will work for a quilt, and I love the feeling of my fingers on the piano keys, but I couldn't get that "feeling" when doing pottery work. Susan felt she should paint because her mom was an artist, but she gave up in frustration because she didn't feel right. Nothing had prepared her, though, for what happened when she took an improvisation class: The exercises captured her imagination and she found an untapped source of creativity on stage.

Thinking back over your experiences, from childhood until now, when did you have *that feeling*? Remembering such enchantments from the past can help you recognize them when they happen again. Recognizing the moment of connection is the first step, but it's not always enough.

Why is it that sometimes a creative endeavor takes hold and you stick with it and other times it passes? I think of it like a romance: There's that initial infatuation, but then conflicts come up, reality intrudes, and the object of your affection may end up not meeting your expectations. Like falling in love, it bodes well for creativity if that initial captivation is powerful. That kind of bonding can happen only if you're open to it. Annie let herself feel the rapture when she first picked up a camera. Once you let yourself go with a feeling of enchantment over a creative endeavor, you're on your way. A certain tool feels just right in your hand. You claim ownership. Ideas seem to pop into your head. What you do with it may seem secondary to the mere act of using it, which suddenly becomes an essential part of living.

Women who have stayed with a creative pursuit often recall the beginnings with a tremor in their voices, followed by a deep sigh over the inadequacy of words to describe how they discovered their creative selves. A singer first hearing "that sound" that comes from within her realizes she wants nothing more than to produce that sound forever. A writer feeling enchanted by her words on the page and instantly becoming addicted to the possibility that she could do it again and again. A seamstress becoming so absorbed with texture and stitch that she is "not thinking about anything else, nothing else."

For Annie, it is the desire to focus her camera, shoot, and see what wonders appeared on the paper in the darkroom. What do you love doing enough that the activity seems to eclipse all else?

Once You've Found It

You can't count on rapture to keep you going, any more than romance alone can keep a marriage together. It helps to have a stubborn will and/or a way to set up some external support system. For example, take classes, as Annie did for photography, or join a group of like-minded people, as many writers do through critique groups. This allows you to set up a system that allows the rapture to come and go, while providing some structure to keep you going when the work gets tough.

Finding mentors is another form of insurance to keep you afloat when your confidence starts to sink. Susan remembers one editor whose influence helped her write: "He said, 'Write for me, entertain me.' And then he'd tell me when I did. Years later, I thanked him for that and he said he'd forgotten, but he agreed it was pretty good advice." Of course, choosing your mentors or support system requires great care. Budding passions don't take kindly to overzealous pruning.

In later chapters, we'll be looking closely at how to assess who you let into your creative world. It may take a while. Annie had the good fortune—or perhaps skill—to surround herself initially with people who supported her work. For those who aren't ready to risk feedback, there are other ways to foster persistence. One way is to develop a special time and place that you declare all your own, during which you can enjoy and protect your creative work the way you would a clandestine lover.

The resilience of the rapture depends on your energy and commitment. Intrusions are inevitable. How do you find time? There are other people to consider: What do they think? There are bills to be paid. Sometimes it seems unrealistic to believe you can make money doing what brings you pleasure. And the creative act itself can prove troublesome, as you dig for inspiration and encounter aspects of yourself that may be painful.

The stories in this book demonstrate different ways that women have managed to integrate their creative life into their "other lives" until they experience more of a continuum than a division. Following the advice in the popular Martha Graham quote that Annie (and, as it turned out, several other women in this book) posted prominently to view daily, the discipline is to "keep the channel open."

How do you do this? For some, it helps to return again and again to the memory of the moments when it first happened. It can be helpful to develop a vocabulary for telling yourself and ultimately others about how your own creative process works. Developing your own creative story—the way the women in this book have developed theirs—provides a foundation for utilizing the unexpected gifts (which at first can look like curses) that your creative channel delivers to you.

When Annie found herself dealing with images that touched the tender parts of her heart, she didn't put up a barrier—she let herself feel the emotions. As with any kind of relationship, challenges involving creativity can take you to a deeper place. If you love the work enough, you'll continue even if you don't know where you're going.

Art or Craft? Or Is There a Difference?

Under the evolving definition of creativity, what you bring to the work defines its creative value more than how it's judged by society. Reporters and photojournalists often put as much effort into a page of writing as magazine or book authors and photographers do— but the paper has a one-day shelf life and out it goes into the recycling bin. Annie says she considers her work more craft than art. Most of her friends disagree and say that Annie's an artist. I'm not sure it matters what you call it. It's intensely creative.

Annie's Pulitzer photo is a reminder of why it's worth it to keep working away, trusting that the dazzling moments will recur. Annie's prize was secondary to the intrinsic value of her work, but it demonstrates the fairy-tale possibilities of dedicating yourself to your creative outlets and sharing the outcomes with a larger audience. Meg says, "Annie's triumph is an example of the magic that can come about any day, in the routine course of work. For journalists at the newspaper where I work, Sunday is a crummy shift—nothing ever happens. We dig in our heels and keep performing, not letting up, trying to do our best, never knowing when the mundane may be elevated to the amazing. Annie's great piece was not like toiling over a book or a sculpture. The toiling came from all the personal work and professional preparation that allowed her to perform at her peak when the time came. Our 'masterpieces' don't have to be years-long projects like the Sistine Chapel."

What does it really mean to "keep the channel open"? Perhaps it's doing the routine aspects of the work and always keeping your awareness tuned in to capture those luminous moments when everything comes together. It seems fairly clear to me from my reading and interviews that creative breakthroughs do indeed come to those who invest in their creativity. But you can't control when or how. It's the "ninety-nine percent perspiration and one percent inspiration" thing. You need to be ready when the moment arrives.

In writing, it's the plugging away that leads to flashes of clarity. In gardening, it's the tilling and planting that leads to blossoms. In painting, it's the repetition of technique that leads to that artistic variation. In music, it's practicing the scales so you can perform the esoteric melodies or compose your own. Annie takes hundreds of pictures a week and she never knows when the right combination of factors will happen to make it a great one.

Sacrifice

As we were developing the themes for this book, Susan brought up the word "sacrifice." This was a bad word when she and I collaborated on the book *Goodbye Good Girl:* We entreated women not to put aside their passion in order to accommodate the needs of others. But there's a different kind of sacrifice that Annie demonstrates—a sacrifice that works for the creative self. It's being willing to endure a certain amount of discomfort in order to pursue a vision. Annie has given up some of her self-protection and has strained some personal relationships in order to immerse herself in photography. She has established boundaries that protect her creative self. Sometimes she gets mad, as she did with her husband when he didn't recognize the importance of her photography assignment.

Anger is something of a taboo, but women who have studied creativity laud it as a breakthrough. Julia Cameron wrote in her book *The Artist's Way:*

> *Anger is meant to be listened to. Anger is a voice, a shout, a demand. Anger is meant to be respected. Why? Because anger is a map. Anger shows us what our boundaries are. Anger shows us where we want to go. It lets us see where we've been and lets us know when we haven't liked it. Anger points the way, not just the finger. In the recovery of a blocked artist, anger is a sign of health.*

Annie doesn't walk around mad, she doesn't hold on to bitterness, but she does set her feelings free in the moment. Over time, she has learned how to tune in to her feelings without expressing anger in such a way as to alienate other people, but she has no interest in squelching any of her feelings. They are guideposts for her. She welcomes the emotional cues that help her read the complex picture of her own life. Anytime she feels strongly, she has something to learn. And often she has something to share.

Have you ever given something up because you didn't want to upset someone else? Gone along with something in order to avoid conflict? Ignored a creative urge because it would be inconvenient to others? It's taken me a long time to learn not to say "yes, no problem" when people ask me to do something I feel wastes my energy and skills. Being a good sport has merits, but it can be costly. Annie is a good model for learning to say no. And that seems to be one of the constants among actively creative women: claiming time. When you want to do something badly enough, there's no choice.

The romance analogy once again might be enlightening, as most women are aware of what happens to their lives when they fall in love—and what happens to relationships when they don't get enough attention. Beyond the initial enchantment, the actively creative life requires regular action. Once you've found it, what do you say to family members who just don't "get it" or friends who are disgruntled because you don't have as much time for them? Or, worse yet, how do you respond to people who say, "I don't think you're going to make it"?

Your response might not be that different than if people were questioning time you spend with your sweetheart: "This is important to me. You are important to me, too, but right now I need to put my time and energy here." In the beginning phases, there are so many ups and downs. Extra energy is needed as you figure out how to bring this new dimension into your life. You may not want or be able to drop your other commitments, but always there are ways to carve out time and give attention to something that sustains you. Throughout this book, you'll see ways other women have done so. It's natural for others to be a little jealous of your new object of affection. But who would begrudge you an activity that makes you feel more alive and at home in the world?

Annie doesn't much like being romanticized, but I can't help seeing hers as a Cinderella story. She didn't grow up in an environment rich in creative encouragement, but she managed to recognize when scraps of inspiration that came her way—starting with the book she received from the nurse. She got down to the hard work of understanding herself, so that she could bring all of herself to the day-to-day chores of her career, all the while responding with genuine concern for others. Even if the glass slipper hadn't come her way, she had found the right fit for her creative self.

Of course, the reality is a lot more dicey than the fairy-tale version, and part of Annie's success stems from the fact that she is not the compliant type; she's not willing to settle in situations where she feels stifled, and she's still facing tough situations in her own life and in the lives of her photographic subjects. There's no happily ever after, but she gets to continue her journey in new places, doing her job while sharpening her creative focus.

Creative opportunities appear if you keep your eyes open and, if you don't turn away when what you see is confusing or difficult, you'll eventually train yourself to recognize the magical moments and seek out supportive people as sources of inspiration. You'll be able to recognize and revel in your accomplishments, whether they manifest as process or product or both.

Onward: Seeing What's Next

Annie's news photographs have been framed and hung like paintings. The photos look different all dressed up and spotlighted against a white backdrop in a gallery than they did against the gray of the morning paper. In the exhibit, there were diving swimmers from the sports page, a gazillion tires from the exposé on used rubber. She's captured on film the faces of migrant farmers, looking haggard and asking readers not to look away. Pictured were the hands of a dead woman, who had invited the press to witness her passing. The pictures are as good as they are because Annie waits and watches until the essence of the image appears. She can see it because she gets herself out of the way, and she's not afraid to keep looking. She'll stay by the river, for as long as it takes.

The alternating currents have continued. Joy and pain, two sides of the same life. The thrill of success has carried a price that the fortunate often feel ungrateful discussing, though it is their truth. She misses her friends, colleagues, and the life she had built for herself:

I'm lonely and excited, and I know this is what I am supposed to be doing. I feel there's a purpose in all of this, and I just have to go with my intuition. When I think about the prize, I see it all connected with Janielle and her girls and my mom and Andy—all of the loss. I don't fully understand it, but I'm open. I'm learning a vocabulary to talk about what is happening with me, and I'm not afraid to take it all in. I wouldn't change anything I've done.

2

Now Starring in Her Own Life: Making the Most of Your Day Job

You either have that knack of doing your job and being satisfied you're doing a good job and making people happy, or you don't.

—Sherry Jean O'Malley,
waitress

Meet Sherry Jean, the Waitress Machine

In her tidy little Berkeley bungalow, as her family yawns into the morning light, Sherry Jean O'Malley already has the table laid for breakfast and has herself outfitted for the day: black leggings topped with a bright little skirt and contrasting top, sensible shoes, and an under-the-eye hint of green liner under her big peepers, which turn bright blue or deep violet, depending on what's she's wearing. She rummages through the closet, where she keeps her collection of no less than three hundred aprons; chooses one for the day; and kisses her two daughters and husband good-bye with a stream of affectionate farewells: "Bye, honey bun," "Love you, darlin'," "I'll be home by the time you're back from school, angel."

Then she's off. In her car, she turns on an oldies rock-and-roll station and catches the classic Four Seasons' "Sherry Baby." She laughs, rolls down the window, and sings out loud. When she arrives at work, she's still smiling. "What are you so happy about?" a co-worker asks. "I heard 'Sherry' on the radio and just knew it was going to be a *great* day!" "You're nuts," her friend says. "Yep," says Sherry.

She calls herself "Sherry Jean, the Waitress Machine." She's worked for nearly twenty years serving bacon and eggs at Mama's Royal Café in Oakland, California, where the customers adore her for her give-all presence—not just the service but the performance that is Sherry's way of just doing her job. "The door opens and it's show time," she practically sings. With her big eyes, red curls, and love-me-but-don't-mess-with-me personality, Sherry is equal parts Mae West and Dolly Parton, a beguiling entertainer who expertly works her tables like a show girl.

Undaunted by mundane chores like cleaning jam jars and refilling ketchup containers, Sherry has elevated waitressing into a performing art, working the antediluvian linoleum at Mama's and contributing to its legend as one of the best breakfast eateries in the San Francisco Bay Area. Crowds line up along Broadway for scrambled eggs and toast with a dollop of Sherry Jean's honeyed sass.

It's not the kind of work that usually inspires bravado, but Sherry has turned an otherwise routine day job inside out. Each shift is an opportunity. She's art in action, treating the timeworn restaurant, with red Formica countertops and pea green shelves, into her own personal vaudeville house. At the same time, she's transformed a back wall above a bank of wooden booths into a gallery space for a rotating exhibit of her aprons—a proud and permanent salute to the uniform of her trade. She has a loyal following and a regular audience, and while she doesn't underplay her job, you won't catch her making too much of it either.

"My mama always said, 'When you're born, you have your mom, and when you die, you have the undertaker, and what you get in between is up to you.'" What she has is a shameless amount of fun and the satisfaction she appropriates in the day-to-day business of waitressing. She spends her shifts bringing laughs to others and entertaining herself with the people who settle into her section every day.

It amazes Sherry how many people she sees who have glamorous jobs and tons of money but look stressed out and miserable. "I feel sorry for people who never smile. One guy was coming in for years and he never smiled. One day I said to myself, 'Sherry will get him to smile.' I walked over to him and asked, 'Do you normally eat nails before you come here to have breakfast and then come here in a bad mood?' He started to laugh."

Each day there are such small victories, along with the occasional dramas and some star-studded moments when famous actors, sports figures—and once even a Buddhist priest she and others thought was the Dalai Lama—make an appearance at one of her tables. It's all in a day's work for Sherry who dismissively shrugs and says, "I don't want for much."

Embracing Your Everyday Work

There's something about Sherry Jean that feels like a cool drink of water, clear and refreshing. What's her appeal? She might be a character from the long-popular television program *Seinfeld*—entirely herself, right there, amusing, amused, visible, and completely unpretentious. She's turned one of the most ordinary of jobs into a long-running stage show. She makes it look like a breeze, but it takes practice at on-the-spot creativity to become a star in your own daily life.

Self-expression for many people takes the form of a quiet, contemplative process, where insights emerge slowly and are polished into words on paper, paint on canvas, acted out on stage. Sherry Jean demonstrates a more immediate form of creativity by bringing all of herself into the moment. She *is* the vision. She gets an internal satisfaction similar to that of more classic artists: producing something uniquely her own that brings meaning to her life and entertains others along the way, leaving them with a bit of herself.

In her humble role with her unstoppable spirit, Sherry Jean has, with a flip of a plastic menu, evolved a model of optimism and style with what life has served her. People feel it in her presence, and sometimes express wonderment, but she has little interest in analyzing it all. She's too busy. Catch her in a time-out, however—even though she doesn't like to sit still for long—and a story emerges about a naturally gifted performer who is content to bring all her creativity into her everyday work. She doesn't really need to do much explaining—to herself or others. She prefers to demonstrate in everyday actions what it means to "be there," in one's life, just as it is, no holding back.

"Pizzazz" and "integrity" are the two words that come to mind when watching Sherry amid the action at work and at home. Her persona is an archetype, the heart-of-gold waitress with a flirty but brick-solid presence, someone you'd go see for cheering up on a bad day. She seems happy and fulfilled.

Consciously choosing how to express yourself is one of the liberating aspects of claiming your creativity. While for some that may involve a change in life circumstances to accommodate a passion—like Annie leaving a law office for a photojournalism job—Sherry Jean demonstrates another model. Instead of "having what you choose," she shows the potential for creativity when you choose what you have.

One thing Sherry Jean has is a clear sense of values. She can be seen as a reminder to keep focused on what's important to yourself. To her, what's important is doing a good day's work and coming home with her energy and spirit intact for her family. That means refusing to deal with anyone unpleasant. Workplace politics are pretty basic, and she likes it that way. She'd rather get her drama by getting home in time for her daily soap opera than in some Dilbert-esque scene at work.

On the other hand, she's not just "putting in her time" on the job. She brings in her wits, her costumes, her history, and her showmanship. She's not doing it for the customers or for the boss. She does it to keep herself amused and fulfilled. She's proud of her job and what she's made of it.

The idea of "appreciating the simple things in life" is cliché, but it's overused for a reason: enjoying the present is more pleasant than suffering through every hardship and stressor that comes your way. Sherry Jean demonstrates an innocent wisdom. How life looks when you focus on what's in front of you. She's not thinking about greater things she might be doing in the future, or regretting decisions she made in the past. She's making the most of her moment, her stage. Creativity may not be something "out there" that you must seek or stretch to grasp: It may be right within reach.

Sherry Jean's Path

A Different Kind of Dance

Sherry landed the Mama's Royal Café waitress job in 1979, shortly after she and her husband migrated west. It was not exactly the kind of regular gig she had imagined, growing up poor, a middle child in an Irish Catholic family with fourteen children. Her father, a river barge captain, emigrated from County Mayo to Pittsburgh, Pennsylvania and taught his children about possibilities. Sherry dreamed of stardom as a dancer while she stitched aprons in her home economics class in junior high school. Her dreams of the future didn't stop her from giving her all in the present. She already had a knack for making the most of her circumstances.

She won her first dance contest performing a mean twist at the age of ten. It gave her a taste of being out front. There was no money in the O'Malley house for luxuries like dance lessons, but when she hit her teens she made enough cash babysitting to pay for a few classes. Even among fourteen kids—all the girls shared one room jammed with bunks—Sherry was a stand-out "go-girl" who just put herself out there, unafraid of disapproval.

At sixteen, she tried out for a local version of *American Bandstand* called *Come Alive*. Legally, she was two years too young and she had no partner, but she didn't let those inconveniences stop her. She recruited her brother, Jimmy. "I made him rehearse with me and I taught him all the dances," she says. "He fixed my hair up so I looked older." Miraculously, they won and became the "Come Alive Dancers," frugging on Saturday nights for a bit of local glory and free concert tickets.

Her fascination with aprons goes back to a time when she was a very little girl planted in front of the TV in the fifties, admiring domestic glamour girls like Alice Kramden and June Cleaver, who filled out kitchen wear with all the right curves. She began sewing her own aprons in junior high. "In home ec class, we always had to have a nice clean apron every day." She didn't mind the rules—she liked making aprons with fussy decorations and perfect stitches—and she didn't mind when the other girls good-naturedly teased her for her scrupulous attention to detail. To this day, her old school chums collect aprons at rummage sales and save them for her.

Despite her love of that old-fashioned symbol of momhood, Sherry Jean didn't have domestic dreams. All of her sisters got married at a young age, but, "I was on a mission from God not to do that," Sherry says. Instead, she got on a Greyhound bus for Philadelphia and enrolled at Temple University. With no family financial support, it was a small miracle that she made it to college at all. Theater was her major.

She was seventeen when she arrived in Philly and rented a third-floor walk-up for six dollars a week, making ends meet with scholarships and waitressing. She took a job at the Oak Lane Diner, where her co-workers were all older Philadelphia matrons with beehive hairdos who tried their darndest to intimidate her. "Can you carry plates?" they quizzed her skeptically. She'd shoot back, "Can you?"

"I wasn't going to let them intimidate me." She claimed her spot among them, but then quit to try something more professional. She took a job at the First Pennsylvania bank, but abandoned it and went back to waitressing. "I got sick of the banking scene and dressing up every day." She dropped out of college after two years, discouraged by the difficulty of juggling work and classes. By then she had also fallen in love with Gary, a fellow student, and decided to act on another childhood dream—getting as far away from Pittsburgh as possible. They ended up in Berkeley, California.

She tried a few other jobs and then one day she slipped into a booth at Mama's Royal Café. She looked around and took it all as a casting call. Instantly, this was her stage. "I came in to eat. I said to the manager, 'I'm a good waitress. I think you'd like to hire me.' And he said, 'Okay, but you have to tell a joke.'" She spun a few of her father's tall Irish tales and was hired on the spot.

Neither of them knew what kind of matchmaking was going on. This would be a long-term relationship, between Sherry and a growing number of regulars, many of whom, it soon became clear, were coming in to see her. Dressing up became a form of entertainment for herself and for her customers. She'd made kitchen accouterments her motif. Her artistic nature was so buoyant, customers responded to her as though she were a star. It was the way she moved, the way she laughed, the miniature silver teapots and spatulas dangling from the earlobes that captivated diners. And then, there were those aprons.

The Apron Lady

When she moved to California, she had brought a few of her favorite aprons; naturally, as a woman of individual style, she preferred them to the mass-produced, restaurant-supply version. The more people commented on her aprons, the more it reinforced her efforts to make and collect them. The more aprons she made, the wilder they got—the patrons at Mama's saw sheer sexy ones or sassy ones with sayings like "To Hell with Housework."

Like an artist watching people in a gallery, Sherry Jean got a kick out of seeing customers' reactions to her apron outfits, often matched to fit her dress or the holiday of the moment. Unlike her long-ago classmates who had gotten giggles from her fussy fabrics and obscure notions, customers were impressed. In this arty East Bay neighborhood, people got the message behind what she was doing. Fabric art had been enjoying a renaissance, from quilts to soft sculptures to tapestries. Sherry had an original twist and showed her art in action. Her apron collection expresses her personality. "I love them and it's me," she says. "They're art in themselves. They've been a part of clothing and fashion since the eighteenth century; they go way back to pinafores, and they're beautiful."

In a way, they were like the work of her grandmother, a southern belle who made elaborate hand-stitched "bonnet" quilts, a different bonnet in each square, no two alike. The quilts were her grandmother's trademark. She made them for her grandkids, for her friends. One hangs on the wall of Sherry's home today in the den. Sherry and her daughter like to just look at that quilt, sitting together and musing with quiet talk about the patterns, imagining what was on Grandma's mind when she chose them. Aprons became Sherry Jean's motif.

Her interest won her the nickname "The Apron Lady," and her reputation began to feed the growing collection. Customers who became fans of Sherry Jean started sending her aprons they'd bought in their travels. Sometimes she'd even get a package from people she'd met only once. "One thing I really like is getting aprons in the mail from strangers. They'll say, 'Dear Apron Lady, I was in Nebraska and saw this and thought of you.' They send it care of Mama's Royal Café. A girlfriend of mine, Mimi, who is a writer who has published five books, collects aprons wherever she sees them. On my fortieth birthday she sent me forty aprons. She spent a lot of time to get them for me. I got this big box in the mail."

As the collection grew and customers started asking more about her aprons, she decided to start displaying them. Showing off one a day just wasn't enough. "I said to the owner, George, 'This room looks naked to me. How about if Sherry just displays her aprons over here.' He said, 'Great idea,' so I did."

These days she has hundreds of aprons, from which she selects a dozen or so at a time to display in the restaurant. She changes the theme, grouping by season or holiday, and cooks up new ways to categorize them by theme and type. For spring, there's red gingham and green gingham, crocheted aprons and aprons gussied up with needlepoint. Darker colors go up in fall. Aprons became a magnificent obsession, so renowned, that the local independent newspaper singled her out for a write-up in their "Best of the East Bay" issue. They at first thought of honoring her for the best apron collection, "But they couldn't come up with anyone to compare me to," she laughs. So they dubbed her "The Best Irish Rose," and waxed eloquently about how she waits on everyone from kings to "nobodies," giving every diner the same royal treatment.

What Do You Say to the Dalai Lama?

Sherry's reputation for being unimpressed is well-known—unimpressed not just with herself but with the most impressive of customers, including actor Elliott Gould, who started going to Mama's Royal Café after his daughter moved nearby. When he first walked into the restaurant, the waitresses invoked their code of politeness—being cool because one simply does not make a fuss over stars. He sat in Sherry's section, and she walked over to take his order. Casually, she delivered her line: "Your voice sounds like Elliot Gould, but you're far too young to be him." The Sherry Jean charm worked again. Gould has been a regular visitor since, always stopping in on his Bay Area visits.

Sherry's tongue is a source of amusement to co-workers and customers, but there was one time when it caused a little anxiety for her boss. Her boss is a Buddhist and invited a priest to dine at Mama's Royal Café while visiting the Bay Area. Assuming it was the Dalai Lama himself, she hinted that he might put in a good word for her with God: "I told him I needed all the blessings I could get."

"He was one of those guys with red robes, beads, and a bald head. I told him I had a red apron for him, if he was interested." Her casual cajoling surprised her boss, who whispered, "Sherry, you just don't get it. This is sort of like meeting the Pope." She set him straight. "I wouldn't treat the Pope any different."

Sherry is also known for not taking any guff from customers. Most not only respect her—they revere her. She describes a typical episode: "I had a party of eighteen, 'cause nobody likes to take big parties. I said okay. I put the food out and they start to eat. I said, 'No one's going to question me on their order today?' They said, 'We've always applauded your memory. You always serve us the right dishes.' And then that particular party, when they left, said they consider me the waitress goddess. I said, 'I've been called a goddess before, but in different situations.'"

Somewhere along the way, Sherry simply made Mama's her theater, an eighteen-year engagement. When she arrives, "It's showtime, honey. The doors are open. Let's go. Everyone knows they can depend on me," she says confidently. At Mama's, Sherry is star and director. That's why she can get away with saying just about anything that comes into her mind. "Everybody says to me, 'If I said that to someone they would slap me. How do you get away with that?'

Well, I tell them you have to put the vinegar with the honey. Last Friday one of the girls came up to me and said, 'Table ten wants their food.' I'm already in the kitchen picking up table ten's food. I walked out and one guy was standing up. I said, 'Sit down and hush up.' And he did. Most people generally are really human beings and they can take it."

Sherry Jean's Life These Days

Working three shifts a week is plenty for Sherry. It leaves her time for sewing Barbie clothes, crocheting baby blankets, and playing with her kids. "You leave with money in your pocket, you don't have any headaches," she says of her leave-it-all-at-work job. When she's in the restaurant, she feels at home and herself. She's trained almost all of the other waitresses: "I feel very well respected in my line of work and as a human being."

She can stand up for herself and is beloved by most customers, some of whom have been known to stand up for her, too. "One day a man in the back room wanted a waffle and some things, and other people had three scrambled egg breakfasts. I brought the three scrambled egg breakfasts on time, but the big guy jumps up and says, 'Where's my food, bitch.' I said, 'Sir, you ordered a waffle. We have two waffle irons. We're having a little back up. It'll be a minute.' Instantly other customers were on their feet, confronting him and telling him never to talk to me like that again."

Her outspokenness helps her feel like she's in control of her life. "Everybody is," she maintains. "They just don't know it. They get lost along the way." She isn't the type to think about what other vocations she might have had. "I have a lot of other things I do in my life. I have a beautiful garden at home—tomatoes and corn—and I crochet. I just do a lot of other things. And one thing I like about this job: When you leave you're gone. You don't go home and worry about what's happening or if something is going to work for somebody. You don't have the headaches and heartaches."

Sherry is unforgettable to the thousands of people she's served over the years. "All kinds of regulars come in. And they go, like, 'Oh my God. I'm so happy you're still here. This makes my day.'" And there are always those aprons to change. "If I look at the aprons too long I'm like, 'Hey. I've got to change them. I'm bored with this.' It's very nice to hear people come in and say, 'Oh, look at these aprons. They're so beautiful.' Sometimes they go on and on. I'll say, 'Thank you.' They'll say, 'They're yours?'"

Sherry adores her children, but teases in her waitress jargon, "You gotta love 'em . . . can't move them to another section." She doesn't really regret not going onto the stage. "I met my husband at school. I made sure he finished. But I wanted to have kids. Now I've got two and I'm happy. I swear if I die today I wouldn't even care. Although a lot more people would be awful mad."

"It's important to be yourself," says Sherry Jean. "It's self-esteem, don't you think? Getting positive action. I like the action, and you get a lot of good people coming through."

Being Creative in the Here and Now: Conversations and Reflections

The Ideal Venue

Sherry Jean has an unofficial but growing group of fans. One of them introduced her as a candidate for this book because Sherry demonstrates one of the most liberating interpretations of creativity yet: You can do it in your own life right now, without changing a thing but your attitude. This was a radical notion to me. Not too long ago, I probably would have thought that a creative waitress was someone who worked her shift and went home to do her artwork afterwards. But meeting Sherry Jean, who has invested all of herself in her daily life, made me rethink my definitions of creativity. Sherry Jean's story brings up the question: "What am I saving myself for?" She lives every moment with gusto, not judging her circumstances or environment, but enjoying it for all it's worth.

You may not have the kind of quick tongue and out-there nature to go through your own life like a star, but there are elements of the Sherry Jean brand of creativity that each of us could borrow as a reminder that creativity is part of our being, not just something we "produce." There's something grand about conjuring up a quick one-liner or costume in a situation where it might least be expected. Everyone has a certain amount of drudgery in a day, but Sherry Jean's message is "Don't let it get you down—give it back." You build creative muscle by seeing the humor and irony in day-to-day interactions and responding with your own take on the situation.

Besides using the kind of brassy charm that lets you say whatever's on your mind, another thing Sherry Jean shows is the power of surrounding yourself with personal symbols. With her apron collection, Sherry Jean is proudly saying to the world, "That's me," and inviting others to contribute. The best part about Sherry Jean's bag of tricks is you can take it anywhere. Maybe you aren't entirely happy with places you have to be at times. It's so tempting to run on "automatic pilot" and hope the time passes fast. But are you missing some opportunities?

Most people at one time or another get caught in the trap of imagining that some ideal venue for self-expression exists elsewhere. Sometimes you need to switch jobs or move to make life changes that allow you to free your creative spirit. But it can be a trap to say, "If only . . ." or "When I finally do this, then I can . . . ," when it serves as an excuse to hold you back from making the most of the possibilities presented by life. Familiar excuses to me are: "If only I'd gone to graduate school in English, then I could have been a great fiction writer . . ." or, "When I finally get a better beat assignment in the newsroom, then I might be able to write something of meaning."

When I look back though, many of my most cherished experiences and accomplishments were practically happenstance, cropping up in the most unexpected ways. A touching human interest story came out of the dreaded night police beat. And, of course, Annie won her Pulitzer for a picture that was not part of a long-planned series, but something that emerged from a routine assignment on an otherwise dull Sunday shift.

Susan writes a twice-weekly column about whatever's on her mind, as well as nonfiction books and fiction. Even with such permission for creativity, for a long time she found herself stashing ideas away for some imagined ideal venue. "I used to think that if I came up with a good idea, character, or truly delicious line, I should hoard it until the perfect time came to showcase it. To wait for the perfect setting, the perfect character to speak it. But now I believe there is no quota on creativity. In fact, you might even get stuck holding on to something for too long and then miss out on the next great thing. So I use a favorite phrase or snippet of dialogue as soon as I can and if they work, they work, and if they don't, they don't. But it leaves me open for more to come in. I trust that there is always something out there waiting to feed me. That is my security and my liberation."

Bringing your all to the moment is a discipline. There's a saying: "Life is what happens while you're busy making other plans." I've traded notes with several different people about the periods of time when we seemed to be waiting for "real life" to begin: "As soon as I finish college . . . when I find the right mate . . . when I get the ideal job . . . when I buy a house . . . when the baby's born . . . when I'm financially stable . . . when the kids are grown . . . " and on and on it can go. One time I had that conversation with a young mother who was terminally ill. "I've just begun to understand the meaning of 'now,' and I wish I had more time to enjoy that," she said. I try to remember her words.

Of course, there's a benefit to steering life in the direction you want to go, especially if you're lucky or skillful enough to have many choices. But the trick is not to lose sight of where you are before you move to the next stage. Anne Wilson Schaef, in her book *Meditations for Women Who Do Too Much,* suggests:

> *When we can participate fully in the process of our lives,*
> *we discover new forms of our creative self. Creativity has*
> *many avenues. Just living our lives can cultivate our conscious*
> *creativity. Can it be? Is just living my life enough?*

You might try remembering the creative moments in your life that you felt most deeply. Where were you at the time? Was the experience something you choreographed or were you caught off-guard? What happened to allow you to be so present in the moment? Sometimes looking back and recognizing past episodes of serendipity can remind you to be open to the present. When I do this exercise, I see that very few of my big aha (or, as fellow scribe Susan says, "dazzling myself") moments came as the result of some direct effort to find them.

In many of the stories still to come, you'll see how many women were practically tripped by their muse when they were rushing headlong elsewhere or stumbling away from a major life experience hardly expecting to feel creative. It's a good argument for attending to what's happening around you, even at the most seemingly unesthetic moments, while at the same time tuning in to your response to the situation. Voicing what you see with a little panache makes it all the more fun, Sherry Jean will tell you.

When Every Moment Is Important

Being in the moment is an essential element for creativity. One concept that helps, discussed by Zen master Thich Nhat Hanh in *The Miracle of Mindfulness,* is seeing life as a continuum rather than dividing time into parts. How many of us think of work time as "their time" and our time at home as "my time"? Or time with family as "family time" and a certain favorite activity as "leisure time." It's that kind of compartmentalized experience, Hanh says, that creates stress and drains life of meaning. As an exercise, Hanh suggests doing menial tasks with full attention:

> *While washing the dishes one should only be washing the*
> *dishes, which means that while washing the dishes one should*
> *be completely aware of the fact that one is washing the dishes.*
> *At first glance, that might seem a little silly: why put so*
> *much stress on a simple thing? But that's precisely the point.*
> *The fact that I am standing there and washing these bowls is*
> *a wondrous reality. I'm being completely myself, following my*

breath, conscious of my presence, and conscious of my
thoughts and actions. There's no way I can be tossed around
mindlessly like a bottle slapped here and there on the waves.

It's a wonderful feeling to be satisfied with your experiences, even the simple ones. And perhaps satisfaction is attainable simply by adopting a content attitude—by saying and feeling so, it becomes so.

Of course, you don't always have the luxury of concentrating on one thing at a time. Sherry Jean might have to juggle two or three different activities at once, visiting with a customer while filling the jam jars, taking an order at one table while looking over to see if people at another table are ready for dessert. She may tune out some activities but still manage to give each customer enough attention that they remember their interactions with her. Having just the right one-liner for every customer isn't something you can manufacture without a lot of focus.

There's something that feels clean about taking each interaction as it comes and then going on to the next, not carrying anything over or taking it home at night. How many of us could find more satisfaction in the humdrum tasks of our jobs if we could feel pride in our accomplishments of the moment? As Angelique Arnauld said, "Perfection consists not in doing extraordinary things, but in doing ordinary things extraordinarily well. Neglect nothing; the most trivial action may be performed to God."

The whole issue of attention deserves consideration. For some, the wandering mind can be beneficial. Doing the dishes can be a time for subconscious brainstorming. But it can be delightful to consider the prospect that doing the dishes is no more or less valuable, in terms of nourishing the spirit, than creating a work of art. There is a balance to be found between musing and just being. Julia Cameron, in *The Artist's Way*, suggests that too much drifting simply leads to more drifting:

Very often, a creative block manifests itself as an addiction to
fantasy. Rather than working or living in the now, we spin
our wheels and indulge in daydreams of could have, would
have, should have. One of the great misconceptions about the
artistic life is that it entails great swathes of aimlessness. The
truth is that a creative life involves great swathes of attention.
Attention is a way to connect and survive.

There's no "right" way to discipline your mind, but recognizing your habitual patterns of attention can help you understand your creative process. If you tend to be distracted a lot, more immersion in the moment-to-moment experiences might leave you feeling clean, blessed, and more open to see art in the everyday.

Just a Job?

In some ways, everyone's job is routine, even those that sound glamorous. The behind-the-scenes work can be drudgery in any profession. In any job, it's what you make of it. I remember my son's fourth-grade teacher, mired in checking his students' papers and models of California missions, laughing over an interview he heard with National Public Radio's Terry Gross. He was well aware of the mundane aspects of his work, but it was a revelation to realize the same feeling was experienced by someone whose job is interviewing some of the most accomplished and famous people in the world. She talked about the "dailiness" of her work and how there were parts of it that felt routine, despite the stellar moments.

It's possible to reframe your experiences so you can find creative fuel in what seems like the routine daily mechanism of life. One way is to alter your routines ever so slightly, changing the way your desk faces at work, making a point of getting to know someone you've never met before, bringing little symbols of yourself to your environment. One city council woman confided to me years ago that she kept herself awake during dull discussions by imagining that her fellow council members were dressed up as various fictional characters. When she stepped down from her seat, I understood why she gave me—the local reporter at the time—a little statue of a gold mouse with big ears. Entertaining yourself is not a bad way of making a private declaration: "My experience of this is important." Making conscious choices about how you view the world and interact with others is, as Sherry Jean observes, a self-esteem builder and a good antidote to the "What will other people think?" syndrome that can be poisonous to the muse.

In my newspaper work, there are the big splashy stories on one end of the spectrum and the rewrites of press releases on the other. When it's my turn to do the dull rewrites, I've tried to make little challenges for myself. How many weird verbs can I use? Can I get every last punctuation mark perfect? Can I bring as much of myself to a conversation with a community event organizer as with a high-profile artist or politician?

Meg plays similar tricks. She considers it a challenge, a game, to take some borderline assignment that barely interests the editor who assigned it and come back with something that's at least readable, if not downright interesting. "I remember an editor, after reading the writing job I did on some loser idea, observing in an 'I told you so' tone, 'See. This is a pretty good little story.' I set him straight. 'I made it interesting.'"

A step toward freedom is to stop thinking of some jobs as creative and others as not. It's not the activity but the attitude that defines what's creative. Deborah has found that to be true because she does architecture work, considered by many to be creative with a capital C. But she also teaches and does union work at a college. Deborah says, "Opening up the definition of creativity in my own life has brought a richness to activities outside of architecture that might be considered 'just jobs.' For example, I now teach adults at our local community college. I try to inspire students to think, to create, for themselves. I sometimes think that facilitating the discovery of another is the highest form of creativity.

"Even more recently I have become involved with collective bargaining, using a creative approach to frame the discussion, prepare the research, conduct negotiation sessions, and deal with our union members. Too often, people expect a 'perfect' expression of their creativity, but it is through the seizing of creative potential in our everyday lives that we create meaning."

In their book *Living Your Life Out Loud*, Salli Rasberry and Padi Selwyn advise people to reexamine their current work situations. Is it the job that needs to change or the person in it?

> *Some people feel they're in dead-end jobs. Even the most routine or seemingly dull job, however, can usually be made more interesting. If you're feeling stuck in a job right now, figure out ways to use the time as wisely as possible for your own growth and sanity as well as those of everyone around you. You never know, that dead-end job might just blossom into something special.*

Sherry Jean has given herself permission to let her spirit fly and has found freedom within the confines of a restaurant. She can be an inspiration for people who feel inhibited by their workaday roles. If Sherry Jean can make waitressing into performance art, what can you do with your job?

People like Sherry Jean show us that the ideal venue is wherever you make it. She's a sage wearing an apron and an attitude. Feeling uncreative? Hints from Sherry: Wear costumes instead of clothing, come up with nicknames for everything in your environment, give whoever's in front of you your full attention, expect respect from others for just being who you are, and start collecting something original—maybe people will help you.

Motifs

Sherry's aprons are an inspiring reminder that we can define ourselves through objects. Anything can be decoration, as long as it's intentional. Years ago in a little cabin where I lived, I hung an antique cast iron pan on the wall, then a few weeks later I added another, and later another. A friend observed, "When you just had one, it looked flaky; when you got two it looked like a pattern; but with three, I'd say you have a motif."

When you display something of your own for people to look at, that's a form of creativity in itself. The benefits are twofold. You get to say to the world, "This is me," and people get to know a little more about you, perhaps your whimsical side, by understanding what you like. I know a minister who collects frog statues, a teacher who collects old lunch boxes, a learning specialist who likes purple shells, and a scientist who likes green Depression glass. My sister collects antique martini glasses, while Deborah collects science fiction books. Every time I see those objects, no matter where, I think of those people. Like Sherry's aprons, their collections give people a way of seeing and thinking about them—and giving something back. I know a lot of children who have collections. Perhaps their collections are a way to define themselves in the world.

Asserting Yourself

As many women in this book have demonstrated, fear is one of the biggest threats to creativity. Sherry's story gives us an invitation to pause and think. If we're in jobs that feel stifling, what specifically is causing that feeling and what can be changed? One thing Sherry demonstrates is that status has nothing to do with job description. She doesn't buy into that. She has no intention of ever being treated poorly. Sherry Jean claims not to be the reflective type but knows that she has in her life a few essential ingredients for peace of mind.

Of course, she says, as she rummages through her apron pockets to make sure she got out all of her tips, "I could always use more money." But she knows she has more freedom than many of the people who walk in with thousand-dollar suits and cell phones. She defines how she is treated by her confidence and quick retorts. People in jobs with greater pay and social status often are less self-assured than Sherry. She's inspiration for throwing your shoulders back, whatever your job title, and saying, "I know who I am, I'm putting myself out there, and I'm not taking any bullshit. I'm proud to be me."

Making a little artistic splash during an otherwise dull moment in some obligatory arena in your life is intrinsically delightful; it also can strengthen your ability to bring yourself into other tasks you may define as more expressive. Taking every chance to express an inward vision—even if it's just using a strange twist of a phrase, sharing a story from your childhood, or making an odd little arrangement of rocks on your desk—is good exercise for building self-assurance and testing the waters. Chances are, others will respond with delight. Most people suffer a bit of boredom in their routine interactions. While you might not be able to push it as far as Sherry Jean does, a few experimental steps out of your ordinary behavior might help you find your own edge.

Onward: Content in the Moment

"When I go home, my brain's clean, and I can focus on my normal life," Sherry says. Ironically, being a small celebrity as Oakland's waitress extraordinaire has brought her status—not that it means much to her. She has what she really wants. "I have a happy life, as a matter of fact."

There's only one Sherry Jean, but other restaurants have tried to get at least a representation of her in their establishment. One apron, maybe? But she turns down offers to display her collection elsewhere. Too much fuss and organization. Is she masking some other artistic drive? She rolls her eyes. "Oh puh-lease," she delivers in her near deadpan falsetto. "I'm busy enough."

3

Unraveling Life's Mysteries: Spinning Your Truths into Tales

My favorite definition of creativity is "the willingness to embrace ambiguity."

—Sarah Andrews, mystery
novelist and geologist

Meet Sarah at Her Country Retreat

Sarah Andrews walks along a pebbled path beneath a canopy of trees. The walkway leads to the door of a wooden building almost hidden in the foliage. This is her writing studio, her getaway. It's right in her backyard, but when she enters, it's to a different zone, worlds away from family, friends, and phones. By the computer sits a picture of the Hindu god Kali Durga, sketches by herself and her son decorate the wall, unusual rocks wait to be touched, and a sewing machine appears poised for action—perhaps used during a break from the keyboard. Everything in here has special meaning—especially, framed on the wall, the covers of her four published books.

Sarah is a successful mystery writer. Five-feet-ten-inches tall and willing to speak her mind, she is—as the men were fond of saying back when she worked full time as a geologist in the oil fields—a formidable woman. At the same time, she has a gentle presence, offering an easy smile and comfortable access to her world. Fiction is the way she unravels her own mysteries, the perplexing personal and troublesome professional encounters she's had over the years.

Through the antics and experiences of her fictional sleuth, Emily "Em" Hansen, Sarah gives readers an entertaining ride through labyrinthine mysteries, but her novels also are her self-described "bully pulpit" for passing on her perspective on human nature, opinions about what's right, and a few insider tricks on how a guileless young woman can take on the bad guys and win.

She enjoys a rhythmic life. On Monday and Wednesday mornings, she takes her cup of tea to her writing studio where she spends the morning. On Tuesday and Thursday mornings, she teaches geology at a nearby university. Afternoons and evenings are reserved for her preschooler son, Duncan. Every Friday she spends a full day with her son and his friend, part of a kid swap with another mom who helps her with childcare. She has a predictable, normal routine—with room for an unpredictable and wild imagination.

Her life appears idyllic today, but Sarah has paid dearly for her wisdom and serenity. Not that long ago, she felt like an alien in her own life. She was the lone female geologist at her job site, a woman who happened to be a spatial thinker with rebel tendencies, trying to make her way in the conservatism of male-dominated oil fields. She learned to assert herself, loudly at times. But what saved her was quietly digging into her own creative source for guidance.

Back then, while developing the bravado necessary to do her job, she confined her observations, insecurities, and questions to notebooks and the backs of napkins, where she scrawled out impressions and feelings she didn't dare share. "I'd see something that would grab me, I'd jot it down, little vignettes." Those notes saved her sanity while she was struggling to make her way in the oil business, and later they became the ingredients for novels. She transformed her real life struggles into literature. Her plots and characters are pure fiction, but descriptions of the nuances of human relationships and corporate shenanigans could only come from someone who has been there.

Sarah Andrews has preppie credentials, degrees in geology, years of experience slogging through muddy oil fields, and an equal number of years drifting in literary circles. She is scientific but comes with an artistic background. She is dyslexic, yet she writes bestselling novels. Her background, education, and experience call up so many disparate images, she's impossible to typecast—a complex study in ambiguity. For her, creativity has been a way to integrate the cognitive and emotional dissonance of her life.

Learning to Blend the Dissonant

For many women, creativity is a route toward wholeness, bringing together seemingly disparate aspects of their lives through an endeavor that expresses with integrity who they are. They've chosen—or feel they've been chosen by—some activity that allows them to blend different aspects of themselves. The goal is something beyond money or a sense of competence. For Sarah, writing certainly was not the most financially rewarding career. And she'd scored enough points in her work as a geologist to have the hard-won respect from her professional peers and a future if she wanted it there. It wasn't glory she was seeking through her writing. She wanted the satisfaction that comes only from doing something that allows for full self-expression.

Many people use the term "healing" for what their creativity provides. Sarah likes the term "integrating." For her that means stitching together her strength and vulnerability, her scientific and artistic qualities, and the feminine and masculine influences in her life. She could just as easily have chosen another discipline. She was labeled as an artist as a child, and she worked as a scientist as an adult. Success in those arenas didn't keep her from feeling confined. "When you have talent, in whatever area that is, people like to pigeonhole you, and you don't feel fully perceived by others." For

Sarah, writing was the venue that could express more of herself, expose more of herself to be wholly perceived.

From Sarah, we learn about the power of the pen to lead the writer to greater understanding of her life experiences. That Sarah's work became a commercial success was not just a fluke, but an application of the lessons she's learned about self-discipline, confidence, perseverance, and networking. The commercial success was a by-product of the personal breakthroughs that came from the writing process itself. Through the writing, she sorted through the barrage of perplexing events that happened in the oil fields and worked through a terrifying personal experience. At the same time, she gained perspective on the multitude of influences that shaped her own emotional and intellectual being. "I think the experiences I've had were not so much formative as educational. I've always known who I am—my experiences allowed me to know myself better."

Everyone is a complex collection of qualities and desires. It's a rare gift to be "fully perceived" by others. And, of course, the prerequisite is to see oneself. Sarah used her writing to explore herself and her world. Now she is a role model for other women, encouraging them to see and share the hidden parts of the self. She also used writing as self-protection. Feeling that others would not or could not understand her, she had to depend on herself in an alienating work environment. She found a tool that can be valuable to anyone who finds herself in a workplace or life situation where other people don't seem to be "getting it." Writing is a way of communing with the self when the outside is inhospitable.

That Sarah has succeeded in so many areas comes as a relief to people who, like her, have a "different" way of learning and seeing. Being dyslexic, she does her problem solving with intuitive three-dimensional visualization before going through the concrete step-by-step process of scientific deduction. Instead of being discouraged by her differences, she honored her own way of perceiving the world. She expected others to do the same. To others, it may have appeared that her attention was elsewhere. In reality, she was tracing the threads of how one idea led to another, following her mind to see where it went when it wandered. She has found a language to describe her process and now invites others to understand her—instead of her always having to adapt to them.

Her story is one of growing confidence. She found herself in the middle of conflicts—even having to arm herself at one point—but she stayed strong and looked for meaning. She looked, listened, took notes, wrote stories, and used the pen as a mechanism for growth. Through Sarah's story, we see that the creative spirit can fly free even in the most stifling moments in the workaday world. As she developed creative distance, she found herself increasingly amused and enlightened by the goings-on around her. Entertained even.

At some point, she realized that her experiences might be entertaining to others, as well:

> I have a very active observer inside. I was a born observer, and I've trained myself on top of that. Even when I am completely engaged in the activities of the moment, my observer is there, recording it all. And she has a great appreciation for irony. When I ask her what she knows, she tells me. The ability to remain detached while engaged is a basic tool for maintaining my sanity under stress.

Even when things turned ugly and her own life was in danger, she was observing her experiences so they could be used later. She started jotting down bits and pieces of her life experience in notebooks in her office, gathering material that led her to remember events from the past. It was all this material, unorganized at first, that took shape when she was ready and found the courage and strength to use her voice.

Sarah's Path

Expectations

Sarah Andrews was born with the academic equivalent of a silver spoon. From birth, there was no doubt she'd go to college. Four generations of women in her family had graduated from college before her. Her great aunt, Constance Warren, who lived up the road, was the woman who built Sarah Lawrence College into a prestigious four-year college. Her mother was an English teacher; her father was an art teacher. Her maternal grandmother directed the Child Studies Department at Vassar; her maternal grandfather taught Chaucer at Bryn Mawr. She and her siblings went to prep schools in suburban New York. Her sister was a straight-A student. Sarah got solid B's.

Sarah absorbed her parent's love of books: "Mother taught us about classical literature but also left paperback mysteries lying around for us." Sarah, though, seemed to show the most promise with painting, sculpting, and other arts. She seemed destined to follow her father when it came to vocations: "I was earmarked for doing the visually artistic thing. I was perceived as the 'creative' one. My sister and brother were 'also rans' in that area, 'only' above average. My father was an artist and an intuitive, and I was like him."

Her father also used his artistic talents in pragmatic ways, building sailboats and even writing about sea craft and model railroading for professional magazines. From her father, Sarah learned about the natural world through pictures and games. She visited his art class on a day when he was teaching physics by having the students send handmade sailboats down a creek. From her father, in ways such as this, Sarah learned to observe things directly to understand principles. From the influence of his Quaker background she came to believe, "that in simplicity, is genius—that simplicity and clarity are hallmarks of intelligence."

Like many visual learners, Sarah "got" information in a different way than other kids. Her parents took her to learning specialists, but at the time dyslexia was recognized only when it manifested in obvious ways like letter switching. There was no recognition of the problems that occur for some who have difficulty drawing meaning and images from printed words. She could catch storylines and make pictures of the novels her mother left around the house, but struggled with nonfiction and technical writing. "The specialists said I was just lazy. That was very frustrating." But art—where everything was color and texture and form—came easily to her. So when it came time to apply to colleges, naturally her portfolio went to schools with strong art programs. She was accepted at Boston Museum School and Cornell University Art School.

Great Aunt Constance balked at Sarah's choice. "My dear," Sarah remembers her saying, "aren't you afraid you'll get through all this artistic training and not have anything to express?" It was perplexing to Sarah that her aunt would take such an interest in her. Though she didn't have a 4.0 grade average, she had aced her SAT's. Looking back, she understands, "I can take tests, I'm good at short bursts of focusing." But before that, she hadn't shown herself to be anywhere near the Phi Beta Kappa level of women like her mother and sister. She felt that she just didn't fit into the academic model. She was becoming an open rebel, rejecting many of the values of her upbringing. She did things her own way.

But her aunt showed a keen interest in Sarah. She made a convincing case for a liberal arts education and wanted to sponsor Sarah's education, so Sarah agreed to go to a regular college and take academic course work. But she couldn't bring herself to compete with all her preppie high school friends who excelled inside the box that made Sarah feel inadequate. She didn't want to stay on the East Coast: "I needed intellectual and emotional privacy from my family. I needed to find out who I was separate from them." So she chose a college far away, in Colorado Springs.

Colorado College: an adventurous place out west, a whole new group of people, hardly a chance of having to do the social thing with the preppies. Or so she thought. "When I walked into freshman orientation, I immediately recognized the clothing, the types . . . pretty soon

I started recognizing faces. I found out that Colorado College had been dubbed 'Yale of the West' because of all the East Coast preppies who had fled there because they hadn't made the Ivy League."

Learning Through Pictures

Fortunately, Sarah had enough self-awareness about her unique learning style that she adapted to the academic scene, carefully selecting only those courses in which she knew she could do well. She did it her way—pass/fail grades only and no declared major. She took a geology course just to satisfy her science requirement.

She remembers her thrill at opening up the geology texts, enlivened by pictures of rocks and earth formations:

> It was wonderful. It was like being able to read the pictures.
> It must be like a florist walking down a forest path and seeing
> orchids in the wild for the first time. The information was
> right there in a form that I could take it in at high speed.

She aced advanced courses in geology—still without declaring a major. The department chair asked her, "Why haven't you declared this as your major?" "Because I'm not in this department, I don't have a major," she said with a laugh. "I have a counselor in another department who will sign anything I give him."

It was a gutsy response. He laughed, and a connection was made. It turned out she declared her major upon the eve of graduation, just so that she could put some discipline on her diploma. For Sarah a lesson was learned: Be honest. Be real. Put who you are out there. Have fun. It will work out.

She worked for four years at the U.S. Geological Survey, long enough to get some good experience and to discover that the money was in the private sector. She returned to graduate school in geology and earned a Masters of Science at a time when women workers were sought after in the sciences. From there she moved into the corporate world of oil, where geological research meant nothing if it didn't produce. It was shortly after the OPEC crisis, when fossil fuel imports had dried up. Oil companies were hot for domestic production, and the oil boom created overnight boom-or-bust economies for towns in the West.

Now she was a geologist facing the ordinary challenges in her line of work: understanding geological structures, making decisions about where to drill, and overseeing the drilling process. She transcended the ordinary—not entirely by choice—because of who she was. She didn't process information or behave the way others did in an arena populated mostly by men, most of whom were linear thinkers. Twenty-something Sarah found herself in barren deserts, in the company of high-rolling corporate dealers, hungry local workers, and a migratory group of roustabouts, mudloggers, and toolpushers. She was the geologist, she knew how to find oil and where. But she didn't always have a way to explain why, and she had to deal with the type of people who didn't want to trust her intuition:

> *I could see what was underground. The way I calculated . . .*
> *people thought it was spooky, a gestalt . . . it's a thing that*
> *women can sometimes do better than men. Men are pretty*
> *good at tracing a logical pattern. Women have a different*
> *awareness. Information is coming in from the side and back,*
> *and sometimes what's in front is incidental. Men couldn't*
> *understand . . . they probably thought I was a witch.*

She remembers one time when she was invited to corporate research headquarters to discuss a sandstone formation—a specialty area of hers. She explained how to interpret the formation in order to develop a drilling plan. She was talking to two men with Ph.D.'s who had struggled for weeks to understand this particular problem, but who couldn't make any sense of the data. They asked her, "How do you know?" She sighed. She knew because she could see it, but it wasn't possible to explain her vision in language they would understand. "The rock speaks English," she finally told them. It turned out her interpretation was right, and she slowly gained the others' trust, but she didn't fit in with her co-workers.

Harassment on the Job

There was an obvious power structure in her profession, and although her mentor, Edwin D. McKee, clued her in on how the game was played, Sarah was often sidelined. Some of the men were hostile—she wasn't one of the guys, but she also wasn't someone they could treat like one of the "office girls." So they often simply left her out of the loop. "The worst of it was when I was working for an independent oil company based in Denver. I couldn't work out of the field office because the guys didn't want me around."

Sarah began to realize that she was internalizing her male co-workers' view of her—not quite a man, but not quite a woman either. Their view of her as some obscure third gender hit home one day when she brought in some soda bread to share in the office. Clerks and the other professionals' wives would bring in baked goods, so Sarah decided to contribute. "At first, no one could believe I made the soda bread. They assumed I couldn't bake. They didn't see me as a whole woman. It was painful."

She had enough savvy, though, that her expertise was needed. The pay was good. She didn't know what else she'd do if she quit. She observed the power game being played and the gratuitous efforts at control and humiliation. The men sometimes exercised machismo with each other, through insults and put-downs. But it took a different form with her: overt sexual harassment, though it wasn't called that because she was an ostensible equal in the game.

> One guy was just plain ill. He was my superior and insisted
> I go to this dinner. I'd been swimming, and I arrived with
> my hair wet. He was furious because I hadn't fussed over my
> appearance. It turns out he wanted me there in the role of his
> girlfriend. Our hosts were salesmen who desperately wanted to
> sell something to the company, so this guy knew he could say
> whatever he wanted. He started telling these awful jokes . . .
> real stomach turners, not funny, not civilized.

Instead of playing along, she called for the tab, got up, put her jacket on, and left. The other people at the table, men and their wives, immediately followed. When the man from Sarah's company caught up to them, he propositioned Sarah in front of the rest of them. "I just laughed and walked away."

She knew she'd pay a price for standing up to him. "Sure enough, he set me up." While on the drilling rigs, her job was seven days a week, but sometimes the drilling schedule left her idle. Sarah got permission, from the man she'd stood up to, to go visit friends. She got a call from the main office. He'd reported her AWOL and blamed her for problems at the drilling site. Sarah didn't have much support from her co-workers. She kept her job, but got a black mark on her record.

Extreme Stress

While she was struggling with relationships at work, she was seeing some patterns of deception in the oil fields—evidence of trade secrets being given away, kickbacks being taken, people skimming off some of the company's profit and putting it into their own pockets. She tried to talk to her boss about both the sexual harassment and the hints of white-collar crime, but he dismissed her concerns as "sour grapes" because she'd had difficulty fitting into the corporate mold. Out of frustration, she began writing down her experiences in detail. At first, it was simply observations, a record of what was real, to help her sort through the stressful events she was experiencing.

> Writing was a way to work through who people thought
> I was and who I really was. A way to express how scared

and incompetent I felt. I absolutely felt like an impostor.
People were telling me, "You're not a guy, but you're not
a real girl either."

Most of her life centered on her job, but problems had surfaced
in her personal life, too. Men she dated in her own socioeconomic
group generally saw her as competition. But when she dated blue-
collar men, friends and family would criticize her for going out with
"losers."

She was losing her sense of self and couldn't figure out why she
was feeling weak and worn down. One day when she was driving
home from work she felt overwhelmed by her life. She pulled over,
called her parents, and said, "I'm coming apart." She remembers her
mom's response:

"You sound fine," she said. She assigned me the role of the
tough one, someone who could take any amount of abuse,
which was not true. I was in trouble, but they wanted to
believe that I was stable, together, tough. That's when I
reached an impasse with my family. Their perceptions of me
were not accurate, and they apparently didn't want to know
who I really was.

It was at this vulnerable time in her life that she met a troubled
man, dated him for a few weeks, and then ended up being stalked by
him. "It was terrifying. He followed me for nearly ten months. There
would be his car. There would be his footprint in the snow. It was
making me crazy." She couldn't get help from the police, as it was
before stalking was a phenomenon recognized as the crime it is
today. On the advice of a friend, she bought a gun and learned how
to use it, even though carrying, much less using, a concealed weapon
was anathema to her Quaker upbringing. But she felt she had no
choice: "I felt like a point man on jungle patrol with no one behind
me."

The stresses at work continued. "It was a fabulous job in many
ways—good pay, company car. I liked and respected the owner of the
company, and he liked and respected me. But, along with the stalking, it was making me sick. I took some time off to rest, but it wasn't
enough."

She began dating a fellow geologist who was so wonderful she
could hardly believe her own perceptions. "I kissed a lot of frogs
before I met Damon," she said. She was independent and not prone
to opening up to others, but Sarah finally confided to Damon about
the stalker. She appreciated his response, which was concerned but
not controlling. "He didn't play 'I'll save you ma'am,'" but after the
problems continued he offered a solution. Why not move to

California with him, at least temporarily? "I had to give up life as I knew it. But it was the right moment. I realized I had to accept help."

She arranged a leave of absence from work and didn't even dare tell her family where she'd gone. The move turned out to be freeing in more ways than just being free of a stalker. Her life became a tabula rasa; she had a clean slate for starting fresh with a new way of life, a new way of thinking. She began studying philosophy and religion and started seeing the world differently. "My rational mind tried me for treason!" she says with a laugh.

Writing became a serious tool of self-discovery in this new environment. "Writing is a way of going deeper. It involves travel to the nether world." She had so much from her past to sort through. The stalking. The sexist workplace. The corporate dramas. Family relationships and expectations. "I figured I needed 100,000 words to lay it all out." She started out writing nonfiction, but decided instead to recast her experiences in fiction. The mystery format worked, in part because of her own past traumas: "Almost every female mystery novelist I've known well has been through some major stuff."

Healing

The process of writing brought her back to herself. She was in love with the man who had helped her escape her old life, and she married him a few months later. And her timing for the move proved good. As her original leave of absence was about to expire, the bottom fell out of the domestic oil industry and she, along with many other employees of her company, were given their walking papers along with a healthy severance package. With six months pay and all that she'd saved over years of working with no time to spend her money, she had enough of a nest egg to take three-and-a-half years to regain her health, polish her novel, learn the publishing trade, and get her first 100,000 words out there for the world to read.

Sarah's protagonist, Em, and secondary character, Alix—very different characters, each encompassing some of Sarah's qualities— "appeared out of nowhere." They took on lives of their own. The people she'd met, the corporate machinations she'd watched, and the texture of life in the oil fields all morphed and took different shapes and unfolded into her first mystery novel, *Tensleep,* named after a sandstone formation.

Sarah set her thoughts free through the writing so she could sort through them to see what had really been happening to her over the years. "To me, truth is a matter of becoming cleansed of untruth." She realized how in the past she had to compromise her truth to make it in the man's world. Creativity was one way for her to reclaim some of the "feminine" she'd denied. For many years, Sarah had to hide aspects of herself that might have signaled weakness in the rough-and-ready oil fields, including the desire for acceptance and any feelings of confusion. Being "feminine" was an open invitation for trouble from men with a lascivious nature or colleagues whose mode of operation involved one-upmanship. Admitting that her scientific methods incorporated a "spooky" visual thinking process allowed others to try to dismiss her.

But through writing, she could express all of herself, without fear of reprisal. Using writing, she began to understand the mysteries of her own methods of perception and how her mind worked. With more self-understanding, she developed a deeper kind of confidence than what came from the play-by-play sparring that looked like confidence in her former world of work. "It opened up other avenues of creativity in daily life beyond the writing itself." She was about to have some new learning experiences and plenty of opportunity to exercise her creativity in new ways. Six years after the move to California, when she was forty-two, her son Duncan was born.

Sarah's Life These Days

Because of the benefits she has experienced from writing in her own life, Sarah's writing is a pleasure to her, not a struggle. "It's freeing to see life experiences as fuel for creativity." The flip side, she says, is equally freeing: "You can use creativity as a filter for perceiving the events of your life." She is tolerant of her own process, honoring the brainstorming as well as the actual production of words on paper. "Writing is not just sitting at the desk. It's when you're out pulling weeds in the garden. It's the time when you're talking about the work. It's driving from here to there and thinking about nothing else."

Sarah counts every moment when she's thinking about her novels as writing time, but she distinguishes between the thinking time and the actual process of stringing together words at the computer. The computer time is sacrosanct, and claiming it involves a regular act of intentional will that many women do not allow themselves. "Creativity is a feminist issue," Sarah says. "You have to have time and usually space to engage your creative self. Many women do not think they can have that in their life. They don't demand it."

These days, Sarah feels comfortable with her own idiosyncratic ways of working. It's natural for her to be thinking of sixteen things at once, including the plot of her novel, what the kids are saying in the back seat of the car, and what kind of plant she wants to put next in the garden. It's equally natural for her to walk to her studio, sit down at the computer, clear her mind of everything, and bring 100 percent concentration to her writing.

In the quest to understand her own creative process over the years, Sarah has felt an affinity with the ideas of psychologist Carl Jung. Jung described two archetypes for functional aspects of personality: "feminine," which Sarah experiences as a world of diffuse awareness and inspiration, and "masculine," which is the land of tight focus and product orientation. Most people respond to both influences to one degree or another, and Sarah works consciously to integrate the two in her creative work.

> As I worked in the male-dominated field of geology, pretty much saturated in male values and work styles, I was able to tightly develop that so-called masculine aspect of myself, but felt unbalanced because I spent too little time in the "feminine." Now I claim the best of both worlds, humbling myself to receive inspiration as I focus on my work.

She takes her son to preschool, goes into her studio where there's no phone or E-mail, nods to the picture of the Hindu god Kali Durga (slayer of the demons), and then sits down to write. "It is such a time apart. It doesn't integrate with anything else in your day." These days, she exults in the flow of words, especially those "aha" moments when diffuse thoughts come together perfectly. "Sometimes," she confides with a laugh, "the creative moment can be almost sexual in nature. There is pleasure and release in achieving that creative high, that flow, that merging with the collective unconscious." At the same time that she delights in the perfect sentence, she allows herself half-formed thoughts. She'll leave something that isn't quite right, making a note in the computer to "go back and fix it," and then she moves on.

It has taken her a decade to learn the rituals that make the work smooth, and it has taken her whole life for her to learn enough about herself to know what to say. "For a long time I didn't know what I thought, I was so busy filling all those roles. I like the line from writer Sara Paretsky, who said, 'It took me a long time to find my voice and even longer to find the courage to use it.'"

Conversations and Reflections: Finding Yourself Through Creativity

Happy Endings

Sarah came into this book through her novels. I met her fictional characters Em and Alix before I met Sarah. I felt an affinity for Em, with her self-effacing ways, and a curiosity about Alix's bravado, and

I wanted to meet the person who could create characters that were so strong and appealing in different ways. Sure enough, there was a story behind the story, a real-life mystery, intriguing in itself, about synchronizing different parts of the self. Sarah's story is one with a happy ending, but as with her novels, there was a certain meandering to get there. In conversations with Sarah, my co-author Deborah and I found ourselves exulting over all the different ways Sarah seems to be living her "happily ever after." She's found a creative tool that sets her spirit free. At the computer, she can let out parts of herself she wouldn't find otherwise. As her creative self developed, so did her love relationship. And all the while, she was conjuring up tales where justice is done.

In a world that serves up plenty that's unfair and perplexing, you've got to love a good story where all the confusion gets unraveled, the villains come to justice, and the heroines are vindicated. Sarah's stories are like that, but more to the point, so is her life. Through her writing, she has unraveled mysteries about her self and the male-dominated work environment where she spent many years.

Writing as a route toward wholeness, of course, is what is behind journal writing, an activity that has liberated the muse for many women. It's something anyone can do to urge thoughts out of their core self, changing abstract images and ideas into something literal that can be examined. In her book *Writing Down the Bones*, Natalie Goldberg talks about how she believes the physical act of writing itself creates power:

> *You are physically engaged with the pen, and your hand, connected to your arm, is pouring out the record of your senses. There is no separation between the mind and body; therefore, you can break through the mind barriers to writing through the physical act of writing, just as you can believe with your mind that your hand won't stop at the wood, so you can break a board in karate.*

For Sarah, writing provides a different kind of access to the self. Talking with her helped me realize how the outcome of writing can be so much different from that of talking. I almost think the brain neurons fire differently to make words come out the fingers instead of out the mouth. I used to freeze when editors would ask me, "Tell me a summary of your story for the budget, one paragraph." I could write it, but I could not say it. Sometimes I think ideas go straight in my ear and out my fingers.

A lot of writers talk about the feeling that they are "channeling" their characters from somewhere outside their conscious mind. I certainly felt that with the short story I wrote about in the introduction.

Sarah has found that she can tap into deeper parts of herself through writing. It's still a mystery as to why, but she likes mysteries.

There are, of course, as many different reasons for writing as there are writers. You may write for the sheer joy of word play, because your heart wants to sing, or as a general purge. There's even a psychology discipline called "bibliotherapy," which relies on the particular type of self-analysis that comes up through writing. At the same time, writing also can serve as what Sarah likes to call a "bully pulpit," a public forum for exercising your ethics and opinions, and the mystery genre has a long tradition for doing so.

Sarah says her work functions as did the medieval mystery plays that her mother told her about when she was young. Rather than seeking closure, like romances, the classic mystery play is what Sarah calls a "hero script where the main character walks through fire, vanquishes the enemy, and gains wisdom in the process." That's why the same hero can appear again and again in a series of books. It's not that long ago that the heroes in such stories mostly were men, but these days female detectives like Sarah's Em are passing on their wisdom.

Most of us at one point or another in our lives slam up against unfair situations and people who take unfair advantage, leaving us feeling powerless. In my testy moments, I like to remember the phrase "Living well is the best revenge." Sarah had to bite her tongue and put up with harassment, but today she has a life that's rich in love, friendship, and freedom. She achieved that through her creativity—transforming the bad stuff she encountered in her life into good material for her stories, the making-lemonade-out-of-lemons approach. Another mystery writer, Sue Grafton, likes to tell about how she started writing because it was a way to kill people legally. Fiction is a great way to act out. For Sarah, it was also a way to discover herself as she figured out how to make wrong situations right.

In a Man's World

Deborah, like Sarah, is a woman operating in a man's profession. For her, being an architect has also meant fighting for a woman's way of doing things.

Women architects often have a way of seeing and doing things differently from the men. I have observed, for example, that men tend to design a building from the outside inward, often conceiving of the building as a sculpture first. Women, on the other hand, usually look at the relationships among people, activities, and the site and design the building from the inside outward. It is a matter of perception—and you have to trust your own.

Deborah's solution to discrimination in the workplace was to start her own architecture firm. "If you don't get the good projects in someone else's firm, take the risk and go it on your own—do it your way. That way the only people you have to be accountable to are your clients, the building department folks, and yourself."

The Jungian typology that has helped Sarah understand the different ways she works can provide a frame for "seeing" the creative mechanism. Women who are most comfortable in the "diffuse" consciousness—or "multitasking," as it's called in corporate circles—may need to have a ritual (like Sarah's bow to Kali Durga) when it's time to hunker down to a focused task. At the same time, honoring the Jungian "feminine" at work sometimes means proudly saying to colleagues, "I need time to process right now—that's why I'm taking a walk. And it *is* working."

When she finally had her own architectural business, Deborah was relieved to feel free to dawdle and doodle openly while thinking something through, instead of having to "look like I'm working." Of course, Jungian types don't necessarily correspond to male/female. Sarah, for example, feels that she was influenced by the "feminine" artistic nature of her father. Just as many women naturally love the tight-focus work that Jung considered "masculine," many men are holistic thinkers. But, unquestionably, the American corporate world—regardless of which genders happen to be working in the office—runs on the masculine model in the Jungian sense. Knowing that can help women understand why they may feel alien at times.

Alone = All One

Often what you write is less important than the mere act of writing. To write is to claim your "time apart," as Sarah puts it. Time apart from the pressures and influences of the often relentless demands made on us. Writing is also a great escape. Later in this book you will see how Donna escapes into the earthy solitude of her garden and how Linda became absorbed in oil colors on a quiet hillside. For Sarah, the magic came from stolen moments in her office with pen and paper. Back before she became a "writer," the time she spent taking notes was a way to disconnect from surrounding influences and reconnect with the self.

In writing, the words themselves can be empowering, helping us to "explain" to ourselves and others what we may otherwise perceive in a symbolic way. It's an imposed order, a discipline that employs a rational technique for sorting out symbols. In her book, *Awakening Minerva,* Linda Firestone writes:

Giving voice to your thoughts and moving your ideas into the universe makes you master over your thoughts. That act makes your thoughts real. The ideas that are positive gain strength through this kind of acknowledgment. Giving voice to your thoughts can alert you to negative impulses and minimize their disruptive powers. The manner in which you give voice to your thoughts and feelings is a manifestation of your personal style.

Sarah demonstrates the universal experience of using a creative tool—writing in her case—as a means to understand her self and circumstances better. Writing works as a sort of therapy for Sarah, a way to extract her thoughts and observations—especially those troublesome or dissonant ones—and lay them out for viewing: "I strive to find that balance point where I can convey my perceptions accurately, so they (and I) can be clearly perceived by others. I write to express myself, to tell my truth, to be perceived."

Onward: The Successful Rebel

In addition to her novels, Sarah also is working on a memoir about her family and her childhood memories. The writing keeps alive the memories of her father, who died shortly before her fourth novel was published. She's also coming to terms with herself as the wayward daughter, who left the family nest and made her own way in the Wild West. Studying comparative religion has given her some powerful symbols for understanding her shifting belief system. Enlightenment, going beyond old patterns of thinking, "means constantly being willing to give up the old map." She has a lot left to figure out.

I can be arrogant, but my work these days is a more humble faith-based activity. One empowers oneself with faith. It's a slow integration of things that don't seem to go together. I hope to move into my later years as someone who can be helpful to those who come after me.

These days, Sarah looks back at her Aunt Constance and sees her in a different light. Sarah thought her the epitome of conservatism, a college administrator entrenched in the establishment. But recently she met someone who knew her aunt, who told Sarah that her aunt was on the cutting edge of education, doing all kinds of experiments. Among other things, she hired Joseph Campbell to teach at her college, bringing his revolutionary thoughts about culture and mythology into the curriculum. Sarah began to see why her aunt had supported her through college, pushing her out into the world instead of wanting her to be a reclusive artist. She'd wanted young Sarah to experience the world, get out there and find something real to feed her art. Something that might change other people's thinking. The wisdom of that guidance become clear in a recent discussion with a mutual acquaintance, twenty-five years after her aunt's death. Sarah shakes her head and laughs softly, "It turns out my aunt was a rebel, and that's what she saw in me."

Ironically, the creative process Sarah found to integrate her own life not only has entertained a growing readership, but also received accolades from members of the profession in which she once struggled to "be seen" for who she was. She won the Rocky Mountain Association of Geologists Journalists Award in 1997. She says:

I have a hard time accepting the apparent futility of expecting to be fully perceived. But I have had some validation for my own perception and observational powers. Instead of "competition," my geology colleagues now have categorized me as "she who writes about the rest of us," and they regard me with some affection and perhaps nostalgia—even some of the men who ignored me before. You see, they wanted to be perceived correctly, too.

4

Rediscovering Old Recipes: Nourishing Body and Soul

Baking has always sustained me. I love being in the kitchen, especially if I feel a little upset.

—Birgitta Schofield, baker and
business owner

Meet Birgitta in the Bakery

It is well past the hurried commuter "bun and coffee to go" hour. But all of the smooth, oil-finished teak tables in the Village Bakery are occupied. Someone idles up to the counter for a look and exclaims with obvious delight at a new discovery. "Pear and ginger muffins. Oh!" It is a common reaction to the unique combinations of ingredients used to make the baked goods. Owner Birgitta Schofield smiles when she sees the looks of delight and surprise on her customers' faces.

She has the requisite blueberry muffins—always baked with fresh berries. But Birgitta also routinely conjures up the unexpected. Bread with kalamata olives. Carrot and sunflower seed muffins, pastries with pear and anise, or her singular cardamom buns, which she baked for her own kids when they were growing up.

She has a knack for putting together new taste combinations, which have won her honors. Instead of walnuts in her carrot muffins, she'll drop in pine nuts. Whenever she gets her hands on some wonderful, fresh produce, her mind goes to work, dreaming up ways to combine ingredients, often dressing up familiar treats with a whimsical new twist, like bear claws with figs. She is the person who, with an enterprising young partner, turned a dirty, rusty old doughnut shop into a quaint Northern European bakery that is deserving of its just-out-of-the oven wares.

Classical piano music plays gently in the background. The Village Bakery doesn't have the intense buzz of a coffeehouse, but the quiet comfort of a family kitchen. At each table is a small pot of delicately blooming white azaleas and a set of woven, straw place mats. The white walls are a gallery of rotating exhibits from local artists. Today we see arrangements of dried flower wreaths and sheaths of bunched lavender and wheat, mindful of a warm spring day even on a chill winter morning. Hanging from the ceiling are a series of nearly identical fabric paintings with simple lines and dabs of paint that evoke fields of wildflowers amid wheat. It is the kind of art that symbolizes this place, where simple ingredients like flour, water, butter, sugar, and eggs—through some alchemy of instinct, tradition, trial and error, and a little bit of creative genius—can be combined into an endless variety of amazing things to eat.

Like her bakery and her award-winning wares, Birgitta is elegantly simple, attractive but unadorned, except for handmade earrings fashioned out of the same copper with which she so loves to cook. She wears no makeup, but her cheeks are naturally pink. She frequently runs her hands through her short, graying blonde hair. She wears soft cotton slacks and flats, attractive yet practical for the hours she spends on her feet overseeing an operation that has grown from turning out a couple hundred loaves a night to producing close to one thousand.

In the middle of a drizzly afternoon it's cheerful inside the bakery, a nouveau cuisine reenactment of Birgitta's old-world childhood experience. Back then, during the long, dark northern winters in Sweden, when human spirits would plunge with the mercury, Birgitta's mother practiced kitchen therapy, treating the blues with something hot out of the oven.

The bakery started thirty years after Birgitta moved to the United States to embark on a new life as wife, mother, and entrepreneur. During those intervening years she gravitated—unaware of what was pulling her—into the realm of food and kitchen. She was at the vanguard of the gourmet food movement in California at a time when professional chefs and home cooks were beginning to shift away from the postwar fascination with anything packaged, processed, or frozen, and reclaiming the old tradition of working with fresh, seasonal produce.

It wasn't one emotional experience that brought Birgitta "home," back to the basics of baking bread. It was a series of events that felt like a calling to bring to others the nourishment and comfort she received back in that Swedish village of Nykoping, with its narrow lanes, charming brick cottages, centuries-old castles, and her mother's oven.

Reviving the Domestic Arts

With a sophisticated background in upscale cuisine, Birgitta is among those who have elevated the simple act of baking bread into a celebrated art form. These days there are prizes to be bestowed—and Birgitta's Village Bakery has received them—for culinary creations that are particularly delightful to the palate. Yet her innovative and surprising spice combinations are just modern-day accouterments for the basic and long-uncelebrated act of producing warm and hearty foods from scratch. Besides the basics of butter and flour and yeast, the main ingredient that Birgitta tasted in her youth was her mother's passion for baking, the pleasure that came from materializing love and care into something that could literally be absorbed by another person.

The most satisfying creative endeavors often are those that evoke the smells, sensations, and images of childhood. Many women come into their richest periods of creativity when a personal crisis leads them on a journey back in time, to find sources of strength and comfort for themselves and loved ones. The interwoven stories of Birgitta's personal and professional lives demonstrate how childhood passions can become powerful motivators for creativity later in life. Birgitta has turned her love of baking into a thriving business, but more important to her are the personal rewards. Baking ultimately was the way she could best comfort her family and express herself. She affirms the intuitive knowledge that brings so many women satisfaction in the kitchen: Being a giver or recipient of lovingly prepared food involves an exchange of more than something physical.

She took a circuitous route to arrive at her own "kitchen"—beginning as a child in her mother's cooking space and moving through the corporate world as a buyer and manager in retail housewares—before realizing she wanted to be kneading the dough herself. Birgitta has always found opportunities to bring some of herself and her history into her environment. Even in the retail business, she put forth a vision and got people to listen.

Birgitta has drawn personal power, as well as a strong identity, from her childhood. She brings into her bakery not just the recipes for good food but also the recipes for good working relationships. From her mother, a homemaker and later a professional baker, she learned about comfort and food; from her father, a typesetter and later a journalist and social activist, she learned about interpersonal politics and teamwork. Her story suggests the tantalizing notion that everyone has the ingredients for self-expression within reach, no further away than the kitchen.

Birgitta's Path

Warmth in the Cold

Birgitta remembers her mother's gentle admonition, a consoling voice from her girlhood, leavening her spirits at a time when she could not have felt more deflated. "If you're feeling blue, bake something." For her mother, inventing endless combinations of baked goods was not only a way of daily life, but also a form of therapy. Life had its limits in their small village, where winters were raw and it seemed there was never enough money. Sweden was vigilantly watching her borders, fearful of a Nazi invasion, when Birgitta was born in December 1941. Her father was away, detailed on border patrol.

They say it was so frigid that Christmas, the coldest winter of the century, that standing water in the flowerpots indoors froze. Nykoping, a nine-hundred-year-old medieval village, was charmingly picturesque under blue skies. But the long winters, when the sun went down in midafternoon and the only source of heat was from wood fires and the oven, took their toll. Birgitta's mother, like so many other mid-twentieth-century women with one foot still firmly planted in old-world ways, had figured out a way to knead the pain, roll out the frustrations, and then feel her spirits slowly rise as she brought forth something wondrous and delicious and perfect, all within a few hours. What other endeavor brings such immediate and satisfying results?

Birgitta recalls:

> I always remember her persona in the kitchen, with all kinds of doughs and cakes and cookies coming out. It was a very nurturing experience for me as a child. It has always stayed with me, coming home to a house always filled with baked goods. Later on my mother went into professional baking, but in the early part of my childhood she was a housewife and took care of me and my little sister. She would bake everything, from the heartiest breads to the finest puff pastries and elegant cakes. She was an absolute artist in the kitchen.

Viking Women

Birgitta comes from a long line of independent women with a tradition of excellence in the domestic arts.

> My grandmother was a weaver. She came from a poor family and had to make everything from scratch. That's what the women in my family did. They trained themselves by doing it over and over. My mother did take some classes and worked with some very good pastry chefs in Sweden later in her life. But she was really so far advanced by that time that I think they got more from her. She really knew her craft.

Birgitta remembers the big round table where she and her sister would gather after school. Their mother would always have something ready for them, even if it was an ordinary roll. In the morning, she'd have something emerging from the oven before the girls went to school and as soon as they walked in the door for the traditional, at-home lunch. She says women have always been strong in her native country: "It goes back to the time of the Vikings when the women were left to take care of the practical things. To take care of the farms and the kids and the food. It has really bred a very strong independent force of women." Economics also contributed to building a strong population of women. "Women have always had to work in Sweden, over many centuries of farm life. They had to put in long hours."

Birgitta never saw women as having a lesser status than men, but when she reached adulthood in the sixties she saw the options open even further, as women around her moved out of the home into the arenas of government and business.

> *Things started to become much more politicized, and women took political power. They insisted on equal treatment. That's when the Social Democrats became involved in family life, as far as giving women money to help them go to school, pay for kids in preschool, and set up a stipend for each child through age eighteen. I think 80 percent of Swedish women work. It was needed because the country was expanding very fast in manufacturing. The welfare state really supported children and also supported women going back to school and getting an education.*

Into the World of Work

Birgitta's pursuit of art and design began in earnest at age fifteen, when she first saw Picasso's famous painting "Guernica" on traveling exhibit in Stockholm. She was struck and inspired by the power and tragedy of the enormous canvas, a critical statement on the horrors of war.

> *I had a wonderful [high school] teacher in Swedish literature. He would always give me an assignment to write about some artist or something to do with art. So I started to write about art and to study it intensively. I went right to the art history department at the University of Stockholm.*

But economic realities intervened:

> *I ran out of money and had to start working. I got involved in an advertising agency. I took classes on the side, but the work became very fascinating to me, too. In retrospect, I probably would have enjoyed going into art, but in those days, money was hard to come by. It was impossible. I had to take a job. I was lucky. The owner of the advertising firm was a great man and he, too, was very creative. He kind of revolutionized advertising in Sweden. He was one of the first that started to advertise bras.*
>
> *He was very quirky and very different, and he gave*

me a lot of responsibility for a young girl. I ran three to four different accounts, with women's magazines that were the Swedish equivalent of McCalls *and* House Beautiful.
I was in my twenties. It was a lot of fun for a young girl, getting involved with a lot of magazine writers. I think it was a very freeing experience compared to sitting with my art history books.

An Alien Environment

Birgitta met her first husband, a scientist, and together they moved to the United States, where he went to work in the aerospace industry. She found herself in the desultory, culinary wasteland of 1960s America, a time when convenience was worshipped above all else. There were few farmers' markets for fresh produce, few fine cheeses with different textures and tastes. Bread usually came white and presliced in plastic bags. It was alien to her rural European upbringing.

After a depressing few years in Pasadena, they moved north to Santa Barbara, a mission town on the central coast. There Birgitta set to work, refurbishing an old industrial building her husband had taken over for a research lab, opening it up with bright colors and windows. This challenge of building something beautiful from nothing revived her spirits, and it would become an activity she would take up often in her life. "That's where the creative thing comes in, seeing what you can do from nothing," she says with obvious relish. "I've loved that, taking dirty little old places and turning them into fresh, life-giving places."

"My husband was brilliant," she says, "but troubled." The marriage fell apart and Birgitta found herself alone with a young son to support. She'd always had a keen aesthetic sense so she went back to school for a degree in interior design. She took a job in the design studio of a major department store, decorating everything from offices to homes. Her work was appreciated, but she found her Scandinavian taste for the clean and simple clashed with the heavy, ornate Mediterranean decor filling up America's living rooms. Unhappy, she switched to retail sales, lending her talents to what would develop into a chain of stores specializing in finely designed home products at affordable prices.

Boldness

It was a fortuitous time for her to be entering the home furnishings field. The simple lines of Scandinavian furniture and home accessories were coming into vogue. Birgitta's tastes suddenly were trendy, and she jumped in with her ideas. "The risk was letting my ambition come to the forefront. I didn't want to just have a job. I wanted to have a voice." She suggested ideas that were wildly innovative at the time. One was to decorate with fabric. The big simple flower patterns that she had seen on windows back in Scandinavia became hip for wall hangings. "I showed these big huge bold prints to my boss and he said, 'You can never sell them.' I said, 'I know I can.'" Eventually he agreed and she imported the bright, boldly designed Marimekko and Boukko textiles from Finland and Almetahl from Sweden and stretched them onto frames. Her success with selecting design elements for the store was the beginning of a career in which she would set her creativity free in the retail business.

At first, she'd decorate offices with fabric and artwork and then send pictures of the finished spaces to her bosses. Her work slowly persuaded her supervisors that her unique sense of style would work in the stores as well. "Little by little, they trusted that I could do it. They asked me to take it over and do all the departments in all of the stores," she says. She didn't get her way all the time, but she was confident, and if someone nixed her idea, she'd just try another angle, figuring the next one might work. "I'd say to myself, 'I'm not going to get my way. How can I make it work for me?'"

She was always innovating. One idea was to bring food experts into the kitchenwares section of the store to give demonstrations and classes to customers. "We had a lot of wonderful equipment in the stores. To sell some of that I thought, 'Why not do a whole class around it?'" That was back when Cuisinart was new. Birgitta became a pioneer of the now common practice of cooking in stores.

Altogether, her approach was successful. While showing what could be done with new kitchen gadgets, she also was getting in on the ground floor of a fledgling food trend incorporating fresh locally produced foods. It was New Age to California but Old World to Birgitta.

She occasionally had to stand up to doubters: "I discovered I could prove myself by showing that things worked." But there were occasional clashes: "I had lots of heated arguments. There were a couple of times I was sure I was going to be fired. I was pretty forceful in those days."

Materializing a Vision

Instead of trouble, she got promotions for asserting her new ideas. She worked in collaboration with a circle of other women managers who set up new stores for the company, brainstorming so that "our stores became known as creative places." Behind the scenes, in her role as manager, she negotiated better pay and medical benefits and a profit-sharing plan for her employees. Supporting women in the workplace has always been close to Birgitta's heart, especially back when "women almost had to excuse themselves if they wanted to go to work."

Birgitta met and eventually married her current husband, Paul, and had a daughter, becoming a working mom with two children. Searching out new items for the stores, Birgitta spent a lot of time in Europe. She enjoyed cooking occasionally, but certainly didn't have the time for long hours in the kitchen. "I can't tell you how many times my husband had to fix dinner for our kids when I traveled. I would go to work, and we had two little kids, and he was in charge of them." But even if she wasn't home making the dinner, she would make sure when she wasn't traveling that she was home to eat. Dinner was a sacred ritual. "We always sat down to dinner together. We ate together and that was a constant. It was a must. That was where we laughed together and cried together. My husband and I both love food, and the family always had a good meal."

At work, she continued her innovations in the food arena and gained a local reputation. Birgitta maintains that her keen aesthetic radar was merely picking up trends that were "in the air." But she was ahead of the curve and other retailers followed her lead. She eventually was recruited to oversee a high-end homewares store. But a change in ownership led to a decline in the work environment. Salaries were cut and employees were not being treated the way Birgitta, with her strong sense of social fairness, expected. Product quality was compromised at every corner. "The only thing [the new owner] looked at was the bottom line." She felt burned out, "bone tired," and ready to downshift.

Homesick

"We sold our home and went back to Sweden. We had quality time." By then her son, Oscar, was in college and one of her deep motivations was to give her teenage daughter, Laura, "a bit of my culture, and to fine-tune her Swedish language skills." It was also a chance to pass on the family tradition of baking. The thirteen-year-old girl became acquainted with her grandmother and her remarkable oven. Just like when Birgitta was a girl, grandma would have something fresh waiting for Laura when she came home from school. "The two of them would bake together," Birgitta remembers. "She taught my daughter a lot. To this day, my daughter cherishes those days and weekends. It gave her a lot of confidence in the kitchen."

For Birgitta, the time back home offered a reconnection with her roots, a reminder of her own girlhood, and an opportunity to learn from her mother's skills and wisdom. Birgitta's family spent a year in Sweden, then returned to the United States. Her mother died a few years later, leaving Birgitta to cherish the memories of her midlife experience of "home."

Crisis and Hope

In her fifties, after enjoying a succession of careers, Birgitta had finally found the time to go back to school and complete her degree in art history, taking up the course of study she had abandoned decades earlier at the University of Stockholm. Her husband's position as president of a Northern California winery gave them enough financial security to permit Birgitta to take some important time for herself. Now she seemed to have everything. She was still a striking woman. She had a large, beautiful new home, impeccably decorated with simple elegant touches, light woods, creamy colors, and woven fabrics of her native Scandinavia. She entertained frequently. She created a lush garden from "absolute dirt."

But the complacency was only on the surface. With her two children on their own, there were empty spaces in her life. Her mother was gone and now her beloved father started to grow ill with prostate cancer. She went back to Sweden to nurse him through his last year of life. But something even more tragic would crash down in the middle of Birgitta's ordered life.

Her son, Oscar, who was completing his Ph.D. in marine biology, had just triumphantly delivered an important paper in San Francisco before top scientists from around the world, and he celebrated the heady moment with his mother over lunch. The pair returned home to a surreal message on Birgitta's answering machine. Oscar's girlfriend had been murdered by a neighbor. "Oscar went crazy," Birgitta remembers. "When you're in your twenties, it's incomprehensible that someone young like you could die. We took him home and spent a long time with him, helping him clean up the apartment and make funeral arrangements."

Her devastated son seemingly managed to move on with his life. He finished his doctorate, met another bright, wonderful young woman and became the father of a baby girl. But Birgitta suspected that he never really dealt with his anguish. "There was a lot of sadness going on. He pushed it away."

Two years later, Oscar was diagnosed with advanced Hodgkin's disease. Again, Birgitta set aside her own life to be with her son and support his small family over the long six months of intensive chemotherapy and radiation to shrink a mass behind his lung. He eventually went into remission, but the maelstrom of family traumas led Birgitta back to the safe incandescence of her mother's oven.

"I always remembered my mother's comment, 'When you feel depressed, start baking.'" As a special gift when she turned forty, Birgitta's mother had presented her with her old recipe book, a dog-eared, disorganized accumulation of kitchen wisdom, carefully typed out by her father in her native Swedish, with her mother's directions and editorial notes: "This is a wonderful fall recipe." "This is one of my favorites." "This is wonderful with that . . ." Birgitta felt revived as she made the old recipes from scratch. She found she enjoyed the labor of working her hands through dough, preparing it and shaping it. She took comfort in the scents that transported her back to that small little kitchen in Nykoping.

During Oscar's illness, Birgitta would cook for her son—the simple, easy-to-digest food he loved as a little boy, like mashed potatoes and soup, with, in the Swedish vernacular, "a little of mother's flavor" added to it. As she nourished him she consoled herself, creating a warm hearth where he was free to talk about the devastating loss he had suffered a few years earlier, the struggles with health, the way the emotional and physical sufferings were connected. The experience took them both back in time, adults looking to their mothers for nurturing. When her son regained his health, Birgitta continued baking, not wanting to leave this powerful source of nourishment from the past.

Choosing the Kitchen

The opportunity to bake on a larger scale came in the form of a proposal from the son of a good friend. Trale was a bread maker, and he knew that Birgitta was a whiz in the kitchen and in business. It seemed like a perfect partnership. He used to come up to Birgitta's home with bread, and she'd show him desserts. "We'd come up with one idea after another," she says. A bakery seemed like a natural outlet for their respective talents. It would be a place to produce the old-world recipes on a daily basis, adding new flavors to the mix. It appealed to Birgitta on a deep level—a chance to stay with her passion for baking and exercise the entrepreneurial skills she had developed in the thirty years since leaving her childhood home.

Her husband, Paul, and other friends and family members warned it was risky. The restaurant business is notoriously stressful, risky, and requires insanely long hours, getting up way before dawn to bake. But she was determined to proceed.

Trale found an old doughnut shop that was closed. The first impression should have sent her running. But Birgitta has always had a gift for seeing the potential beauty in the most hopeless of places.

> It was fall, so it was cold and damp, and when we first opened the doors the smell hit you—old, rancid fat. It was very dirty. Old equipment broken down, dusty and rusty and just thrown everywhere. That was the first challenge. It was such a horrible building when we took over, dingy and dark and miserable looking. But I wanted to take the challenge, and I was looking forward to working with Trale.

The oven was an old, revolving model made for pastries, not bread. Birgitta and Trale set to work, cleaning up, remodeling, and adapting the old oven for bread baking. The partnership worked, the products began to gain a following, and slowly, discriminating patrons started discovering that the old doughnut shop now offered fresh new flavors, healthy breads, and decadent cakes. The bakery raked in gold medals and sweepstakes awards at the local harvest fair, a success for which she credits inspiration from her mother and the bread-baking wizardry of her young partner.

> It wasn't like we took the awards too terribly seriously, but I was extremely proud and elated. Since there are so many good bakeries in the area, it's certainly a nice pat on the back. The judges are all professional and feel we are as good or equal to the artisan bread companies.

Birgitta's Life These Days

The Sensual Pleasure of Food

On an ordinary day, there is excitement in the Village Bakery. One afternoon, after much experimentation, Birgitta is thrilled to come up with an improved bread, using high gluten flour. She inspects the product, pleased that the color is more golden and the outside crustier, with a fine split running like a fault line down the middle. "It's beautiful. Just perfect," she declares, comparing it favorably to its more basic predecessor, made with regular flour. This new bread takes much longer to rise, but the extra time is worth it to Birgitta, whose mind is always turning over ways to improve her product.

"What we've tried to do is change with the seasons, so when we come into spring, we'll do much lighter morning pastries. We'll have strawberries and rhubarb and incorporate that into our morning pastries and fine desserts." Her creative style includes working through the community. She uses as much local produce as possible, buying from nearby farmers. Several elderly couples come by with rhubarb, blackberries, figs, pears, and lemons from their backyards. "We have a little trail of people coming in with their wares. I will do exchanges for bread. That's really rewarding."

She displays the bread in the bakery as a potter might crockery, using it as decoration. Along the wall behind the counter are shelves of thick peasant bread, stacked artfully to show off their geometric variety—from chunky ovals and circular wreathes to baguettes as brown and sturdy as small tree trunks. She is daring but not reckless in her experimentation, coming up with tastes that are new and combinations that blend well without necessarily screaming out.

Creating Community

She acknowledges many of her customers by name. It's not a boisterous greeting but soft and lightly conversational, really like the small town village baker—reserved but personable. "I know when their kids are born. I know what is going on in their lives. I'm totally involved with my customers." This customer involvement is one of the quotients of her creativity and success. "It makes this bakery, that the customers built it and they're tied into it on a personal level. We have a group of people that have followed us for the last four years, on a daily basis, so it becomes a community, a family. That was part of our original philosophy, to really try to have an impact on the community. We give a lot of bread away to the different schools and to the old folks' homes."

When people come into the bakery, they frequently exclaim how it's the closest they've seen to an authentic European bakery in the United States. "I guess that was my vision, really wanting to re-create something that I was brought up with," she reflects. While her mother's influence lives on in Birgitta's kitchen, she credits her inclusive management style to her father's influence. A social activist as well as a journalist, he taught her the value of respectful teamwork. Birgitta was using "team-based" management long before it became trendy in the corporate world. She intuitively sees the value of supporting other people's ideas.

> One reason I think a lot of my staff feel really good about being here is that they do have a sense of autonomy. A sense of freedom, of doing and trying, and knowing they can have a couple of days off and relax and know it is okay. It's important not to be overly dogmatic about how you run the personnel side of it. I was very young when I was entrusted with management, and I guess through the years I developed a style I sensed worked very well.

It's being able to listen to people. I always try to take a little time and be part of their families, and I also like working with women who really need a job. People who have kids at home. I know what they're going through. They have come from all walks of life. They often have struggled. They come in, and I give them a chance to go up a little bit and get some more money. They still can go home when their kids are sick and take them to school and doctors. It is so important.

One of the most wonderful things you can do in a company is to assemble a group of creative and talented people and let them have the freedom to be what they are. I've always been fortunate enough to have had that in my own life, and that's how I want to run this company. I don't want to be overbearing and critiquing constantly.

Brigitta looks hard to find the right people, "originals" who come in with their own ideas. She asks prospective bakers to come in and do a test bake and show her a few new recipes. "I am interested in how they get along with the other people, how organized they are, if they know exactly what to do with the butter. I have such good people who have been with me for a long time." There are "taste mornings" where everyone sits down and critiques the products. "Everyone gets involved. Even the maintenance people. They have become very picky," she says, laughing.

Birgitta is clearly satisfied by the part of her work that involves working with other people to make their ideas happen, drawing on the skills and experiences she learned as a leader in the corporate world of retail housewares. At the same time, she has come to deeply appreciate how much she gets from doing the nitty-gritty work of the home, the hands-on kind of creativity learned in childhood and understood with age. For all of her business savvy and vision, the kitchen is the place where she feels fully herself. Cooking for her is "soothing for the soul because it's creative and you use your hands at the same time. I like that combination. It's not just sitting and reading and trying to grab a concept. It's doing. I love the 'doing' part of life when you get your hands dirty, when you create something with your mind and with your hands."

Birgitta's story yields an assortment of ingredients for the creative life: Connection with childhood memories. Willingness to plunge in and get your hands dirty. Confidence in your vision. Knowing when to risk and when to withdraw. Facing crises by drawing on personal resources that can transform your life from the inside out. And, as a foundation for it all, identifying the activity where you feel most "yourself."

Conversations and Reflections: Finding Ingredients for Creativity at Home

Intrinsic Goodness

Birgitta achieved no small amount of local fame when she burst on the food scene with her healthy, yummy breads that looked and smelled as good as they tasted. But she didn't have much time to chit-chat or accept kudos when the awards started rolling in. She was busy in the kitchen. Birgitta isn't in this work for the pats on the back. Her work in the bakery warms her soul. The cooking is what she likes best. Her story validates what many of us feel in visceral memories of our mothers and grandmothers: What happens in the kitchen consti-tutes significant creativity.

Of course, few of our sisters, mothers, or grandmothers received "outside" recognition for their domestic feats. What sets Birgitta apart from all the unsung domestic heroines is the way she has asserted her vision in the world—taking basic dough and elevating it to food art-istry—possibly due to her many years' experience in blending the creative with business activities. In Birgitta, we see a model for pro-moting products—the fabrics, housewares, and now, baked goods. And as any good marketer will tell you, the key is believing in your product. She loved the fabric and food and cleanliness of her child-hood home, and by making that good business she is among those bringing meaning back to the term "domestic arts."

I think about the phrase "practicing the domestic arts." In some ways, the daily chores of cooking and gardening can be "practice" for keeping creativity going during the ordinary routine of a day. One person's drudgery is another person's creative outlet. Certainly this is not an argument for "women belong in the house," but rather a sug-gestion that we value the time we devote to homemaking—at least the parts we enjoy—not as an outtake from achievements but as an integral and proud part of life.

In Praise of the "Domestic Arts"

Recently I have begun hearing more and more professional women trading stories about revived pleasure in all the things that makes a house a home. One woman talked about the tingly feeling she gets when she goes to the sewing machine floor of Sears. Another has begun carting around her knitting. Several are pumping their moms and aunts for recipes for family meals they grew up with. Bir-gitta is used to being in front of the trends, and once again she is a leader—inspiring other women to take pride in the creative domestic arts of their girlhood.

My mother has a black-and-white photograph in her kitchen of her grandmother baking a pie. So many of my family traditions have to do with food, such as the ancestral, "Oh, let's have a little lunch"—which is when a guest comes over and you casually bring out a four-course meal, with pie of course. A fair number of women in previous generations of my family had careers, as nurses and teachers. These days I wonder, how did Aunt Garney find the time to make a "little lunch" when she was teaching kindergarten?

After college, when I was beginning my career, my mom gave me one of those serious, heavy glass rolling pins, along with a recipe explaining that pie crusts were best if they "weren't too short"—that is, not too much butter or shortening. Making pies always seemed hugely daunting to me. I've lost the rolling pin, one of those things that disappears when you've neglected it for too long. Recently I've been hanging around my friends' kitchens when they bake, watching and learning, remembering being a little girl standing on a stool, waiting for the dough pieces to make tiny doll pies. I think I'll get another rolling pin and see if this time it feels right in my hands.

If you cooked alongside the women in your family or played house or dolls as a girl, you probably have memories of making little cakes or sewing little dresses and feeling that rush of excitement at knowing you'd made something important. Indeed, these were complex projects, and these memories are part of our heritage. As Julia Child once said:

> Cooking is just as creative and imaginative an activity
> as drawing or wood carving or music. And cooking draws
> upon your every talent—science, mathematics, energy, history,
> experience—and the more experience you have the less likely
> are your experiments to end in drivel and disaster. The more
> you know, the more you can create.

After the feminist revolution, a lot of women didn't have time—and some, in reaction to the social powerlessness of being a house-wife, didn't have a lot of respect—for the domestic arts. Cooking and sewing seemed to many like holdovers from a time when women didn't have many professional options. Now, with many women balancing a career, parenthood, and home life, who has time to crochet a baby outfit or bake a cake from scratch? Efficiency is paramount, and the men in the house need to pull their share or the whole scene falls apart. But something may be lost for women who found joy in the household activities that seemed fun in childhood. Ideally, you could pick and choose—not having to be responsible for managing the

whole house, but getting to indulge in the domestic arts that feel creative and evoke happy memories.

Deborah, a single woman, architect, and college teacher, is
hardly a housewife. But she paints sweatshirts, makes jewelry, creates
little water gardens in her yard, and bakes strawberry and rhubarb
pies. She always has stacks of drawing projects to do and papers to
grade, but she feels like she needs the time for baking and fabric
painting and gardening, activities she's enjoyed since childhood, to
keep her balanced.

> It keeps me sane, it's expression, creating an environment.
> I sometimes get so absorbed in doing my jobs, I need to find
> my equilibrium and my home projects use a different kind of
> energy. It's not a performance. It's for myself . . . and for
> friends and family when they visit.

Although history trivializes the domestic work of women (literally, the word "trivial" comes from the Latin word for "three roads,"
the place where women gathered to do the laundry and talk), in
recent years there has been a blessed shift in perception. Much of
society now celebrates the complex creativity involved in the maintenance of hearth and home. Many of those elaborate old quilts our
grandmothers made are hanging in art galleries today. Some of our
matrilineal culinary tricks are now the stuff of gourmet food trends.
The corporate world is embracing teamwork: that age-old collaborative style of getting things done that women know by heart. The
day-to-day accomplishments of our foremothers are now testimony
to how creativity has always thrived in the fabric of women's daily
lives—ordinary women, not just those with brilliance, bravery,
and/or bravado (but viva those who have all three).

Women like Birgitta are winning awards thanks to the unsung
efforts of their mothers and grandmothers. Birgitta descended from
Viking women proud of their ability to warm families from the cold,
and she has become a torch bearer for a broadening definition of creativity that encompasses the unsung homemakers of days past,
women like her own mother and grandmother. Although poor, her
grandmother made simple but beautiful new clothes, even weaving
the fabric, so that her children could be the best dressed in school.
These women brought so much care to their daily duties that they left
lasting impressions on others.

House Goddess

Even today, despite the trend to honor the domestic arts,
women who don't work outside the home may respond with

downcast eyes to the question, "And what do you do?" For a couple of decades, the word "housewife" was often preceded by "just a." That's changing, too, as society and individual women are recognizing how much creativity is—and always has been—involved in the domestic arts. In *The Women's Book of Creativity*, C. Diane Ealy writes:

> *The woman who chooses to stay at home creating a nurturing environment for the entire family has frequently been dismissed. The assumption has been that she is fulfilling a role put upon her and if she had a choice, she would have a different career. Her efforts are grossly undervalued by society, so she may also have difficulty finding value in her work. But when she discovers she is passionate about homemaking and it allows her to express creative energies, she can learn to honor her activities.*

Bread and Company

Besides bringing belated appreciation to our hard-working female ancestors, it is validating that today there is an ongoing discourse about the meaning of food in our lives. I'm beginning to see how many women (and men) share the mysterious satisfaction that comes from poring over a new cookbook. The excitement goes beyond imagining the food itself, but involves a sense of possibility, the re-creation of a picture we see on a page, bringing to our tables this glossy image of perfect nourishment (not that it always turns out looking that way, but there is that hope . . .). At home, this is how Birgitta gets her inspiration. Sitting alone, reading and staring at the pictures in cookbooks, the ideas start to percolate. I like thinking about cookbook dreaming as part of a creative process and not just as the practicality of figuring out what to eat each night.

Meg, a newspaper reporter whose work seems to consume so much of her week, doesn't consider herself much of a cook, and finds elaborate, three-course meals wasted energy when her husband is rushing off to teach a college night class and her young son refuses to eat much beyond pizza, peas, and macaroni and cheese. But cooking has still become a creative point of connection in her family. She says that after thirteen years of marriage she still can't see her way to spending two hours in front of the TV to bond with her husband over baseball. But she likes to snuggle up beside her husband, who values the kitchen even more than the garage, and watch videotaped cooking shows on PBS: Jacques Pepin, Julia Child, Biba Gaggiano, Burt Wolfe. Cooking together on weekends is a shared project, picking fresh vegetables from their garden, poring over cookbooks for recipes, and mixing up risotto and pastas to eat with a glass of wine, while a bel canto pours out of the stereo. It's the contemporary home arts, with cooking as a creative outlet, not just a chore.

Food has so much to do with our connections to one another. Sometimes it's a healing agent, as Birgitta found with her son. Sometimes it's a form of communication, as when we take a dish to a friend or serve something special for a celebration. In my family, cooking a hot breakfast has always been a symbolic way of sending kids out into the world "full." Cold cereal is the usual fare, and most people can't believe I cook eggs and pancakes every morning, even though I'll make frozen dinners on busy nights. Each of us seems to have a certain food thing that's symbolic in our relationships to each other. I love it that the word company literally means "with bread."

Homemade

All of this is not to say that we should or could prepare elaborate meals on a daily basis. Any guilt that comes from using prepared food is silly—of course most of us can't live our busy lives and make everything by scratch. But preparing a homemade dish or meal can create a feeling that speaks to our instinctive sense that homemade transmits care.

A visitor from Germany once asked about a sauce I had served. "Is it self-made?" he asked in his language's version of "from scratch." I had to say no, but quickly pointed out another dish that I had prepared myself. I pride myself on the ability to put together big dinner parties on short notice with little fuss, using various "tricks" of pre-prepared food. But I also like to have one offering that I make myself. Looking back, maybe that was Aunt Garney's "little lunch" solution—not everything homemade, but one thing you made yourself that people will remember.

Why is it so important to some of us to have something that is your "own" to offer people? You can get all the vitamins and food combinations in pre-prepared foods, but intuitively we know there's something more to it, something that comes from the hands and heart. It's the chicken soup syndrome. Cooking is so primitive, so linked to survival. We're no longer confined to rigid expectations that daily cooking is required "women's work," but we can enjoy the freedom to appreciate the phenomenon of hearth maintenance— whether we choose to perform it ourselves, even if just once in a while, or simply resolve to honor those who provide it.

In her book *Awakening Minerva*, Linda Firestone urges women to see the domestic duties not just as individual acts but as a collective composition, together comprising the creation of a hearth that nourishes the self and others.

*Within the realm of the hearth and under your protection
exist those aspects that influence your everyday life and feed
your extraordinary creative actions. Though the power of the
individual elements of the hearth is fleeting, they do nonetheless color your perceptions and influence your creative
expression. Women do not create in a vacuum.*

Comfort Food

Passion is what elevates our creative work—whether it's of the
"bread-and-butter" daily variety or fine art—bringing intrinsic meaning to the process and communicating with others. Intuitively, people
can generally sense when they are being given something created
with passion, whether it's a piece of poetry or a piece of bread.

What gives rise to that feeling?

Passion is a joyful motivator, but again and again we see it
emerge out of personal crisis. Passion is an internal force, often aris-
ing from loss, that seeks a form to manifest. For "passion," once again
I look to word origins for understanding. And I find that it literally
translates to "suffering." One day I was talking to an artist who said
he no longer felt passion but felt at peace. But perhaps passion isn't
positive or negative. I like to look at it as something that comes up,
often as a constructive approach to a difficult situation. For Birgitta,
the passion of baking resurfaced from the need to nurture a suffering
loved one. Her story demonstrates how we can go back into our own
histories, not just to uncover the demons, but to rediscover the angel
of comfort who appeared when we needed her.

The late and legendary writer, M.F.K. Fisher, who herself elevated food writing to a respected literary genre, wrote in her book
Alphabet for Gourmets:

*S is for Sad . . . and the mysterious appetite that often surges
in us when our hearts seem about to break and our lives seem
too bleakly empty. Like every other physical phenomenon, there
is always good reason for this hunger if we are blunt enough
to recognize it.*

Nourishment can be an antidote to sadness—perhaps that's why
people take hot dishes to friends when they've suffered serious illness or a loss. We may stumble over the words to console and worry
about intruding, but we can communicate care in the language of satisfying physical hunger. In a short story about a baker attempting to
console parents who had lost a son, author Raymond Carver wrote
about the "small, good thing" that a fresh baked bun can represent in
an abyss of sadness. When we're overwhelmed, in pain or under

stress—wanting to hide from the world—our friends may coax us over for lunch or dinner with the admonishment, "Well, you still have to eat."

Slowing Down

In her introduction to *The New Laurel's Kitchen*, author Carol Flinders, who wrote one of the seminal cookbooks for vegetarians back when the whole health foods movement was just beginning to flower, suggests we should view cooking as not just a source of comfort but a meditational activity to cure the "hurry sickness" from which so many of us suffer. Carol's friend made an observation about a shift in consciousness that occurred when she walked into the kitchen one night.

> *I don't know, really, what changed. I just know that one evening I walked in there grim as usual, determined to get it over with, and instead I found myself relaxing—accepting that I was there and willing to do it as well as I possibly could. And ever since then, it's been completely different. You know, partly I think it's the food itself. If you watch, so much beauty passes through your hands—of form and color and texture. And energy, too.*

Flinders, a university lecturer, former newspaper columnist, and author of three nonfiction books, describes the kitchen as a sanctuary for connecting with the spiritual sources of creativity, comparing it with a garden.

> *Cooking involves an enormously rich coming-together of the fruits of the earth with the inventive genius of the human being. So many mysterious transformations are involved— small miracles like the churning of butter from cream or the fermentation of bread dough. In times past, there was no question but that higher powers were at work in such goings-on, and a feeling of reverence sprang up in response. I wonder sometimes whether the restorative effects of cooking and gardening arise out of similar—though quite unconscious—responses.*

Like Birgitta, Flinders also came to a point in her life where she brought her girlhood enjoyment of kitchen activities into her professional life. First she wrote cookbooks and a food column, then she combined her interest in the hearth with her scholarly work as a Ph.D. student in comparative religion, weaving together the themes of women, spirituality, domesticity in two books. For both women, integrating the hearth with their professional careers has provided comfort and inspiration in sorting through personal and philosophical issues.

Are there any household activities that nourish your spirit in some way? If so, how can you make more room to explore that activity? How does it connect to other aspects of your life? For women who "do too much," it can be a relief to spend time reflecting on daily tasks, doing a checkup with ourselves to see what's bringing us satisfaction versus what tires us out. Choosing where to put your energy can be an antidote to the feeling of being pulled in all directions.

You can clear away some of the domestic chores you don't like to revel in the ones you do. Often this works by making trades with those you live with: "I'll make dinner if you will . . ." Just identifying the activities where you feel "yourself" can be freeing. As you bring yourself more fully to tasks that are self-expressive, you're "practicing" creativity. And in the odd way that happens when you least expect it, those baby steps may lead to one of those "aha" moments that delivers inspiration about the next leap you'll take in the creative life.

Connecting the Dots

Along with many of the women in this book, Birgitta took a roundabout route to arrive at what felt like "home" in the creative sense. After interviewing and writing about Birgitta, Meg reflected about how Birgitta's history and long line of jobs seemed to lead to the bakery. Meg said:

> We can all look back, perhaps from some point of success, and see how the various steps led us to where we are, sometimes not even realizing we were following a path. Annie [the photographer] called it "connect the dots." She meant that the path seemed random. But perhaps we create our paths by our choices, even if we aren't consciously aware of what we're doing or where we're driving ourselves. Each of Birgitta's occupations and ventures gave her experience that she brought to her own business: interior design, remodeling, and marketing.

Often there's an overemphasis on the "planned life," in which one plots out an education and career and retirement chart. That can work, but there's freedom in honoring the serendipity. I'm certainly not doing what I predicted I'd do when I started college as a pre-med student, but a rare essay assignment in a biology class got me going on an analysis of religious versus scientific approaches to ideas, and the instructor said I sounded more like a candidate for philosopher than physician. I ended up with a degree in philosophy.

Susan, a columnist, likes to tell about how she took her first high school journalism class because she couldn't get into driver's ed. Writer Sarah had no clue that her geology degree would take her into the world of mystery novels. Looking back, each of us can see how one thing led to the other. Making those links can help you identify the choices you made, with or without knowing it, leading either to a greater appreciation of being where you are or to the awareness that you still have choices.

Onward: Continuing to Bake

As a professional woman in the mid-twentieth century, Birgitta was at the beginning of a social movement that set women free from enslavement to the kitchen, but now she is an eloquent spokeswoman for celebrating the choice of hearth as a place of self-expression. Here is a woman with a degree in art history and an incredibly impressive professional resume, and yet for her it all leads back to bread. She's pleased that her public display of those prize-winning rolls and loaves of bread offers permission for all practitioners of food alchemy to acknowledge the kitchen as a zone for creativity.

Her bakery has grown, with more demand. She has opened a second and is planning to open a third. She takes an annual summer trip back to Sweden, where she recharges amid the memories of where it all began. But you'll still find her back in the kitchen as often as not, and she's still home in time for dinner.

5

Doing It for Yourself: Sharing It with Others

*Creativity is, at its core, energy. When we no longer
need that energy to protect or defend ourselves, then
something from our true self can come bubbling up
from that stream just below the surface—if we let it.*

—Linda Kammer, poet,
painter, cosmetologist

Meet Linda in the Salon

Coconut shampoo, clove, and flower-scented shampoos fill the air with a familiar mix of aromas in Linda's salon. This is the place for fixing hair, attitude, and spirit. The same pictures are always posted next to Linda's mirror, one a turn-of-the-century photo of a woman with hair so long it touched the floor, another a portrait of a young Hopi woman, hair arranged with a traditional squash blossom at each ear.

Linda Kammer is tall and thin, bookishly hip with wire-framed glasses, streaky blonde hair, a long skirt, boots, and lacy socks. In a voice like a feather, she asks "How are you?" and customers know it's a real question, not just a nicety. So they tell her. And sometimes she'll tell a truth in return. Customers often learn something while in her chair. This is a "salon" in a larger sense of the word. It is a mini-mecca for a whole community of writers, poets, and artists of one kind or another who, individually and usually unbeknownst to one another, have somehow found Linda and continue returning to the place in front of her mirror. There is nourishment to be found there, and not just for split ends.

Why creative people have been drawn to Linda's chair was a long-standing mystery, although not a coincidence. She's great with hair, but elements well beyond expertise with scissors seemed to assemble this particular client list of editors, novelists, journalists, painters, and craftspeople. Parts of the explanation emerged over the years, as Linda began sharing her insights with her grateful clientele. The full picture finally came clear when Linda staged an art show, her first solo show, where she displayed her paintings accompanied by her poetry. Her clients were among those who became her audience. Through their conversations with her over the years, they had sensed something of this creativity in Linda, having traded dreams, experiences, and insights—and they often left her salon feeling more inspired in their own work.

Now it all unfolded in framed oils and drawings on the wall, alongside words that were plucked from the same source. What was inside Linda had emerged: abstract paintings with a quirky but luscious interpretation of the surrounding landscape and poems designed to carry you from the landscape into her dreams. Had she been hiding the work all these years, fearful of exposure? Or waiting until just the right time to reveal what was inside her? Or was the art itself secondary to how the creative process had enriched her life—in a way that put her in a position to enrich the lives of others?

Learning Creative Courage

Linda gracefully demonstrates the ideal way for creative people to move through the world—free to express the self and earn respect from others—without any special credentials, socioeconomic privilege, or access to a major art market. Simply by going through the daily steps of raising a family and working for a living, with a certain consciousness, Linda accomplished great leaps of self-expression through her artwork and poetry—right in her own hometown. She commanded an audience when she was ready.

Linda is a role model particularly for introverted women who are most comfortable exercising their creativity in private spaces, and who may see their work as art but hesitate to show it in public. Linda is the archetypal "shadow artist," the tranquil and unassuming persona who finds herself surrounded by artists before she gathers her courage and claims her rightful place among them. Today, she is serene where she once feared criticism.

Climbing into the spotlight as an artist sometimes calls for a certain amount of willfulness, extroverted pushing, and even belligerence, but those are not qualities you see in Linda. She has what she calls her "crazy woman" inside herself, but she found safe ways to let that wildness be "seen" by others. And she has found subtle ways to tune out the critics in her life while surrounding herself with nourishing influences for her creativity.

Harsh personal questions have arisen along her creative path. Some of them may sound familiar: How do I keep my creativity alive while I make a living? How can I express my creativity when I'm busy with a family? If I reveal my creative expressions, will I alienate people who see me in a different way? Will people think or say "Who do you think you are?" if I call myself an artist? If I can't travel in big-city artistic circles, how can I learn my craft? Where can I find encouragement for my work? How do I tune out discouraging messages? How do I know if what I'm doing is any good . . . and who is the judge?

Linda pulled counsel from her dreams and meditation and from people who regularly entered her work space, which happens to be a hair salon. The answers she has found in her own life hint at exciting possibilities for all of us: If you follow your inner voice, trust your instincts, relax, and look around you for teachers, one day you'll be ready to show what's inside yourself to others.

In Linda, we glimpse the elegant simplicity of the creative life. Fame and fortune are no greater goals than confidence and composure. Linda's accomplishments have occurred within the context of ordinary life. Amid the dailiness, she found something deep within herself, gave it form, and ultimately gathered the courage to share it with others. She left them wanting more. You can sit in her chair and listen to her story, ask her advice about how to move forward, and in a voice that is almost a whisper but can carry across an auditorium, she will tell you: "Don't do it perfect. Do it anyway."

Linda's Path

Pristine Pastels

Linda grew up in a small northern California town, surrounded by nature's opulence: pastures iridescent green in the spring and golden brown in late summer; apple orchards where the trees were mist-shrouded, black-on-white silhouettes in winter and colorful, fruit-laden foliage in autumn. It was only a short drive to the rugged Pacific coastline, where high-powered waves slam against granite rocks so hard it propels spray onto the roadway. It is those landscapes she now paints.

She was the second of five children with two working parents. "We did not have much one-on-one time with our parents by today's standards. But paradoxically, the busy chaos functioned as a privacy screen and allowed me time to explore my inner landscape, to experience who I was." The everyday aspects of creativity came to Linda as part of growing up in a large family: "If we wanted something, we had to make it." Toys, clothing, and games started out as raw materials that were assembled by hand.

To experience more lofty aspects of art, she only had to go next door. Her neighbor, Lois, was a high school art teacher who welcomed visits to her home, where artwork hung on the walls and other works were in progress on an easel. Lois always had art supplies available for her young visitors, and there Linda formed plaster into sculpted shapes and dipped her hands into brightly colored, viscous finger paints. Her child's heart quickened as she reveled in texture and movement and the gratifying results. She thought to herself, "I'm going to be an artist like Lois." She was about six years old.

Then, within a couple of years, came some artistic tools of her very own. But with these first artistic tools came the beginnings of her fear of using them. She recalls, "I had another neighbor, Jo, who gave me a box of pastels. 'Don't tell anyone I'm giving these to you,' she cautioned me." Perhaps Jo said the words so that Linda could have something she didn't have to share with her four siblings, or maybe Jo believed that Linda needed to be private in her art. Whatever the reason, that box of pastels became a symbol to Linda. She didn't use them. Forty-plus years later, she still has them. She tries to understand what kept her from opening them: "I felt that if I used them, they would be gone, and I didn't have, and wouldn't have, the resources to replace them. I loved looking at them and feeling the powder on my hands. That was the beginning of my lifelong fascination with color."

The pastels represented something Linda wanted to hold on to, not use up. She felt an inkling that there was some part of her artistic spirit that, once materialized for others to see, might vanish. The coming years would demonstrate the wisdom of her childhood concerns—that there is risk in exposing the childlike sense of artistic mystery for others to see. Because of her shy ways, perhaps the risk seemed greater than to others. Nonetheless, her task would be to overcome her fears in order to go public with her art.

Art for the Self or for Others?

As the box of pastels sat untouched in her drawer, Linda took art classes in school, experimenting with various forms. In high school art classes, she became fascinated with drawing human figures. She thought they were good, but one semester she got a C. That was deflating, and then something happened that was confusing. Her teacher inexplicably raised her grade to an A. To this day, Linda suspects her parents went to the teacher and convinced him to change the grade. The A was a mixed blessing. "I felt I had to live up to the expectation of the A, and I tried very hard to do my best." Best for herself or best for the teacher, though? She became aware of a schism: What you create for grades is often different than what you create just for yourself.

The rewards of creativity faded after high school. Linda went to beauty school, married, divorced, and had her son, Jason. "I was twenty-one with a year-old child, working in a beehive beauty salon, when blow dry cuts came into style. It was like a breath of fresh air. Within a few years, I had my own successful salon. Even then, artists would come to hang out. But I became restless."

Her wanderlust drew her to an isolated rural community, where she met and married her husband, Joel, a man who responded to her eccentricities and creativity, allowing her the emotional and physical space she needed to explore the unformed but increasingly urgent desire to somehow express the feelings that were beginning to take form. Two years later, she gave birth to their daughter, Tiana. "At that time I was doing cloisonné work [making metal jewelry with enamel designs baked on top] and cutting hair on the side."

But the back-to-the-land lifestyle was becoming old, and the family returned to Sonoma County, bought a house, and turned the garage into a studio for Linda. The studio allowed her to move from cloisonné to sculpture. In order to get some basic instruction, she sat in on classes at the local university and community college. Her studio work was part of a comfortable life routine that also included swimming, golf, and traveling, in addition to studio time and hair cutting.

Just about that time, Linda decided it would be rewarding to make a living as a graphic artist, and she started taking classes at the local junior college. Working in the field was a disappointment. "I was never satisfied with graphic arts . . . it all became 'work' . . . the mystery was gone . . . the artistic joy was muted. Art is not other-directed for me." It wasn't a wasted learning experience, however, as she feels the principles she learned there have informed her drawing and painting.

Later she would come to understand what had been missing in the graphics arts arena. In her workaday life, she was mild-mannered Linda, following the rules and aiming to please. But in her creative life, she was driven by what she later would name her "crazy woman"—the wild, internally driven muse that would not conform to rules aimed at a particular end result.

> I need art to be my connection to my heart and soul. This
> is the thing that allows the crazy woman to sing. In so much
> of my life I care for others. This crazy woman, when I let her,
> cares for me. Late at night, she leads me down the hall to the
> computer to tap out a harmony in words. Or she drags me
> out of bed before sunrise to sing with my paints in the
> morning air.

Beginning Conversations

Linda was too frustrated with graphic arts to continue, but she had practicalities to consider. She had consistently kept at haircutting, so Linda decided to open another hair salon. That provided a work environment without too many rules and would give her some freedom to explore her creativity when she was ready. She found enjoyment in the strange intimacy of the salon environment, as people brought her their opinions and experiences and sought out hers. She often found herself involved in deep conversations with people who came back every few months or years. Many would confide their creative hopes, their insecurities, their goals. And bit by bit Linda would share hers. She found continuity in these long-term relationships, casual but not insignificant, and they inspired what would prove to be a valuable exchange on both ends.

As the conversations with people in her chair continued, Linda began sharing glimpses of her dreams and offering words—when she could find them—to describe her creative endeavors and her view of life. Her quiet and carefully chosen words, punctuated by silences, would draw out revelations from her clients.

> *Our discussions were wonderful. No subject was off limits.*
> *Stories were told. Ideas were explored. It was a beauty shop,*
> *so the talk often began with hair, or cosmetics, like "Have you*
> *used Retin A?" But then the conversation would spiral deeper,*
> *into external image versus internal growth, and "What are we*
> *trying to hide?"*

The women would reveal parts of themselves to Linda while feeling the warm water pour over their head and her fingers washing their hair. They would question their full calendars, wondering aloud what happened to quiet moments and freedom. Linda listened carefully, gathering nuggets of truth and wisdom.

Work with hair requires attention to detail. At the same time, Linda was exercising a broader artistic vision within the social context of her work, and she found herself also consciously exercising creativity through ceramics and drawing. She had shows, and she sold her work. She maintained her hair salon and her artistic life separate from each other, and both grew. "I felt like a creative person, but there was a deeper part of my creative self that had not been touched, until my unconscious brought me a message."

The Naked Dream

> *I remember a dream I had about seven years ago. In this*
> *dream a new pair of shoes was being made for me. My*
> *wardrobe no longer fit. I realized that the activities I normally*
> *did lacked something. Everything dropped away. I was left*
> *naked, with only a new pair of shoes, and nothing went with*
> *them. I took the dream to mean I had to find my way of being*
> *in the world.*

That was the end of the neat and predictable balance she had created in her life. She was no longer settled. She was restless. She stopped playing golf, stopped swimming, and gave up ceramics. In another dream at about the same time, "I dreamed that the army was no longer needed, it was time to teach them how to paint."

She spent more and more time painting, now with a teacher, learning about the landscape in the great outdoors. She felt playful, almost reckless, trying out new experiments with paints, seeing poetry in the words that came to her in bits and scraps during the night. There was a wildness about the work that did not look like the quiet, self-possessed Linda that others knew. This was her crazy woman, who began to command attention every day.

Since then I've become a poet and a painter. I've created a new self, or maybe I've simply found my real self. I know now who I am, and I have security in that. This self-knowledge allows me to be in the world more fully. In the past I had a tendency to be influenced by others, but now I can stand on my own with my self intact. Before, when I kept the artist separate from the rest of my life, I would do my artistic work, then pull back. I'd hide. But my inner process has changed, and I will not allow that to happen again. I will not apologize for what I am or what I do. My art speaks for itself.

Linda began to cultivate her dreams and talk about them more with other women. The visual power that took over her paintbrush seemed connected to the subconscious forces that materialized in her sleep. She came to trust them. She says:

I believe that dreams are a window to the soul, and I look to dreams for direction about what to do. In my dreams, I find inspiration. My dreams define my need to do a painting or to write a poem. My paintings and poetry are a way to "get home." My dreams validate my experiences. Often the reason I paint is to complete something. In my dreams and in my paintings, I see myself being in the moment, not totally responsible to the outside world but to the inside world. "In dreams begin responsibility." I love that quote.

Moving Out of the Shadows and Into the Light

Linda found her voice, artistic style, and confidence once she realized she was painting and writing to complete something for herself rather than for others. She tuned in to an inner voice that seemed to select certain words and phrases. Wanting to learn the tools for the work better, she enrolled in a poetry class. She immersed herself in her painting with the same energy, depicting on canvas what she saw in a way that intrigued her. "My paintbrush became the vehicle for moving between the inner and outer worlds, between the known and the yet to be discovered."

Yet, as with the poetry, she realized she needed feedback and some creative exchange. She slowly began to involve other artists in her process—looking at one another's work and sometimes sitting side-by-side to paint the same view of the ocean. Slowly, she learned that she could maintain her vision, even as her art was being exposed, without losing her confidence.

There was a difference, though, in sharing with other creative people she knew and opening up her private world to strangers. A defining moment came when she participated in her first poetry reading. The event was part of her poetry class, and it began with readings by established poets. She was nervous, listening to the others—published poets, educated poets, poets with "credentials"—as she waited her turn, trying to focus on their words instead of her own fluttery stomach. She gathered her strength, only to have the audience disappear before her eyes.

The featured poets read to each other. Then they left, taking the public with them, without listening to what the students had to say. I realized that although my contribution was little valued, I had to do it anyway. And my perception of those poets, heroes such a short time before, had changed. I no longer idolized them.

That experience represented for Linda the meeting of the public and private. Her inner voice had been ready to speak aloud. She'd had the anticipation of response and then received nothing. That could have been a white-flag moment of surrender: A visceral real-life unfolding, in all its horror, of what happens when you open that little box of pastels. It can all disappear, just like that. The effect might have proven devastating, but the opposite occurred. She realized that the words she had written did not lose an ounce of meaning to her, whether others perceived their value or not. Her conviction—that the work was ultimately for herself—was not just wishful thinking; it was real enough to hold her up happily on a stage, reading to a handful of fellow students, without a public audience. "I believe that the way I do my work can be a road map for other women, showing that there are many ways of being successfully creative in the world. Simply expressing yourself is proof that there is value in doing things your own way."

Lack of response from others wouldn't stop her from doing her work. She spent more and more time doing her poetry and her paintings. The work was an end in itself. Then one day came another challenge to go public—this time with her paintings.

My teacher told me it was time for a show, that you're not an artist until you are "seen." The advice resonated with something I felt inside. That art was meant to be experienced by others. It felt a little dangerous. But I decided to take the risk.

Linda decided to share her poetry and art with friends, not looking for artistic feedback as much as looking to open her creative self and be "seen" by others. An invitation from a coffeehouse owner gave her a forum for a short poetry reading.

Linda mounted a one-woman show of paintings and drawings. There was a full house. Among those there were many of her clients, thrilled to see this other "side" of Linda. They commented to each other on the loveliness of her landscapes and nudes, as well as her own graciousness. Sometimes artists are awkward about saying "thank you" praise, but Linda was delighted to hear the responses. "My dad was impressed and so was I, to see everything up there on the wall, being presented."

She received the kind of recognition she didn't expect. Not only were friends and family proud of her, but some of her paintings were sold to people who didn't know her, and some of her poetry made its way into literary publications. Objective feedback hadn't been Linda's primary goal. But her poems and paintings moved the audience to laughter and tears, and seeing and feeling their warm response to her. "That was my validation as an artist." She discovered the fine line between needing external approval and enjoying the effects on others of her artistic gifts. She didn't need approval, but she loved the recognition and appreciation she received.

At a subsequent presentation, Linda stood in front of people to read her poetry, with her paintings as backdrops. One of the poems showed that interplay between personal history, dreams, feelings, and art—the interplay so often discussed in the salon. She read it slowly and looked up occasionally to meet the eyes of her listeners. The degree of self-revelation was far greater than with anything she'd done before. The poem received a standing ovation.

Linda's Life These Days

Some years back, Linda came upon a quote from painter Cecil Collins in his book *Vision of the Fool:* "Creativity runs just below the surface of humanity." Since then, she has consciously sought ways to let that impulse rise in her daily life, aware that it cannot be forced. "If creativity is just below the surface, then if we work too hard, if we try too much, we'll go beyond that stream . . . we'll miss it entirely. To be successful, we must listen, we must trust, we must allow."

Linda values her interactions with others, but at the same time sees her essential self as separate. She is aware of the ongoing pull and push between her desire for connection and her need for solitude. "I love that push-pull, and I use it in my painting, taking that energy and directing it into the creative flow." For her work to thrive, she needs detachment from the external world, which seems to her more competitive and goal oriented than the inner world she must protect for her artistic vision to flourish.

> It has taken me years to value that private part of my existence. I think it is how women exist. We live in the private. We live with a sense that "being" is value enough. Often we do not always organize our lives around "goals." Women generally have an easier time with not knowing, with mystery. I am now comfortable with seeing what comes. I value the privacy that allows me to simply "be" with whatever I am doing.

The Crazy Woman

Linda's persona is so sane and soft-spoken, you almost want to laugh when she calls her muse the crazy woman. Her paintings and poems, though, vibrate with a free spirit that adheres to only the most minimal control. That freedom of expression comes from giving herself permission to create in the wild, doing it for herself, expressing herself playfully, and refusing to ever call her poetry or art "work." "My mind jumps around, and inside these jumps I find my creativity. The crazy woman is free from society's strictures, she has freedom not to think like others think." Linda's conscious task is to allow a safe place for her crazy woman to live and get as wild as she wants. Linda is a strong and grounded guardian, who has spent a lifetime protecting her muse from the external influences that might thwart her.

The task is not easy. Externally imposed rules, expectations, criticism, and competitiveness are poised and ready to intrude at any time into the creative life of anyone who is not alert. Linda says she continues battling external intrusions and does her painting and poetry because she has no choice.

> It's painful not to do it. When I write poetry, I meet with the crazy woman whenever she rises. I am willing to go with the flow, even when it means getting out of bed to record a word or a thought. Poetry expresses the truth of who you are, although sometimes it seems only you can understand it.

It is an extra gift when you share it and someone lets you know you have also spoken a truth for them.

Interior Life

Linda replenishes her creative well through regular meditation. "Meditation enables me to develop a container to hold my self. This provides the safety to be exposed and not be eaten by people's responses. Meditation also provides me inner strength to be myself, to be imperfect." She meditates both on her own and with a group. Meditation has become an instrument of her creativity, offering opportunity for finding the meanings in her thoughts and actions.

Linda also gains strength and confidence from sharing her dreams with others, listening to their dreams, and perceiving the similarities in the struggles people face as they seek ways to keep dipping into the flow of creativity. She has talked about dreams with some of the women, now friends, who come to her salon for more than a haircut. The conversations served to enforce her belief that "creativity has a natural ebb and flow, different for each person, there for those who work at paying attention."

Creative blocks are no longer a worry now that she has defined her attitude. "If not now, then later. I just have to relax, not try too hard, and allow myself to find the current below the surface." Linda says she has grown comfortable with not knowing what's happening in a logical way. Without the worry, she can drift with her impulses until something emerges. Linda's development of an internal safe place has allowed her art to thrive, giving her self-validation in a world that she believes places too much emphasis on the external trappings of success. "Society's values are based on credentials. What our culture really needs are values based on creativity."

Conversations and Reflections: Risking Self-Exposure

Many women who know Linda turn to her for ideas and inspiration because of the way she has demonstrated her creative muscle. After all, this quiet woman, who readily acknowledges her insecurities, has stood up before hundreds to read poetry and has displayed her paintings for the world to see. She didn't naturally gravitate toward the limelight. Instead, she was pulled by her creative spirit, her crazy woman, who seems to have a mind of her own. Like Annie, who found herself in the Pulitzer spotlight, Linda has an introverted and private nature. It wasn't easy to exhibit the essence of her self for all to see. But she did it. A close look at her creative path provides some clues about balancing the risks and rewards of revealing your creative self to others.

Maintaining a secret, private space can be a way to nurture the work (Linda would say "play") in a safe, criticism-free environment. And yet sharing what you have created is like giving a gift: You're showing something to others upon which you have bestowed great personal care. In so doing, you are transmitting that care to another. Spend too long with your creativity stowed away in a place apart from the "rest of your life" and your muse may feel stifled. Connecting with others can provide motivation, replenishing your creative source.

Are you someone who protects your work from exposure? If so, how do you know when vigilance becomes irrational fear? Becoming attuned to the balance often is a matter of bravely examining your fear and joyously imagining your hopes. What is the worst that would happen if you revealed your creative work to others? And what is the best that could happen? Writing down your visceral response to those questions is a good beginning for an exploration of the push-pull between self-nurturance and self-revelation.

Delicacy

Linda's story demonstrates the paradox of sensitivity: If you allow yourself to be "open"—vulnerable enough to respond to the creative spirit—you're probably also making a gaping hole for damaging intrusions. We've all heard stories about evil, callous, or just thoughtless people whose harsh words, rolled eyes, or stony silences were delivered in a vulnerable moment, wounding the person risking creative expression. There's the tentative poet, the fledgling painter, or the nervous musician who takes the criticism as a crippling blow. Or there's the shy performer on shaky legs, trying to make her debut, who retreats behind the curtain after a bad review or lack of audience response. Linda's story about people walking out before her first poetry reading is one of those tales that could have ended badly. But instead, she stuck it out and returned with a tale of courage.

The risk is real, as Linda sensed even as a small child, when you put your heartfelt work out for the world to see. At the same time, there's a lot of creative juice that comes from an exchange with others. The challenge and the joy of creativity is, as Sarah said about her writing, to be "fully seen," by one's own self and then by others. With Linda's unassuming nature and childhood fear of criticism, she was an unlikely candidate for creative warrior. Yet she bravely marched out to the public light—that place where everyone can see you and anyone can take a potshot—and she emerged unscathed. A graceful guide for creative courage, she has demonstrated it can be done.

The Secret Place

Your creative self will demand a certain amount of safe play-time if you are to end up with self-expression that is relatively pure—undiluted by what others think. But how much time do you need to explore your own vision, judgment free, before you can share it with others? Long enough to materialize what you see in a clear enough form that—though you might benefit from some polish or additions or corrections—you won't be tempted to lose the essence of the work once other people have their say. Creative connections can bring meaning and fun to the creative pursuit, and sometimes reaching out can net opportunities for making income from your work. But as the desire for recognition shifts the focus outward, it's critical to already have integrity in the work before stepping too far out of the safe zone.

Emily Dickinson, who lived all her life in the same small town and only had her poems published posthumously, actively shunned the spotlight. She wrote one poem called "I Am Nobody," in which she castigated the fame-seeker who is "public like a frog . . . to tell your name the livelong day to an admiring bog." Her reclusiveness and defense against public intrusion seems excessive; still, there is a certain nobility in the way she protected her creative spirit from judgment by the masses. Wouldn't it be glorious to have time and space to revel in the intrinsic value of your creative work, free of concerns about how others will react? Most of us desire ultimately to share our creative work with others—while we're still alive to enjoy the exchange—but we can remind ourselves about the value of that time apart and cherish it.

There's a delicate imperative: To continue production from the deepest parts of the creative well, you can't let the reactions of others interrupt the flow, as it might be extremely difficult to get it started again. Julia Cameron's book *The Artist's Way* helps explains why:

> *Creativity flourishes when we have a sense of safety and*
> *self-acceptance. Your artist, like a small child, is happiest when*
> *feeling a sense of security. As our artist's protective parents,*
> *we must learn to place our artist with safe companions. Toxic*
> *playmates can capsize our artist's growth.*

Taking time away from the influences in the outer world can allow an integrity to come into creative work. Often the internal work is a private matter. Sarah, in her writing, fled to private moments with a pad and pencil to work through experiences that were puzzling to her when she worked in a "man's world." Birgitta's time-out from the business world allowed her to sort through her feelings and memories, which led her to the bakery. In Linda's artwork and poetry, she worked privately to get the quiet, gentle aspect of her persona to accept and enjoy her inner crazy woman.

Most creative people need periods of repose to reflect upon themselves, giving them a firm footing before they walk out in public. Being able to say with some resolve, "This is me," makes it possible to bring your creative offerings to others. As you embark upon—or go deeper with—your creative work, are you consciously bringing all of yourself to the endeavor? Is there anything you are holding back from yourself? What kind and how much of private "playtime" does your creative self need for exploration?

Stepping Out of the Shadows

The timing of letting others see your creative self has everything to do with how comfortable you are with what you see. Once you feel secure with what you find inside, the authenticity of what you create shines through. While writing this chapter about Linda, Deborah and I attended one of her events, an art exhibit and poetry reading. That Linda's quiet voice filled the room was no less remarkable than the fact that a woman so seemingly self-contained could have created those bold-brush abstract paintings on the wall. "Linda's honesty is in all of it," Deborah said.

Linda had originally set out to do the painting and poetry for herself, and as she grew more confident, her life began to transform in ways that allowed her to show it to others. Seeing Linda's family members, clients, and friends among the strangers in the room underscored the personal nature of the work. "She is doing what I consider one of the most pivotal reasons for any creative act—creating meaning in her life. It's the payoff for taking risks," Deborah said. The first risk was personal, letting her inner self out through words on paper and paint on canvas. The second risk was showing that to others. At some point, Linda decided she didn't need to hide behind anything.

It's natural to keep much of yourself hidden in certain aspects of daily life. I once heard somebody say, "If everybody told the truth all the time, we'd all go nuts." There's a reason why we say "fine" in the office when somebody asks us how we are, even if we've just gone through a root canal or a breakup. It's the same reason why you don't do cartwheels down the hall when you're feeling joyful (although I do have one colleague who routinely slides down the banister): There's a time and a place for both the muse and the dark side. To get around in most social situations and professions, you may follow certain rules and expectations and avoid letting day-to-day interactions touch your heart. But to also lead a creative life, you can't let detachment from the self become habit forming.

Over the years, I've found refuge in the rules of daily journalism. I could trip outside the format from time to time with feature writing, but I could always retreat into a I'm-just-doing-a-job frame of mind. Professionalism can be a convenient cloak against the cold breath of criticism. In a newsroom, half your story may be lopped off because of eleventh hour space limits. You learn quickly that it's nothing personal. I learned to detach, most of the time, from the responses of others. But I was fortunate to maintain an intermittent connection with an intuitive, vulnerable part of myself that led to my "other" writing, the kind that exposed some raw and real parts of me. I kept that to myself for years. Eventually, sharing my poetry with my husband felt safe, and then I slowly began showing some of my essays to people, inviting criticism. Sometimes it stung. I told myself, "Maybe this is a good thing. At least you know it's important to you."

I thought of a friend of mine, the queen of cool, who was going through her first real heartbreak in a relationship after years of keeping emotional distance. Crying and laughing at the same time, she said, "Well at least I know I'm alive." I think of her each time I want to protect my work from harsh criticism. It's comforting to know that some of my words and ideas remain dear to me, even though I've marched so many other words out into the world with a job to do.

I probably wouldn't have volunteered to show anyone my poetry or short fiction—other than friends—but when the publisher of a women's fiction anthology invited me to submit, I decided to send in that story from ten years earlier, the one inspired by my friend Susan Amato's painting. The story was accepted into the collection *Saltwater/Sweetwater*. What made it bearable for me to have it in print—this odd story that seemed to come out of nowhere—was having my friend's painting reproduced in the book as an illustration. Somehow that seemed like bowing to the muse, sharing both credit and responsibility with an unconscious force.

If I'd kept my story to myself instead of showing it to my friend, I would not have gotten that delicious zap of personal affirmation that came from knowing that she and I had independently received a similar visitation by the creative spirit. Such intimate "recognition" held more meaning for me than objective responses that I received to subsequent work that had more commercial or literary value to others.

Creative schmoozing whips up its own kind of energy. The alone work is crucial, but it doesn't always have to be lonely. Finding out what others go through when they're playing or wrestling with the muse can give you some new ideas and maybe a few much-needed laughs or tears over shared experiences.

I'll Tell You Mine, If You'll Tell Me Yours (Truth)

Telling our stories to each other helps us to deflect the external influences, keep them at a distance. As Carolyn G. Heilbrun says in *Writing a Woman's Life,* "Women must turn to one another for stories; they must share the stories of their lives, and their hopes and their unacceptable fantasies." For Linda the chance came with a creative circle, a supportive group that she developed almost unconsciously in the course of her "day job" and her artistic "play," ultimately joining together the separate facets of her life.

Linda's work allowed her to develop slow, long-term relationships with people who were just as likely to come back to see her because of the interesting conversation as for the good haircut. Linda could reveal as much of herself or ask as many questions as felt comfortable with each person. Through this careful rapport with artists, writers, craftspeople, and other creative people, she was teaching, learning, and developing community.

How can you find creative community in your own life? There's no secret handshake or any other obvious way to identify other people who are struggling with the deep, personal kind of creativity that can be so isolating at times. Some people look to the world to have it "all together" while they're secretly struggling to understand themselves—and be understood by others—through the creative process. Some of the least likely candidates along your daily path may be looking for just the right kind of personal connection to cajole or inspire or entertain them between the lonely times of hunkering down to a challenging task.

Once you make a decision to seek out other people, there are formal and informal ways to proceed. You can take your first step in any direction. The formal route is through classes, associations and already-established groups. For most of the arts, you can find courses through universities, junior colleges, night school programs, or private tutors. Many county or town governments have some kind of arts council that can direct you to organizations. For writers, there are national organizations for almost every kind of writing—from journalism to romance—that have local chapters. Libraries are another good place to find what's already happening in your area. If you have already tried some of these routes, it may be helpful to try them again and focus on the more subtle possibilities of connecting with like-minded people—rather than focusing solely on the ostensible goals of the formal setting.

Another route involves focusing on the circles where you find yourself every day, whether that's your own or your children's school, the workplace, where you worship, or the errand stops you make in the routine course of the day. Look closely at the way people decorate themselves and their spaces. Look for symbols of creativity and ask questions about them. Be prepared to talk about aspects of your creativity you are ready to share. At first it will be small talk, but bit by bit you may start unraveling one another's creative stories. Pay attention to your responses. If the words you hear in response to your revelations make you feel threatened, this isn't the right kind of connection for you. If the exchange leaves you feeling open and safe, you're on your way to weaving a mutual support system.

Sometimes you can embark on long conversations and build relationships based on creativity without necessarily revealing all of your creative outlets or endeavors, which is what Linda did. You can let out some of your ideas, take in the thoughts of others, and work up to the nitty-gritty business of revealing your creative self. Becoming attuned to your comfort level, you can gauge the timing for opening your creative self up to others. I like Julia Cameron's analogy of the "protective parent," which she describes in The Artist's Way. Lovingly tuned-in parents know when their children need to be kept close and when they're ready to venture farther from the nest. Pay attention to how you are feeling about your creative work after a certain kind of contact with another—whether it's in a class, group, or one-on-one conversation. You'll know whether or not you should continue or withdraw for a while. There is nothing wrong with caution. And, as Linda did for many years, you can enjoy the company of other creative people without immediately declaring the whole of your creative self.

The Shadow Artist

In The Artist's Way, Julia Cameron uses the term "shadow artist" to describe those who find themselves drawn to—or attracting—creative people before they declare themselves. She urges people to take the hint if suddenly they seem to be surrounded by artistic people.

> Shadow artists are gravitating to their rightful tribe but cannot yet claim their birthright. Very often audacity, not talent, makes one person an artist and another a shadow artist—hiding in the shadows, afraid to step out and expose the dream to the light, fearful that it will disintegrate to the touch.

Sometimes fear is a healthy response, as it can allow you to protect yourself when your self-confidence is fragile. For Linda it worked to wait. Maybe it's not such a bad idea to stay in the shadows long enough to gather confidence in your own vision before stepping out. One can enjoy a quiet incubation period for nurturing creative expression, then find a collaborative environment where mutual respect allows the delicate tendrils of one's growth to absorb nourishment from another person's understanding.

Only you know the difference between "waiting for the right opportunity" and "just waiting" to embark on creative exchange with others. How do you know when it's time? It could be that you get to a place with your private work where you say to yourself, "I'm on the right track ... this looks like I envisioned it." You're delighted and you want to transmit that delight to another. Or the impetus to connect with others may come from the opposite direction. You're stuck, bored, or frustrated with your work, and you're feeling abandoned by the muse. In these critical moments, when you're feeling decidedly "on" or decidedly "off," you're likely to seek feedback. Maybe it's, "I accomplished this, finally, and want you to see it." Maybe it's, "I'm feeling like all my work has been wasted, and I'm looking for some reason to go on." You usually don't get to carefully plan the moment when you're so thrilled or so desperate that you need immediate feedback, so it's all the more essential that you've laid some groundwork for the moment when you're ready to lay your precious offering or dying embers at the feet of another.

Caring Feedback

You need feedback of the right kind. Sorting through criticism, recognizing the difference between denigrating feedback and gentle but honest examination of your work, is an issue that came up with almost every woman in this book. Each of us does the sorting differently.

As a writer, I look for feedback from people who are honest, caring, and secure in themselves. Mark Twain once wrote something that hints at a selection process for choosing who's in and who's out of your creative life: "Keep away from people who try to belittle your ambition. Small people always do that, but the really great make you feel that you, too, can become great." Twain's point brings us back to the protective parent analogy. As the guardian of your creative self, pay close attention to how you feel about the feedback you're receiving. It's pretty simple in theory, but difficult to remember, especially if you tend to be self-critical. If someone makes you feel energized, that person is worthy of inclusion in your creative life. Those who make you feel inadequate don't belong. You have the gift of creativity. It's yours. No one can take it away. Gentle encouragement can inspire you to go in new directions. Overt or subtle put-downs can hold you back. You can choose who to include.

Sometimes it becomes easier to sort through the feedback from others once you see that the harshest critic may be yourself. For a long time that was the case for Linda, who could paralyze herself with harsh self-judgment. But these days Linda has ways to quiet her self-censor.

I follow the advice of painter and writer Cecil Collins.
He suggests giving the internal critic the job of protecting
your best quality, so that it will remain available to participate
in the creative process. For Collins, that quality was a pure
heart. For me, it is a playful heart. By giving my critic the
job of protecting my playful heart, it won't interfere with what
I'm doing. Plus it provides assurance that if something comes
up to threaten my playful heart, the critic can neutralize it,
allowing my playful heart to remain untouched.

When you start examining your fears about exposure, try to identify which critical voices are coming from outside and which are from inside yourself. Does fear of harsh criticism prevent you from moving your creative self out into the world? You can put that fear aside once you are secure in your own work. Security doesn't come from outside approval, but from self-acceptance. That means quieting your own nagging voices. Linda's got her internal critic to work for instead of against her creativity. Can you turn your critic into a faithful watchdog? Instead of yapping at your efforts, get your critic to bark at those who threaten you and your creativity.

Teachers All Around and Inside

How much easier it would be to learn if each of us had a wise and generous teacher to guide us when we hit the rough water. I've heard a number of women recently talking about how their lives might have been different if they'd had mentors, the way many girls have today. Linda believes she has always had mentors and that everyone can, if they just open their eyes. "I've always found a teacher when I've needed one," Linda says. She perceived even as a small child that she could learn from other artists. As an adult, she recognizes that people are all going in different directions, and the goal is not the same for each of us, but we have our perceptions to offer each other. Instead of looking for one mentor, we can surround ourselves with peers who collectively teach one another.

Many of Linda's relationships were casually begun but evolved intimately over decades, contributing to the metaphorical "kitchen table" of women's shared knowledge. With conscious effort, each of us can nudge our supportive friends into a community. Someone just needs to set a time and a place. Make appointments. Linda wrote about women's gatherings in a poem: "It is there, that we who never learned to sew, remember the delicate art of stitching together the fabric of our life." At a recent art show and poetry reading, many of Linda's friends and customers began exchanging stories about how her "salon" has become a trading post for creative insights.

Dreamy Images

One insight that Linda talks about is how she draws inspiration from dreams or meditation, activities outside the noise of daily activity that allow her to listen to her unconscious. She consciously cultivates her dreams. There are different techniques for "dream mining." Some people keep a dream journal, others ask their dreams to answer questions, and still others look for specific symbols to guide them in decision making. C. Diane Ealy believes we can control what comes out of our dreams by deliberately creating a sort of dream language that allows the conscious and subconscious to communicate. In *The Woman's Book of Creativity,* Ealy writes:

> The assistance our dreams can give us doesn't have to
> arrive haphazardly. By communicating with the dream reality,
> we can orchestrate its responses to our needs. Rather than
> trying to discover the meaning of a dream, we put our efforts
> into building a rapport with our dream world. . . . Instead
> of waiting for our dreams to come up with an image and
> then trying to figure out what it means, we can suggest to
> our dream reality that it use particular images to represent
> certain things.

Ealy suggests that women can give their subconscious concrete symbols to answer questions, symbols as banal as a red light for "no" or a green light for "yes."

One sign of creative conversation is when dream language is spoken. Images from dreams are traded along with suggestions for good movies or restaurants. Talking about the images with others helps to turn them over, discovering new aspects of potential meaning. Dream imagery is nonlinear and irrational, something ultimately understood only by the dreamer. But talking about dreams is illuminating, a language of creative community.

Onward: Growing Comfortable in the Light

The haircuts are still needed, but the ruse has ended. These days when Linda's clients make an appointment, some say only half-jokingly that they're going "for therapy" or to "get their creative tune-up." Many credit her with helping them with their own creative breakthroughs—urging a poem out of them, inspiring an image for a painting, developing an idea for a book. No longer keeping her art life separate from her workaday life, these days Linda is settling comfortably into a place at the center of an artistic circle she helped create.

> When I had my first art show, I sold half of my paintings and many drawings. I realized I had done what I wanted to do and people loved it. I didn't expect that. I thought that because the vision that I portray in my work is so personal, it would not be desired. But I think the playfulness, freedom, and mystery that exists in my work was grasped by many more than I had anticipated. I don't want to "explain" my art. It needs to resonate with the perception of the viewer and be free to create meaning for them, independent of me.

Linda plans to continue both kinds of work, not interested in giving up her salon. She likes having a job that keeps her in touch with people and promises an income that allows her to protect her paintings and poems from the pressures of the marketplace. For a long time, Linda didn't want to be a hairdresser—she wanted to only do art; but now she says: "I have learned to value my path, to accept what I've done, as well as what I've not done. All experience is part of learning to know yourself."

Linda reminds us that you do not have to have degrees or credentials to be creative. "You do what you can do—instead of thinking you have to do it perfectly, or the way others do it, or the way tradition would have you do it." The childhood fear that someone could take away the box of pastels is gone. She feels safe from critics, those inside and those outside, because she can speak the truth about herself. "For many years I did artistic things and received recognition for them. And I always thought of myself as creative and artistic. But now I think of myself as an artist."

6

Seizing the Opportunity: Accepting Your Imperfections

Around here, I've often got mess upon mess. It makes me feel great to be in the middle of something and have these pieces of it all around.

—Nancy Jenkins, volunteer director of a children's talent show

Meet Nancy at the Show

Nancy takes a slow, deliberate breath. She tells herself, "Okay, so this is just a middle school talent show, and you're just a volunteering mom. Whatever happens will be fine." For weeks she has cajoled and comforted nervous children. Her house is strewn with paints and cardboard and costume materials. Fueled by adrenaline, she smiles reassuringly for the kids, all the while laughing at herself as she teeters intermittently on the edge of hysteria.

The overhead lights dim and the chatter in the gymnasium settles into a hush, and then there is darkened silence. The spotlights go on, beaming down on tall screens surrounding the stage, painted with the faces of history's famous movie stars—Marilyn Monroe, James Cagney—their likenesses captured in a few well-placed brush strokes. An old Broadway show tune begins. A velvet curtain parts and the show begins. Tonight, there will be twenty-five-foot-high dancing puppets, not to mention the gymnasts tumbling to the beat of old-time songs. There will be the collective adult breath holding while a child struggles in front of hundreds of people to get all the notes right in Beethoven's "Für Elise," and cheers for dozens of other kids who will each get their three minutes of fame.

Forgiving audience members would be satisfied simply to see their favorite middle schooler appear on stage and survive the act. But Nancy and her co-producers have turned the prosaic school talent show into dazzling vaudeville. Parents and kids, their entertainment expectations calibrated low, blink twice in disbelief at the old basketball court's overnight transformation into a professional-looking theater. The overall effect presents a calculated and considerable statement: "What these kids are doing is important. Watch and listen."

At one point in the evening, Nancy appears on the stage with her two daughters to sing a ballad and there is wild applause. Kids and their parents are screaming, "Nancy! Nancy!" When the hoopla fades, the guitar notes begin and bell-clear voices blend in pure, three-part harmony. The song is about family love and ties between the generations. By the refrain, half the people in the room have tears in their eyes. They have been touched not only by the song, but by what Nancy has given all of their kids: a chance to shine.

It has taken seven months of set painting, costume making, organizing, music recording, and careful encouragement of nervous young performers to prepare for this ephemeral event. Two nights and that's it. Portions of the show will be recorded on videotape by proud parents, but for the most part, all of that vision, work, and fuss is gone in a poof of gleeful applause. What endures from the talent show is the by-product of the process itself—for Nancy, her collaborators, and the students involved. This is collective creativity in action.

Nancy doesn't pretend for a moment that she only participates in the talent show for the kids. The annual talent show at her daughters' school was the key that unlocked the door to her own artistic life. A high achiever, Nancy has a streak of perfectionism that once tyrannized her, manifesting in bulimia and anorexia. Now she knows to ignore the inner voice that tells her something has to be done "the right way." Instead, she dives headfirst into activities, inventing as she goes along, making lots of messes and showing her daughters how a woman looks when she feels free to be herself.

With her long, wavy, red hair and cowboy boots, living in a home filled with art work and musical instruments, Nancy brings a casual glamour and sophistication to the role of "just a mom." She's smart and pretty, and she has the kind of self-mocking humor that allows her to get away with being a little wicked. She's a "cool mom," as the kids say. You can't miss her. And for that reason, she helps spotlight the work unsung maternal heroines always have done: plunging into their children's world, turning ordinary activities into magical events, making fun, making memories, and starting something new. At the same time, she's teaching herself and inspiring others to forget the perfect product and image, and to instead laugh and learn during the creative process.

Growing Wherever You Are

Especially for people with a perfectionist's nature, it's tempting to postpone the creative urge until that "ideal outlet" presents itself at a point in your life when you finally have the time and are free of distractions. Nancy demonstrates that the time and place are the here and now. She's a role model especially for women who see the child-rearing years as a time to let their own creativity lie dormant while they support their children's developing talents.

During life stages in which responsibility to others defines your commitments, many women feel that it's best to put their own desires "on hold." In actuality, the busiest times in life may be when it's most important to find a creative outlet that's conducive to self-understanding. For Nancy, it was the chance to create artwork, play music, and turn the house upside down for the sake of a project. The simple act of making a mess turned out to have great symbolic value for someone once overly concerned with having everything "all together." Rather than being selfish—the big "no-no" to many caregiving women—finding meaningful work or play can be beneficial to everyone. Nancy has learned to pursue her own vision, sometimes stubbornly, and that has proven to be positive, not just for her own sense of fulfillment, but for her daughters. Since it's clear that Nancy derives a great deal of pleasure from doing these shows, they have for a role model someone who can joyfully nurture herself while being responsible to others.

Many people today are replacing thwarting societal messages to women and girls with affirmations like "You can do what you want," "Don't worry what other people think," and "It's okay to make mistakes." Nancy figured out that the best way to give those affirming messages to her daughters was to demonstrate them in her own life.

She had to overcome a lot before she realized that, even though she was always the "academic type," she could be creative, too. She learned to honor her own peculiar method of doing art work, and she developed a confidence in her skills that made it fun to work with other people. She's recovering from a perfectionist streak that once manifested in serious eating disorders. Now she's making up for some of the experiences she missed in her high-achieving childhood. At the same time, she has grown sophisticated in teamwork interactions. Another demonstrated lesson for her daughters: You can assert yourself while working companionably with others.

What began as a school production as community service has evolved into a series of life lessons—some completely unexpected—and Nancy's emerging awareness of a goal she has for her daughters' creativity: "I want them to bust loose earlier than I did."

Nancy's Path

Aiming High

Nancy grew up in Louisville, Kentucky with loving, cultured parents and a belief in possibilities. It was a time when most mothers stayed home, and Nancy's mom did, too, even though she was a concert pianist who in another era might have had a career on stage. Nancy remembers her mother's playing as exquisite: "I'll spend my whole life trying to figure out my mom. Being that good at something is kind of unusual." Despite her talent, Nancy's mom never expressed any frustration over the "might-have-beens" and seemed content with having her two daughters as her main audience. Nancy remembers her mother at the piano playing Rachmaninoff and Debussy. She also remembers her mom going out with her girlfriends, listening to country music, and drinking beer: "My mom loved every kind of music."

The drive for perfection began at an early age for Nancy, and she doesn't know why. "I was the kid at the birthday party, where they'd have a game like 'How many words can you come up with for this?' and I'd come up with twelve and still be going after the other kids would say two or three. I was driven, but I was very good at keeping that from view." She was working like mad to keep ahead, while at the same time making everything look easy: "Typical upper-middle-class, high-achieving female."

An academic bent led her to the college track via advanced math and science classes. She was known as a brain. "My typical line was, 'You want it? Oh, I can do that. I can do it better than anyone.'" There wasn't room in her course schedule for much art or music, and Nancy's self-image didn't include being an artist, though as a child she was surrounded by artistic opportunities that she absorbed without giving it much thought. "As a child I did artistic stuff, all kids do, but I would never have dreamed of taking an art class. I didn't give the creative life any headway. It was all AP English."

Even though she didn't think much about art, Nancy was inadvertently learning the tools of creativity through play. Her mom had art materials and building supplies and paints and glitter available for whatever she and her sister wanted to do. Without calling it art, the girls would paint and build things: "We had a mess all the time. It was our fun, making messes with paint and junk." As long as it was playing she could relax and have fun—much different than her almost obsessive approach to the other challenges in her life.

Letting Go

Besides doing everything the "best," Nancy wanted to *be* "the best" and—after her mom made comments about her sister's weight gain—being thin became primary to Nancy's image of perfection. Her obsession with being the "good girl"—smart, accomplished, and trim—led to her becoming anorexic and bulimic in her teens. Starving herself, then overeating, then throwing up gave her a feeling of control over her life, much of which revolved around meeting the perceived expectations of her parents and teachers. Little was known or discussed about the disease at the time. She liked being thin and never talked to anyone about how she stayed that way: "I didn't know what it was—that was before anorexia was a household word."

Her bingeing and purging continued when she went away to college. The first school she attended was Mills, a women's college in California. Creatively, it was a fruitful time. Surrounded by supportive female mentors in an atmosphere that valued the arts, she thrived, loosening up enough to declare a major in drama, do choreography, and take dance classes daily. Among other dancers, anorexia was not that uncommon: "I was following my heart," she reflects. "Unfortunately, I was still starving my body."

Nancy continued to battle the inner compulsion to control her eating, surviving on a ritualistic daily meal of one turkey patty, a container of frozen chopped spinach, and cottage cheese. Five-feet-four-inches tall, she dropped to a skeletal ninety pounds, just enough to keep her anorexia from becoming life threatening. She was hard on herself, expecting and earning As.

Around this time she made a romantic mistake, carrying it through to the altar. He was another high achiever. Older, he swept her off her feet. He was as hard on her as she was on herself. She felt unloved, stung by his criticism, and more nervous than ever. The union lasted less than two years.

She was accepted to Stanford as an upperclassman, where she decided to take the opportunity for grand-scale academic achievement. She studied science and decided to become a physical therapist. At Stanford, she met the man who would soon become her second husband. She felt like herself with Bob. He had a sense of humor and no rigid expectations about how she should behave.

She remembers one time when she was driving with him in his sports car and, in a moment of luxurious stretching, she put her bare foot against the windshield and it popped out. The rush of air was frightening, but more than that she expected fury for having damaged his car. Instead of upset, he was just puzzled: "I was amazed at how calm he was. I couldn't believe it." She felt a swell of appreciation for her new mate and a sharp reminder of the old fears of judgment.

After college, Nancy embarked on her career and established her independence, finding creative fulfillment as a physical therapist: "It's very creative," she explains. "It's using your brains and your hands in the same way as an artist." But she still battled her disease. The end of her anorexia and bulimia came with her first pregnancy. Taking care of the baby growing inside her was incentive to take care of herself. She began gaining weight and feeling more at ease. With savings and her husband's work, she was able to stop working in her physical therapy job, and she turned her attention to her home, family, and community. She had two daughters, three years apart, and became active in her church.

Seeing Herself

One day, a friend asked her to join a sculpture class, in which women were encouraged explore themselves through the art. The idea didn't appeal to her at all: "My impression was you were supposed to go into it with something you wanted to work out. It was about rituals: passing around symbolic objects and burning different things . . . I grew up in Kentucky and I came fairly skeptically to New Age thoughts and ideas. I didn't feel I had a lot of issues to work through or explore." In retrospect, she sees that she had plenty of issues around perfectionism, but she hadn't yet begun to sort them through.

In an odd way, Nancy felt she didn't qualify for the class. Her initial thought was that she hadn't suffered enough to be an artist and that with her academic background she didn't qualify for entrance into the creative club. But later she would come to see she was wrong on both counts. She allowed herself to get talked into doing the class and soon found herself squishing and molding clay. She began working on a life-size woman. She didn't intend the sculpture to be of herself, but she studied her own body to learn how to shape her creation. It developed into a red-haired, thin being with green eyes— much like herself.

Through the sculpture class, feeling herself stretch the ever-so-thin skin over the statue's frame, Nancy began reflecting on her past anorexia. She was no longer bingeing and purging, but she still struggled with her high standards. Now she could finally face the significance of her past eating disorder and even talk to her husband about it. She parked the sculpture under the piano—where it remains today—as a reminder of a creative breakthrough.

Her initial resistance to taking the sculpture class taught her something about herself: "I want to know how to do something before I start. I want to be good at it before I start." She didn't want her daughters to feel those limits. She resolved to encourage her daughters to explore their creative talents, giving them guitar and singing lessons, and filling the house with art supplies and various pieces of interesting junk that had potential for becoming part of a creation. She began to teach herself to "just start doing something." She still didn't like failing. She still didn't like not knowing how it would turn out. But she kept going.

At her daughters' schools, she was known as a mom who would help out. She was mostly in the background, a helper, until the day she found out that the talent show at her eldest daughter's middle school was floundering for lack of someone to produce it. Both of her daughters were showing their musical talents, and Nancy had hoped they would get to participate in talent shows during their school years. She recalls how she signed herself up during a chat with another mom at a sports event.

Connecting with Others

"Linda [a different Linda from the poet in chapter 5] and I were sitting at a soccer game. She had worked on a talent show before. The school was desperate for someone to do that year's talent show. Anything we did was going to be good because the baseline expectation was so low. It was just one of those things you fall into. I told myself, 'Whatever you do will be better than nothing.' That attitude gives you this wonderful cushion." She agreed to co-produce the talent show, and she and Linda assembled a group of women.

Pretty soon her house was turned into a wall-to-wall studio with props, set parts, and costumes. She found the work alternately maddening and gratifying. She didn't always know what she was doing. One time she was doing some painting in a slow, mechanical way. Part of her mind was thinking, "There must be a faster way to do this," but another part of her mind was leaping ahead to the other jobs she had to do. She realized that her flashes of inspiration erupted while she was doing the humdrum mechanical parts of the job. She allowed her ideas to form where and how they wanted to. She'd start to paint a set without knowing exactly how it would come out.

Nancy had never worked so closely as a team with someone else before, but she quickly began to see that it worked when she and Linda respected each other and had the confidence to put forth their own ideas. The women would laugh about how they had to take turns indulging their egos and then helping the other. One minute they'd be the diva, the next they'd switch to being the supporter: "We started calling that being each other's art slaves."

Nancy might not have discovered the benefits of teamwork if the task had not presented itself in the beginning as being practically risk free—and for that she thanks her friend and collaborator. How can you fail if you step up to fill a void: do a little fund-raiser, enable children to perform, and have someone to lean on in the process? They were a good match. Linda enjoyed the organizational aspect, dealing with school officials and staying in communication with parents, while Nancy liked the art and music. They turned out to be creative in different ways, and they used their strengths to help each other. For example, Linda gave Nancy the encouragement she needed to pull off the complex business of coordinating the schedules of dozens of kids and families.

Somehow the talent show came together. Nancy may have felt like she was in the middle of chaos, but when the lights dimmed and the sets appeared, she realized that she had gotten past her obsessive perfectionism and was actually enjoying things, just as they were. For once in her life she wasn't dwelling on the little things that had gone wrong here and there. This was a success in the larger sense. The show itself was just part of it. She was also having a great time.

Nancy found herself volunteering for the next year and the next. Each year, she started with a theme, and from the theme emerged ideas about songs and ways to present the children's talent within the concept. Each year, the decorations became more elaborate. Giant golden replicas of Oscar trophies stood at attention for the Hollywood theme. For the cowboy theme, she got kids together to make giant cows.

Nancy got more than a few unexpected perks in return for giving her time, energy, and enthusiasm to the school—she discovered some of her own talents in the process of showcasing the children's. When she got the job of designing sets, she had no idea that when she got a paintbrush in her hand, she would find herself lost in creative bliss for hours on end. She sang along with her daughters to help them practice and ended up allowing herself to be drafted into a musical performance with them. And while working on the production, she discovered the creativity involved with teamwork, experimenting with what some have called "creative ecology," a group effort where the collective vision takes on a life of its own, beyond the individual contributions.

Wicked Witches Welcome

Over the years, Nancy worked with many people and collaboration helped her recognize something special in other women that might not have come to her attention otherwise; one woman she worked with didn't have any "credentials" or training as an artist or musician, nor was she sophisticated or educated in a traditional sense: "I don't know if I'd say I'm a snob, but I didn't recognize her abilities."

Then the woman displayed artistic skill that took Nancy's breath away. The expressions she brought to the faces of sculptures and the ideas she had for costumes were among the most original Nancy had seen:

There are people who love to make things. Maybe they can't spell, maybe they lack formal education. Creativity knows no bounds. It certainly doesn't know educational bounds. If you have it, there's nothing that can block it. With her, I realized it took some guts to put her ideas out there. I realized then that if you want to do it, it's all a matter of hiking up your trousers and doing it.

Not all of Nancy's working relationships gelled. Problems came up with one woman who Nancy perceived as being emotionally delicate, "as though she had some deep hurt." Nancy felt she had to constantly protect her. That made Nancy hold back some of her own creative ideas, investing energy in second guessing the woman's response, taking care not to cause hurt. There was an element of emotional fear in the relationship that ended up working both ways, preventing the development of the trusting bond that's necessary for collaborative creativity.

Mostly she found that her fellow volunteers were tolerant of each other's ups and downs, "wicked witch days and all," and were confident and willing to speak up. During the Hollywood talent show, for example, she had decorated her giant replicas of the Oscar trophy with little mink stoles: "Right before the show started, another woman whispered, 'Lose the boas!' and she was so right."

Nancy's Life These Days

Making Messes

Nancy's life is different from women who must make a living by going to work, combining their child-rearing years with jobs and tight schedules: "Almost everything I do now has to do with the school and children's activities." But the hours she has committed to projects may not be that much less than a mom who works outside the home.

Perhaps the main difference is that she has a clear flow and connection between her "work" and her "home" lives. It's all happening together, in stacks and piles around her. With the level of organization necessary in a household where both parents work, often there's an emphasis on order. Nancy's approach goes against all the lessons about reducing clutter and the conventional wisdom of "when in doubt, throw it out." She saves stuff because she never knows when it might be useful.

Nancy's house can look Martha Stewart perfect, but open any given closet and there are the ingredients—fabric, containers, tools, and buttons—for making just about anything.

> *One time we needed wheels for a car one of the girls was building, and I thought, "What about the lids from old spray paint cans?" For some reason, I had all these empty spray paint cans in the shed. There's a lot of value in not throwing things away. There's every possible creative thing around here. The kids are always saying, "Mom do we have . . . ," and*

usually I can say "yes." Both of my daughters are proficient at taking on a creative project.

Having designated areas for a continuing mess seems to work for Nancy. Sometimes the designated area is the whole house, sometimes just a table, other times a corner of a shed. But her kids know they can start a project and not have to pick it up before they're finished. In giving them permission to enjoy the messy aspects of creating, Nancy ended up giving permission to herself.

For Nancy, the creative chaos is a reminder that she can let go of perfectionism. It's ironic, she reflects, that her bulimia was a function of wanting her self and her life to be "together," since "it's so gross." The talent show allowed her to see that a certain amount of messiness, confusion, and uncertainty is healthy when trying something new. Telling herself it's "just a school project" has given her a "cushion" so that she doesn't have to impose her straight-A perfectionist's standards on herself. To the outside observer, the event may look as perfect as any school production can be. Nancy still has high standards for herself, but along the way she revels in the freedom to laugh or scream and let go during the many stages of production, during which everything is pure chaos. The lessons from the talent show have also rippled out into other aspects of her life.

Nancy has discovered, as many women do, that relaxing your standards can actually yield higher results than when you're feeling perfectionistic or nervous about end results. She started talking back to the inner voice that was telling her, "You have to know what you're doing so you can get it right the first time." She's found that she can experiment with ideas and skills she was afraid to try before. Instead of seeing mistakes as something to be avoided, she sees them as necessary to move to the next step. She turns the disastrous moments into good stories, which gives her more creative freedom and gives the children permission to experiment, too. One student caught the freedom bug. In the middle of the final production, he thought of a skit to ad lib for his James Cagney character and a friend's Marilyn Monroe. Nancy said, "Go for it," he did, and the result "was the funniest thing."

Real Teamwork

To a casual observer, the two main producers of the annual school talent show couldn't be more different. Nancy is the flamboyant, effusive one, Linda more inclined to be carrying a clipboard. They started out with the advantage of clearly defined roles and goals, but as anyone who has worked with a team knows, good planning alone doesn't necessarily make for smooth relationships. What has worked for them is mutual tolerance, giving each other a wide berth for their differences and reminding each other often how much they appreciate each other. The kids know Nancy for her words of loving encouragement, but her partner knows Nancy can be mischievous—funny about it, but wicked nonetheless—crossing her eyes and shrieking when things aren't going right.

Nancy says trust has helped strengthen the bond between her and Linda. A friendship has grown from that. "Part of it is that she is so secure, happy in herself," Nancy says. Trust allows ideas and feelings to take shape; for women engaged in holistic creation, which often starts in the middle and works in whatever direction the ideas go, there aren't necessarily words to describe the mental process under way.

Nancy and Linda aren't thrown off by each other's reactions and know what's truly important to their process. If there's an administrative issue and Nancy says, "I can't think about that right now," her friend understands. And if Linda doesn't want to get caught up in the details of Nancy's eccentric process of making sets, Nancy understands. They know their parts, encourage each other, and don't fall apart during the occasional meltdown. "You know you're going to get there," is the way Nancy describes it. "Trust has to work both ways. The other person may not be taking the same path you would or even be able to explain theirs to you." Nancy has learned to be patient with others and with herself:

> Women need to be able to express their worst and their best. I like being able to say anything that comes into my head and know that's safe. When I first started working with Linda, I thought she was all sweetness and light, but she can get down there . . . We all have to let some of our witch come out. We have to be polite and say the right thing most of the time, but sometimes you've had it. When I lose it, the children really get off on it. When my dark side shows, they say, "She's your evil twin." I remember one day there was a problem with the set and I jumped off the stage and was screaming, "I hate it. I hate it."

Nancy remembers the response: "Linda laughed." Perspective returned.

Making It Up As You Go

Since Nancy first decided to let her imagination go wild for the annual talent show, she began to encounter more chances to play with art. All philanthropic—supporting charitable organizations—but at the same time, an expression of herself. There was, for example, the collection of life-size puppets she created for her church's Christmas pageant. Among the nativity characters, there are two women on either side of Joseph. They have similar features and clothing, but there's a slight difference in their rapturous expressions. One looks more innocent, the other has a couple of laugh and worry wrinkles. "We decided to have two Marys," Nancy explains matter-of-factly, "one before childbirth and one after." An extra Mary in the pageant was a small innovation, perhaps perplexing to others, but a gratifying act of creative irreverence for Nancy.

Nancy's confidence grew as she realized there aren't always words to explain her inspirations and they needn't always make sense to others: "Sometimes when I'm working, there's this linear-mentality voice that says, 'This is taking you way too long, come up with a way that's faster.'" But Nancy has learned that while she is meandering along the circuitous route toward one part of the project, she is synthesizing other ideas, getting a picture of the whole, and very often enjoying herself in the process. "When that voice speaks to me I say, 'Shut up, we're having fun.'" Nancy's favorite collaborators are women who take her side against that linear voice and let her have her fun.

Conversations and Reflections: Losing Perfectionism, Finding More of Yourself

Redefining Perfect

Having watched Nancy in her role as talent show producer over the years, I had a view of her as the "perfect" mom and wanted to bring her into this book to help other mothers explore the possibilities for close, fun interaction with their children. But over the course of the interviews, a shift in theme occurred. Being perfect was not the goal; rather, Nancy's work with her daughters' school events had finally provided permission for her to do something and *not* be perfect.

As it turned out, the reality of Nancy's process carried a more profound message about creativity than the image I'd witnessed from afar along with the other talent show audience members. Nancy didn't manufacture all that dazzle and opportunity for the children on stage by following some secret "cool mom" formula. Rather, she pulled it off by making it up as she went along.

Creativity involves a high tolerance for mistakes, acknowledging your strengths and limitations for the sake of teamwork and talking back to the inner nag that tells you to follow the rules. These are lessons Nancy continues teaching herself and demonstrating for the children.

Looking a little closer at Nancy's creative story, I began to see more of the mechanism for change. Resisting perfectionism and being committed to facing all of yourself requires honesty, not as a vague concept but as a discipline. For example, Nancy's willingness to reveal the "messy" parts of her creative growth and personal history was an act of honesty in and of itself. She could have just talked about the surface of her life, but when Meg and I got to her house to interview her, she chose to go deeper. It happened when Meg saw the statue under the piano. Meg's eyes got big as she stared at the statue, the red hair and green eyes. Meg looked back and forth from the statue to Nancy, struck by the likeness, then Meg reached out and touched the arm of the statue. "She is so thin," Meg said. Nancy whispered back, "Her skin barely covers her bones." Nancy's eyes clouded over and we all sat down on the floor around the statue. And then she began to tell us about her battle against anorexia and bulimia and how having her children helped save her. I was moved by her honesty, and said, "I would never have had any idea." Nancy shook her curls and grinned. "Of course not. I like to present well."

The Bad Side of Good

The plight of women who strive to meet the expectations of society—to be beautiful, thin, smart, and competent, and to make it all look easy—is the subject of the book Susan and I wrote, *Goodbye Good Girl*, which was the foundation for this book. Being "good" and following the external "rules" is stifling. Real creativity—the kind from the inside out—requires all of the self, including parts we may have trouble acknowledging.

Nancy's anorexia was one manifestation of the social illness that demands that we "present well." It's not unusual that it wasn't until years later that Nancy began to understand the dynamic between her eating disorder and her perfectionism. Most women have had friends or family members over the years who at some point learned how to intentionally throw up in order to stay thin and became sicker and sicker. Susan wrote a column about a friend's daughter who is a high achiever, with lots of friends, a good body, and what started out as a little obsession with weight that led to bingeing and purging and eventually a dangerous weight loss. The most shocking aspect of the daughter's illness was that "she didn't know how serious it was . . . she didn't seem to have a clue."

Throughout the stories in this book are examples of how women manifest their frustration with external pressures—feeling lonely or ill, using drugs or alcohol, and, as in Nancy's case, trying to assert control by starving her body. For many, the creative process has been healing, as it was for Nancy. The more she relaxed and had fun with all the artistic and social aspects of the talent show, the more easily she could laugh, cross her eyes, or scream as she bumped into her perfectionism. It's particularly poignant that Nancy is the mother of two daughters who are now able to model a creative process that will allow them to express themselves freely—mistakes and all—rather than strive to please.

Jumping In

The tightly wrapped good girl avoids situations where she doesn't immediately know how to be successful. Shedding those bindings can be scary, but there are ways for perfectionists to take small steps. For Nancy, it was taking on a creative project that was close to home and seemingly "safe," because she had support and the bar was set fairly low (school talent shows can be pretty funky and parents and students will generally still be happy).

If you have perfectionist tendencies, you probably know that throat-tightening feeling that comes with a voyage into the unknown. Some women practice loosening up by deliberately tackling activities that symbolize fears—as photographer Annie did by taking calculus to overcome the math phobia that to her symbolized low self-esteem. Is there anything in your life that makes you feel tense and say, "I don't want to go there"? Often, that's an opportunity to meet face-to-face with your perfectionism. If you wade in, fears and all, you'll find yourself in that nether world of insecurities. Can you handle the moments of "not knowing" long enough to discover what's on the other side? Nancy found that the phase of feeling out of control ("Yikes, I don't know what I'm doing! I've never done this before") is a necessary part of finding her own way.

Children as Teachers

Watching Nancy in action—seeing her with the glow of health and good humor—is inspiration to let loose. I once had the idea that being a grown-up and modeling good behavior for children meant keeping feelings under control. There's that unspoken rule that tells us parents aren't supposed to have needs, but they should always tend to the needs of their children. Nancy is clear about her likes and dislikes. When something isn't going right, she does a mock motion of pulling her hair out, making fun of herself and her worries. I've watched her do this with the kids and they grin. It doesn't seem like anger directed toward them. It's Nancy expressing herself, and they seem fine with that. She laughs with gusto, from a deep place. The personal drama is a part of her she developed as an adult, but it seems natural, as though she was always an expressive child, rather than the quiet good girl she was.

Nancy is learning from the kids as they learn from her. She interacts with not only her daughters, but with dozens of children. They'll tell her what they think and make her laugh if she's getting caught up in details—especially when it interferes with their fun. Nancy is teaching herself and the kids that projects are just as successful when you take a relaxed approach, letting the paint drip on the linoleum, wielding a jigsaw without a pattern.

Her perfectionism will probably always be there in the background—and the grand scale of the talent show is an example of her incredibly high expectations—but she's learned to say "shut up!" to those negative internal messages that say achievement has to come from following the rules. She's constantly working to overcome her "good girl" instincts. Getting these lessons from kids requires dropping old ways of thinking and really listening to what they have to say. It's the same kind of "getting over yourself" that helps with performing, music, art or any kind of creative endeavor.

There is reciprocity when parents let go and become more fully themselves—kids respond. Children have a sixth sense about what's honest and real. When Nancy started expressing herself, her daughters seemed to grow more free to do the same. A recent survey showed an increasing number of women prefer being at work to being at home, because at work everything's more predictable and it's easier to feel successful. It's the difference between trying to meet standards defined "out there"—by work and society—versus getting down into real interaction. Wading into creative projects with children can be a reminder that healthy growth has more to do with discovering the self than following the rules.

One of the biggest challenges for me during the years when I worked full time was coming home after spending a day in the newsroom, having worked through a long list of stories and phone calls and meetings, and finding my son in the middle of a game with his caregiver and the other kids. I learned not to interrupt and try to put him on my "schedule" ("time to go now and get dinner"), but to watch and wait and, on rare, lucky occasions, be able to figure out the game and perhaps even participate. It took a lot of gear shifting to get into that pace and mind-set, to be able to play after working all day.

Playing with the Kids

It's worth the effort to learn to play, which is really the work of childhood. Doing creative projects with kids can show them a different side of themselves. It's a chance for them to get away from the classifications they may get at school, where kids tend to be categorized as brains, artists, or jocks. Why not do it all? I grew up in a family where we painted, sang, wrote poetry, played sports, and looked at the stars through a homemade telescope. Thankfully, we weren't required to do any of it perfectly or even well. The activities were more like games than lessons.

I didn't realize until I was an adult how unusual it was to have such a wide range of activities going on under one roof; I now see how my parents made a conscious decision to include us in their fun. Soon after my son was born I realized that having kids is a good excuse to play, experimenting with creative projects you enjoyed as a child, finally getting to do some of the things you didn't get to do then.

For the big projects, like school talent shows, few parents today can make the time to take charge. Parents like Nancy are all the more valuable because school funding in many areas is shameful. Art is often considered fanciful, extra, unnecessary. Band and art teachers can talk until their throats are sore about how doing music and art helps brain development, but school boards drop those classes first when it comes to budget cuts. The prevailing attitude that "art is optional" makes it all the more important when parents whip up energy for creative projects at their children's schools—it's telling children art is important.

Some parents, like Nancy, are lucky enough to have the time and resources to volunteer at their children's schools, which so often need help in maintaining an emphasis on the arts. However, all parents can take the time to engage in creative projects with their children at home. For example, spreading out paints on the kitchen table, playing charades and other games that use improvisation, writing a play or story together, staging a neighborhood or family talent show, or having joke-telling marathons. The only rule for these activities is: No judgments allowed! By doing this, both children and their parents can claim their creative selves in a fun, safe atmosphere.

Even though I'll never sing or write poetry professionally, having grown up doing those things has given me a couple of extra ways to make myself feel good during an otherwise ordinary day. My son writes poems for fun, even though he's also a jock: "I don't know where it came from!" he exclaimed one day about a lovely piece he wrote in an almost archaic language. He got a glimpse of the power of the unconscious. He might benefit from that experience in many ways, but feeling good is reason enough. I can lift my own spirits by singing in the car, rekindle feelings by writing a love poem to my husband. Using your creativity to express yourself, your experiences, and your emotions—and sharing those creative expressions with others—is how memories are made. These fun exercises also are practice for emphasizing process over product.

In the *Woman's Book of Creativity*, author C. Diane Ealy urges women to know they have permission to enjoy their art for the sake of it: "I find many adults expect that if they develop the natural gifts they had as a child then they have to begin earning a living from that talent. I'll let you in on a secret: your innate abilities can be nurtured for pleasure and pleasure only!" Doing things "just for fun" does help exercise the brain in a way that ultimately helps with more goal-oriented tasks, but the playfulness works best when it's for no reason at all.

The Quilting Bee Effect

People who've been involved in collaboration may be able to relate to Nancy and her pal's term "art slave." Any activity in which you choose to be part of a community rather than emphasize individual effort involves trade-offs. You get the fun and perspective that comes from working with other people, but you have to give up some control and the purity of your vision. The "art slave" joke refers to one approach to the issue of control: Take turns being in charge of different projects and be available—on a practical and emotional level—to help your collaborators complete their projects.

Being able to joke with your collaborators requires perspective. Nancy figured out how to navigate those tricky waters, in part by recognizing the balance between her need for creative space and her need for interaction. She communicates clearly about that and expects others to do the same.

In the early 1990s, corporations began to adopt the teamwork approach and see it as a key to productivity, but not all managers had the disposition or skill to give up control and share the power over decision making. In his book *Creators on Creating*, Frank Barron talks about the fundamental challenge of teamwork:

> As in all creative phenomena, the relationship between the creative person, the creative product, and the environment is

full of seeming paradox. Creative persons benefit from support, from encouragement, from even a lone voice backing them in the face of adversity. Many creative persons have benefitted from mentors, role models who guide them along the way to developing their own uniqueness. And yet the creative mind also needs a degree of solitude to match its immersion in the world, a time to mull things over . . . in that solitude we can shape them, reorganize them, work with them, digest them, and make them our own.

Nancy has found that this push-pull between the need for solitude and interaction can happen in an atmosphere of trust. She has developed warm feelings toward her collaborator; they've become true friends. The friendship developed out of a cooperative environment where they respected one another's roles, having exchanges but not stepping all over each other in the process. The talent show provided the best of all excuses for indulging in whimsy. It was infinitely practical. After all, it was for a good cause. It had to be done. "It helps to have a clear goal that everyone shares," Nancy says.

When collaboration is working it's like executing a good dance: you know each other's moves, urge each other on. In the writing of this book, which has been a collaborative process, what has seemed to work best is an agreement that we can all say and write whatever comes to our minds, and each of us has permission to edit anything out that we see fit. Similar to Nancy's observation, I've found that my collaborators and I need to first feel safe about getting our ideas out there and then be thick-skinned when someone wants to remove something of yours (in Nancy's lingo, that would be "lose the boas!"). The sublime part is when everyone agrees, ego and control issues have dissolved, and everyone's focused on the outcome. The vision is shared and everyone seems to know what works and what doesn't, what belongs and what should go. The work has a life of its own, a vision beyond that of the individual participants.

It helps when everyone has the same goal. The "quilting bee effect," a sort of community building, often happens during collaborative projects. Part of the new conversation about women's art involves the connections between the practical and the artistic—for example, feeling pride and satisfaction from the results of a service-oriented, group creative endeavor. There was a time, not long ago, when professionals sniffed at people whose lives revolved around what seemed like amateurish volunteerism and service work. But we're seeing revived appreciation of the "village" and "community." The synergism and good will—the joy of working together— ultimately becomes more important than the product itself. Wouldn't it be wonderful if, as an added bonus, children learn the value of collaboration from watching their parents engage in group creative efforts?

Onward: But Not Too Far from Home

Motivated by her sense of philanthropy, Nancy at first saw the development of her own artistry as a secondary gain from the work on Christmas pageant puppets and talent show props. There's no denying the depth of artistry in the faces she paints on sets and puppets, but for now she is content with the multilayered nature of what she is doing, lingering somewhere in the middle between art and craft. She surrounds herself with other women's art, supporting and enjoying the creativity of the women in her community.

Yet there are hints of new paths ahead. She and her daughters recently were asked to perform as an opening act for a well-known band that was visiting her town. And it wouldn't be surprising to find one day that Nancy is painting on canvases instead of pressboard or exercising her considerable production and design skills on a larger stage. Whether or not Nancy takes her creativity farther out into the world before a larger audience, she will be content with the gifts she has received for her efforts so far—hearty approval from her daughters, the students she works with, and herself. For now, her focus is on creating what's necessary for the next talent show. She says, "I'm so glad to be involved in a creative process that involves my kids."

7

Dancing with the Kids: Teaching without Words

I suppose I consider myself to be creative. After all, everyone is. And teaching is a very creative activity.

—Vera Aubin, teacher
and folkdancer

Meet Vera with the Children

Old oak trees cast a cooling shadow over the sun-toasted stage, where eight small children are moving in a circle to a Central American folk song with a staccato beat—boys in black slacks, girls in black skirts, and all with black vests trimmed with gold rickrack over white blouses. Their blonde, redhead, and jet-black-haired heads bob up and down. Some children flow easily with the music, others take awkward steps, but with some nudging and pulling and laughing they manage to coordinate their movements.

It's a warm afternoon at the harvest festival, a gathering taking place in a rural northern California town. The audience sits on bales of hay—some clapping, all smiling. Those who don't speak Spanish might not catch the meaning of the words that blare out of the loudspeaker, but soon they recognize that the song's about a chicken: When the kids get to the chorus, they all put their hands on their hips, flap their elbows back and forth, and make chicken noises, cackling and cracking up because this is their favorite part.

Some children miss an occasional step, then scramble to catch up with the others, not seeming to mind. No one would guess that a couple of these kids were too shy to get on stage a couple of months earlier. The girl who steps up to the microphone to announce the dance speaks in perfect Spanish, even though she's a *gringa* who spoke only English until she started school.

Off to the side of the stage stands their teacher, Vera Aubin, a woman with short brown hair and a radiant smile that reflects what most people in the audience are thinking: These children are irresistible to watch. They're performing the dances they've been practicing in their kindergarten class for the past two months, immersed in the activity of a foreign culture that now feels natural to them. Vera is watching them closely, offering encouragement with gestures and smiles. "That's good," she mouths, her head nodding. The children can't hear her, but they look to her and know what she's saying because she says it so often: "That's good, *muy bueno, niños y niñas!*"

Her snappy brown eyes are focused intently on the stage. At first she doesn't see the two teenage boys in baggy pants and backwards caps lumbering toward her with a quasi-awkward gait. One touches her arm and she turns around. "*Hola!*" she greets the boys, smiling and hugging them one after the other, though never taking her eyes off the stage. "We, uh . . . we just wanted to say hi," one of the teenagers tells her. "I am so glad!" she responds in her soft Costa Rican accent.

These boys, now in middle school, are normally the essence of cool, but they decided to suspend their new habit of not schmoozing with teachers when they spotted Señora Aubin at the fair. She was their first teacher. Their favorite. They sidle up beside her, near the stage, remembering the music and the dances they performed seven years ago, back when they were kindergartners—Anglo boys immersed in Spanish culture, learning the music first, the language second.

Vera teaches Spanish at a small alternative school, mostly to English-speaking children of parents who want their children to become bilingual. Some of the parents, if sending their first child to kindergarten, may assume all teachers are like Vera: easygoing and devoted to their children. It might not be for years that they realize how special she is, and they may never be able to explain why.

"She's the teacher who speaks only Spanish, except for the Pledge of Allegiance, which we all do in English with a Costa Rican accent. We had fun in her class," one teenage boy reflects. Even though their children move on to other schools, families continue to come to events at Manzanita Bilingual School because of the community that has grown over the years.

Señora Aubin is at the center of this community, which she has helped create, because of the positive energy she stirs up, inspiring parents to open up and learn along with the children. Vera cared about the students, and they knew it. This is why they seek her out years later, a little embarrassed, but still giving her a hug in front of everyone. In Vera's class, there is a shared innocence. She explains: "We don't need to speak the same language, but we can communicate. And we can dance."

Teaching Culture, Creativity, and Community

Vera has turned the celebration of her own history into an impressive learning experience for others. By embracing the ways of her culture—particularly through dance—and bringing that into her classroom and into her friendships, she has tapped into a source of enthusiasm and energy that is contagious. When they're with Vera, children and their parents find themselves receptive to new information and experiences.

Vera's story shows how different cultural values can become the basis for creative communication and can cause energy to flow from one person to another as they learn the ways of the world. California has been embroiled in political wars over issues of immigration and bilingual education, but Vera has kept her focus on what people from different cultures can learn from one another. Optimism and a true appreciation for other people are central to her work.

When called upon to do so, Vera will reflect upon and explain her teaching methods; there's theory behind her methodology, but the main ingredient of her success is her own love of life. What we learn from watching her in action—and seeing the responses from children—is how volumes of information can be shared without language. Vera's story is a reminder of what it takes to be a good teacher of children and of adults. She models creativity, using humor and patience. Because the program she teaches is kindergarten immersion Spanish for English-speaking children, she has learned to use visual materials, gestures, and kinetic activities as teaching tools. The tools themselves, though, are not as significant as how they are handled in the classroom—with care for the children and an awareness that each will respond differently.

Vera maintains a vivacious good-spiritedness that communicates the excitement of learning—largely through dancing and singing and art: "You have to be willing to play with the children in kindergarten. That's how they learn—through playing and having fun." Her attitude is not one that can be faked, nor derived specifically from good teacher training, good intentions, or good skills. It's a way of life that requires practice outside, as well as inside, the classroom. Vera spends her free time nourishing herself with activities that bring her pleasure: dancing, gardening, writing, baking, and getting together with friends for intellectual discussions, adventures, and—a word that comes up often in conversations with her—"fun!"

It's hard to say if she dances because of her sunny disposition or if she has a sunny disposition because she dances regularly. Either way, with her physical grace and high energy, Vera is inspiration for making dance a regular part of life and for remembering all the ways people can connect with each other without words. She grew up with music and movement in Costa Rica and has made that her gift to her students.

Vera's Path

Elvis and America

Vera's earliest memories are of listening to music, swinging side to side, and dancing with her mother in the kitchen while her mother prepared food. The radio was always on. She grew up in Costa Rica in a large family with seven children:

> *Where I come from, there was always music and everyone danced. Dancing is as natural to me as breathing. Whenever the community would get together, we would have dances— simple dances that everyone could do, old people and children. In our culture, the whole family would dance. You would hear the music and dance and twirl around. Dancing was not just about girls meeting boys when I was growing up. The girls would dance with their parents. The fathers would dance with the children and swing them around. All the children would go to the dances.*

Her family lived simply, in a rural area near San Jose, with little money and an emphasis on education. Teachers were respected and at the center of activity in her town. She always knew she would grow up to be a teacher. When Vera was growing up, Costa Rica was peaceful, with a stable democratic governmental system, though surrounded by countries torn apart by civil wars. Still, people were moving to the United States, including some of her family and friends.

From what others said, Vera grew up with a mixed picture of America. There were economic opportunities, but there wasn't much to recommend the people: "When I was growing up in Costa Rica, people would say that Americans do not have feelings, do not love, do not have emotion." Still, eventually she would follow other family members to California.

"It was actually my older brother who came first, he was only eighteen, to meet Elvis and ride big motorcycles. I was young and was accepted into a teacher's college in Costa Rica and wanted to complete my training. My mother and youngest brother were also still at home and not interested in moving." Vera stayed to graduate from normal school and to teach in Costa Rica for three years. But it wasn't easy; teaching was hard work and didn't pay well. "Letters were coming home about the opportunities in America, and eventually we all made it here."

Vera, her mother, and her youngest brother were the last of her family to arrive—joining three sisters and two brothers who had already made the move. She decided not to go with her brother on his motorcycle travels; she lived with family in San Leandro, though she visited her sister in San Francisco as often as she could. She still remembers her first sight of the city. "When I first saw San Francisco and all the lights, I thought I was dreaming. All those cars, the buildings, so much happening. It was beautiful. I will never forget it."

Learning the Language

She was shy and didn't speak English well, so her sister advised her to exchange Spanish lessons for English lessons. That was how she met her husband. William was a teacher in San Francisco and wanted to learn Spanish. They traded languages and hung around together as friends for more than a year before they married, and Will introduced Vera to places around northern California.

This new culture was sometimes enchanting, sometimes shocking. They happened to visit Berkeley on a day when antiwar protesters were swarming the campus. Will and Vera were walking near the undergraduate library when trouble broke out: "All these people were marching. They were very angry. Police started drawing their guns. I started crying because I thought it was a war." They safely ducked into the library, but the whole scene left Vera aware of how much she still had to learn about the nuances of American culture.

After she and William married, they moved to a farming town where Will held a teaching position. During this time their daughter was born. Vera took English and cooking classes at the local community college. Then Will took a job teaching at San Quentin Prison. They moved again to a town near the prison. Vera was focused on family life. Four years after their daughter was born, they had a son.

Vera made friends easily. She and Will went out dancing, and cooked and entertained friends at home. She made friends from Mexico and Central America, some of whom talked to her about their experiences with acts of racism, so she was on the alert. "People would tell me, they don't treat us well because we are of a different race. There is a lot of discrimination."

On several occasions she experienced this kind of mistreatment. Once, when somebody made a racial slur, she turned on her heel, looked him in the eye, and demanded, "What did you say to me?" She remembered the lessons from her youth: "I came from a very poor home. We were taught to be nice to people, to have respect, but not to let people kick you."

Vera continued learning more and more English through conversations and at night school. She finally felt settled when they moved to a rural town in northern California, an antidote to William's stressful job with the prison system. The commute, during which he passed vineyards and orchards, allowed William the time to decompress after his day, and to Vera, it felt like the perfect home for her young family.

In her daily life, Vera was just as likely to say "*hola*" as "hello." She was determined to speak both English and Spanish at home. It was a matter of pride and practicality that her children would grow up knowing the songs and traditions of her Costa Rican culture: "I decided, 'These kids are going to feel proud of me and my culture.' I'd say 'We are important, we have good customs, we have good families, and we have a good future.'"

Her conviction moved into action when her children started school, and Vera decided to become involved. She volunteered to bring some of her native culture into the classroom: "At home, we were always putting together Latin American music and food for celebrations, so I suggested we do that at the school. The teacher said, 'Great, you can do anything you want. You don't even have to ask me.'"

The first dance she taught the children was a tropical dance called the cumbias, with roots in African and Puerto Rican cultures. "They would say, 'Do we have to dance?' but then they would do it, smile, and say, 'I like it.' I saw happy faces." She began to recognize the children's initial tendency to be put off by something foreign, but she learned that the initial bristling reaction was only on the surface. The children really wanted to learn about something different: "I wanted them to understand there was something besides the American culture they knew. It was good to see them widen their horizons."

In her own way, Vera was helping dissolve the barriers between cultures. She knew by her own feeling of warmth and ease that she was doing something valuable. She knew it when she saw the children change as they began to dance, becoming more open to other cultures—and, for some of them, more open with each other.

Becoming a Teacher—Again

Teaching again felt like the calling she had first felt in Costa Rica. She decided to get her California teaching credential. She took classes at the local community college and transferred to the local state college to complete her training. She started teaching at an alternative Spanish immersion school on a very part-time basis while she was completing her training at college. She was teaching to English-speaking children who didn't understand her very well, and she found herself using all kinds of facial expressions, hand movements, and props. Naturally, dance became part of the curriculum.

When she had volunteered in her children's classrooms, she had seen how dance had opened the children's eyes to a different culture. Now she saw that it also was a way for children to absorb the language—through the songs and movements accompanying the words. The English-speaking children were quickly picking up Spanish, and at the same time they were learning not to feel threatened by different traditions, but to instead appreciate different customs.

She found children in the United States to be different than in her native country: "Children here are more aggressive, more independent than in Costa Rica. Costa Ricans are more affectionate, maybe too affectionate." But she came to see how these raucous American kids settled down and got into the rhythm of dancing. Besides dance, she also brought into the classroom her native country's tradition of hugging children at school. She brought some of the gentleness of her culture into their lives, while getting satisfaction from having the delights of her childhood experienced by her students: "I believe that touching is good, and dancing is one way to incorporate touching, the music I love, and physical activity. I think it's good for the kids."

She knows that a lot of what has worked for her in the classroom are traditions that stem from her native country:

I credit Señora Lia in my Costa Rican teaching college for helping to form the way I teach. From her, I learned to be responsible and to be organized. Like her, I try to engage the hearts and minds of my students. I let them lead me into their areas of interest. And I think it is important for them to have the experience of performing. To be recognized in a formal setting.

At first the dancing was an after-school enrichment program. Then the parents asked that it become incorporated into the school program, for the whole school. The children wanted to perform the dances they learned for their families. In the beginning, it was quite simple. But over the years the performances evolved into "productions" with costumes made by Vera and the parents. Often the dancing by Vera's class was the highlight of the school productions. In addition, the children participated in local festivals, dancing on the beds of trucks in parades and on stages at outdoor fairs and community shows.

Dancing as Teaching

Folk dancing was not just for show, it developed into a teaching medium for Vera. Students learned the dances; they used the dancing to compare and contrast cultures, appreciate different rhythms, and study maps, geography, and social studies. Dance became a core part of Vera's teaching: "Not only is dancing a very friendly social activity and fun, it is a way to communicate and, of course, it is also good exercise."

Vera remembers one student who was so shy, she hardly talked at all, in any language: "With the dancing she started to feel more confident." Vera asked her if she wanted to announce the dance at one performance and the student said "no." Vera asked her again before the next performance and the girl said "no" again. "But," says Vera, "at the next performance the girl walked up in front of the crowd and announced the dance in Spanish." Vera believes the combination of music, dancing, and lots of hugs has helped many shy children blossom. It worked for her in her own youth, making her the person she would become. And it worked for the children she taught.

The parents of Vera's students were pleased with the results. Vera would always be invited to social get-togethers with the parents, and after a certain amount of food and drink, she would suggest dancing or singing or both. Manzanita Bilingual School parties turned out to be like those she remembered from when she was growing up: parents and children together, dancing to records or instruments. Vera's enthusiasm was contagious. Vera was happily involved in exercising her teaching skills in an environment where she could share so much of herself, her love of children and her culture, and her sense of fun. But outside the doors of her classroom, the school itself was in the throes of change, with conflict brewing between the owners and parents. Parents wanted more involvement in curriculum decisions in the upper grades, and they wanted more power in making administrative decisions about the school. Vera managed to avoid taking sides. The founder decided to close the school rather than permit the parents to become more involved in its operation.

It turned out to be a new beginning: The parents started their own school, and they wanted Vera to teach dancing. By then, she had her teaching credential, and she became one of the first teachers at the new school. The organizational challenges of the small private school were complex, and in a new school where parents were actively involved, often there were interpersonal and political issues to resolve. Vera managed to assert her positive ideas without getting pulled into conflict. She didn't give attention to complexity that seemed unnecessary and tried to keep focused on the school's cultural and teaching goals.

The school began to attract families with similar values, people more concerned with tolerance and making connections than competition and conflict. The families developed a community, spending time together even after their children went off to middle schools and high schools: "We're always putting together music and food. I don't understand parties where people just eat and talk the whole time. I always want to dance."

Life Outside the Classroom

Costa Rica's reputation as a haven has grown over the years, and these days it is a popular vacation spot for bird watchers, naturalists, and people seeking the humid heat of the rain forests. Vera started taking her students and American friends on trips back home to Costa Rica. Then she and her husband began to organize trips with friends to Costa Rica:

> These are really fun. Lots of hard work to plan and arrange, though. We took a group of people—nine families, thirty-one people mostly associated with the school—to Costa Rica. I arranged things to do and places to visit. Yes, we go to village dances. I was so proud to share Costa Rica with my friends.

Another way Vera found to stay connected to her roots was through a Latin and South American women's group that she started when her children were small. They started holding monthly meetings at each other's homes to discuss local and international politics and current events, as well as to meet people of interest in their community. The twenty woman originally performed folk dances: "We performed at festivals, in schools, and for friends." They have been meeting for seventeen years, providing one another with regular contact with the culture of their youths and a safe place to contemplate the changes in their lives.

> We function as a support group for each other now. One woman goes through a painful divorce and we all take turns calling her and making sure she has someone to do things with. It's not so much orchestrated as spontaneous. We all want her to feel wanted and welcome in our lives. And we talk about interesting things. Occasionally we will invite guests to join us—mainly to share something of interest. I remember inviting someone from the school to talk about how to relate to abused children. It was very interesting.

Each month two women team up to plan the monthly get-together. They organize the menu, cook the food, decide the music, and determine what will be discussed. They still dance, but they stopped performing a few years ago: "This group has become a family. Some of the women in the group don't have a family—so we have each other."

Vera's Life These Days

Integrating Work and Home

About her teaching, Vera says: "It's something I would do any-way. That's how jobs should be, not 'I'm doing it because I'm getting paid.'" Her life is integrated. Her work feeds her home and social life and vice versa. Without fanfare, she derives great satisfaction from her daily activities. She doesn't make a distinction between "work" and "play," and she passes that attitude on to her students.

In their book *Living Your Life Outloud*, Salli Rasberry and Padi Selwyn talk about enriching versus draining work. One sign that work is enriching is feeling energized and wanting to engage in other creative activities at the end of the day.

> *From our research and interviews, the evidence is overwhelm-ingly clear—people who engage in work that is meaningful feel it is one of the most rewarding areas of their lives. They look forward to each day knowing they are appreciated, productive, creative, contributing members of society. . . . Uniting who you are with how you earn your living opens up an exciting, creative world, a vitally enriching part of your life.*

When she's not teaching, Vera enjoys creating new recipes and making breads: "Bread is so basic, so nourishing." She also is a gar-dener: "I love the color of fresh flowers. In the summer my house is surrounded by flower boxes overflowing with color." Vera also con-siders her letter writing to be a creative outlet.

> *I remember my mother always wrote thank-you notes: "Always acknowledge when someone has done something nice for you," she'd say. I still write thank-you notes. And I write long letters to my family and friends in Costa Rica. These letters tell my friends stories of my life here so we can remain connected, though we aren't physically close to each other.*

Dancing is not just something Vera does with the children. It's part of her life, something so important that she schedules regular time to dance in formal settings, in addition to dancing around the house and at school. At least once a week, she dresses in brightly colored skirts, peasant blouses, and dancing shoes—sometimes for a class through the community college, sometimes with existing groups, and often less formally at the public monthly dances arranged by the folk dance teachers in the county:

> *Dancing is a social activity. You dance with others. We have met many of our friends through folk dancing. I love dancing!*

It is a universal way to communicate without language. The music talks to the body and the body responds. I can't imagine not dancing.

Encouraging Children

Vera's creativity comes out in her interactions, in allowing children to find their own way. She provides the paints, the music, the books, the clay—and occasionally brings into the classroom such things as a functioning model of a live volcano or live animals. What brings all that to life for the children is watching the teacher's face light up for them. And seeing the pictures framed, and the dance moved on stage for public approval.

There's a lot of "free time" in Vera's class, when kids can work at their own pace, sit on the floor instead of at desks, and spread out and play. Vera believes students need the discipline of a scheduled routine in the classroom, but within that schedule, she feels they need time to play and stare out the window—to go in and out of focus.

In *The Creative Spirit,* authors Daniel Goleman, Paul Kaufman, and Michael Rae wrote:

> *Children more naturally than adults enter that ultimate state of creativity called "flow," in which total absorption can engender peak pleasure and creativity. In flow, time does not matter; there is only the timeless moment at hand. It is a state that is more comfortable for children than adults, who are more conscious of the passage of time.*

Vera quickly assesses the learning style of students, knowing who needs quiet time to work and who enjoys group projects. She provides a mirror for them to see their developing learning styles, occasionally speaking in English to make positive observations. If a child is obviously struggling with a project, she'll praise what's working and offer a suggestion for how to proceed. She provides a comfort zone for their work, motivated by the second part of her definition of creativity: "everyone is." With children, she believes, it's a matter of stepping aside and allowing their personal approach to develop, untouched by judgment.

Dancing has become one of her most precious teaching tools. Practice time means the students have a chance to get up and move during the school day, stretching their bodies and laughing. They get to touch one another. They must coordinate their movements. And they are absorbing some cultural savvy that they will carry with them long after they leave this school. Music is an international language: you can feel the beat and move even if you don't understand a word.

Reflections for Your Creative Journey: Sharing Joy

Back to Basics

Do you ever wish life were more simple? Do you ever look at someone interacting with a child—laughing, open, and undistracted by the complexities of the "adult world"—and wonder how it's possible to be so unabashedly comfortable in the moment? Children have great antennae for knowing when people are really with them versus times when adults have their minds elsewhere and are doing some kind of obligatory pat on the head. Adults don't really get away with faking it with kids. I think that to be able to be truly present with children is to be in a state of grace; the same applies to creativity. I often find myself trying to sweep extraneous worries away, getting back to the childlike awareness of the moment—without judgment, but with an appreciation of what is happening. In Vera's class, the kids can dance freely, without self-consciousness. Being able to find that state of being in your own life can allow you to let your creativity unfold, taking you where it will.

Some of the things that get in the way of free-flowing dancing, writing, painting, or any kind of creative endeavor are strictures of time; activities that require your periodic attention; and those internal voices that say, "This isn't cool. . . . This is different. . . . This is too revealing." The way Vera lives her life and what she encourages in the children is at once simple and profoundly wise: She turns a deaf ear to static. She doesn't allow herself to be bothered by the ego problems or ignorance of others, whether it's racism, self-consciousness, or embarrassment at showing feelings. She just continues every day to live her life according to her own values, giving other people room and time to be themselves and expecting them to do the same for her.

Too Much Fun

The word "fun" came up so often in Vera's story that when Susan read the first draft of this chapter, she started circling the word each time it came up. "Too much 'fun'!" she wrote in the margin. I looked back and started counting how many times the word showed up in this chapter, and I had to laugh. It was repetitive indeed, so I tried to take some of them out.

However, having watched Vera in action for years, I understand how many definitions there are for "fun" in Vera's vocabulary. It's like the way the Eskimo language has a lot of words for "snow" and Native American languages have a lot of words for "green." There are many aspects to fun in Vera's life. There's fun in being with children, dancing, being with friends, and relaxing with creative projects at home. Then there are the nuances: fun as in belly laughs, and fun as in that delightful moment of recognition when a child makes a breakthrough.

It's pretty basic. There is nothing flamboyant about Vera, except the greetings she gets from current and former students and their parents. She is enthusiastically absorbed in the day-to-day business of her life, feeling no need to "move up" or even "go deeper," but just to continue enjoying each new day, each student in her class, communication with a friend, flower in her garden, loaf of bread from the oven, and opportunity to share her cultural heritage with others.

Dancing

As Don Campbell explains in *The Mozart Effect*:

When we dance, we are like hobos who jump on the freight train of the beat. Swept along, our bodies automatically adjust to the pace, pulse and rhythm of the sound; the music evokes an organized pattern of responses. The emotional pulse of great concert music entrains an entire audience. The beat of disco music entrains a group doing aerobic exercises.

So, too, with folk dance: the rhythm, the music, and the words inform our bodies about the culture that produced it. Many of the people who make time for dance in their lives seem to be pretty sunny people, even optimists. Dancing can temporarily transport you into another world, where the most minute movement gives a signal that sets off a huge motion. So much is intuitive, and anticipating another accurately can affirm that communication is on track. Using dancing as a creative outlet is another way in which you can continue your creative flow.

Music and Education

It's popular for educational number crunchers to call music and dance something "extra," but there's plenty of evidence that it's valuable both as an end in itself and as an enhancement to other kinds of learning. Campbell discusses some of the educational benefits of using music and dance with children in his book, *The Mozart Effect:* "Playing an instrument or participating in a music program in school (or incorporating music into such areas as history and science) has been shown to have broadly positive effects on learning, motivation, and behavior."

Following are a few examples selected from his long list of those benefits: Students with experience in musical performance scored fifty-one points higher on the verbal part of the SAT and thirty-nine points higher on the math section than the national average . . . University music and music education majors had the highest reading scores of any students on campus, including those in English, biology, chemistry, and mathematics.

Clearly music and dance enhance the educational experience and have long-lasting effects. Research is finally catching up with what Vera has always known and used in her classroom.

Not a Wallflower

There are all those hidden benefits of music, but Vera demonstrates one of the most obvious: You can be the quiet type, but dancing allows a way to connect with others and be in the spotlight. Susan observes that dancing is a way for some to overcome shyness. "You give yourself over to music and visibility. You have to push back something of your self-protection. Vera is modest and almost shy but she engages in dancing, which is an unselfconscious act. She goes out into the middle of the floor, and that takes a lot of confidence." So for children, Susan says, dancing is a way not only of learning music and rhythm, but also how to feel comfortable with being expressive in public. It's a way to break down inhibitions—a lovely lesson to learn young.

Onward: More Fun

Although Vera's hair is gray now, her eyes still sparkle, her enthusiasm is unabated, and there has been little external change in Vera's life for the past twenty years. She has a happy home life, her now grown children stay in regular contact, and her sisters and brothers gather several times a year. There are friends with whom she has been dancing for almost twenty years, and she's still as close as ever to the women who continue to meet and share their lives each month.

A life of creative continuity is a blessing, but it also involves a series of skills that can be learned. At times in life when your environment seems alien or you feel far away from your "self," one exercise is to remember the sources of joy from your childhood. Writing about your most pleasurable memories or sharing those memories with friends can bring your past joys back to life. For Vera, the sources of comfort she brought to a new country were dancing, her cultural heritage, cooking, and gardening.

You can find opportunities to exercise childhood creative traditions in your current context. For Birgitta, who was nourished by memories of her mother's kitchen, the antidote for a bad day was as close as her own kitchen, where her mother's recipe book provided prescriptions for feeling better. Most of us have memories of some "comfort food" from childhood. Vera also served her native foods to new friends, symbolically bringing part of her self into her relationships.

Finding people with similar interests is a way to establish creative community. If your pleasant memories involve dancing, for example, you can take a class to find others who share that interest. Or, as Vera did, you can gather together friends who have similar histories and establish regular times to meet, reinforcing one another's memories within a shared context. What are your family traditions? If your family sang together or went fishing or went to art museums, you'll probably have a lot of unspoken simpatico with people whose families engaged in the same activities. Once you've established your creative community, you may decide to act on the shared memories.

Of course, getting to know someone who has far different traditions and trading ideas with them can also revive old sources of creativity. Birgitta's corporate employers benefitted from her Swedish aesthetic in designing their stores. Vera's children's teachers welcomed a chance to bring aspects of the rich Latin American culture into an American classroom. Whether you are learning new traditions or sharing old ones with other people, you are exercising the skills of creative community building.

Vera is still at her first teaching job, in the little Spanish immersion school. The school has moved, and some of her original students now have graduated from high school. They've had a lot of turnover among teachers and administrators, and they've restructured as the budget and number of students has expanded and contracted—but Vera's kindergarten class is still there, along with that same stack of vests and those old folk dancing records. Same old thing, new and different every day.

8

Singing for Yourself: Saying "Yes, I'm Good"

What I think of as purely creative is when I'm writing a song and I don't even know where it's coming from—it's just a thought or a melody or a phrase. It seems as though I'm tapped into something else, my energy is attached to something greater.

—Sara Pond Poyadue,
singer, musician

Meet Sara in Concert

It's Valentine's Day, and Sara and her all-woman band, High Standards, take the stage dressed in vintage black dresses, shoes, and hats to perform their swing music magic, combining the rhythm of the forties with the harmony of a heavenly choir. Their voices blend in complex chords and rhythms and they live up to their name. High standards, indeed. Each song has taken months to perfect. And Sara has been polishing this harmonic musical style for eighteen years, long before the revived interest in swing music brought forties music back into vogue, drawing crowds of all ages to jitterbug and dance cheek-to-cheek at places like this swank California coastal club. This is High Standards' first regular gig after almost a year without performing.

Sara is recovering from cancer surgery. A lot of things look different to her now than they did before she got sick a year ago. Her life and her musical talent seem so precious. No matter how sick she feels, she keeps on singing. She believes that singing is a healing influence in her life and hopes it will help her overcome cancer. On stage, she is less aware of the audience than she is of the notes blending, just as she and the three other women in the band had practiced. The songs seem to go by so quickly, after all those rehearsals.

During the performance, Sara knows the music is right, but something feels wrong. It's time to introduce the band, but something's stopping her. She's the leader of the band: the concept, the arrangement, and the harmonies are her creation. She wants to take the microphone in her hand during a break between songs and proudly announce "We're High Standards. I'm Sara Poyadue." But she's been dealing with some personal issues that make it hard for her to introduce herself and the others as band leaders do. She's held back by what feels to her like a power struggle with another band member and within herself.

Sara is feeling defensive and a little uncertain—feeling that it's still not okay to really shine, to be a leader, to claim her place as the driving force of the band. An old nagging voice from the distant past sounds in her ear, "Don't set yourself apart," "Share equally with everyone," "Don't be too full of yourself." She's been brought up to be modest. At the same time, she has paid a price professionally for avoiding self-promotion.

As she stands on stage, she feels a physical response to the emotional hurt she has over a story that appeared in the local newspaper about a previous performance. Sara's name wasn't mentioned in the headline, and another band member came off in the newspaper story as if she was the leader. Whether the misrepresentation was intentional or a journalist's mistake is irrelevant to Sara; it is yet another in a series of slights that make her feel invisible.

In the clarity that follows a brush with death, Sara realizes that she's given others credit for her work for too long. She has always downplayed her part, wanting to make sure everyone is recognized. But this was her band, her vision, and now she wants acknowledgment for that. It seems essential to her health that she find a way to embrace the talent she was born with and take credit for the results that have come from pushing her musical and vocal skills to the limit.

Sara Pond Poyadue—or Sara P., as she's known on her children's recordings—has perfect pitch, the ability to pick up different instruments and play by ear, and an intuitive knack for composing tunes and lyrics that stay with you. Music has been a source of joy for as long as she can remember—a way to express herself and connect with others. But something has always held her back from acknowledging her talent and promoting her work.

A few years earlier, she wrote, performed, and produced a children's music tape, *Tot Rock,* that had children and parents singing along. Friends of friends, who bought the tape because of word of mouth reviews, were amazed when they learned that the composer and lead singer of these engaging songs wasn't a recognized professional. In retrospect, Sara sees how *Tot Rock* might have taken off if she had invested as much energy and money into promotion as she did in production.

In a way, Sara's proud of the way she's done music for music's sake, going for an artistic vision instead of following trends or becoming a slave to marketing. Detachment from the opinions of others gave her the freedom to follow her own internal score rather than seeking outside approval. In and of itself—even if no one had ever heard her sing—music always has been a source of health and joy for Sara, even in times of illness and sadness. Now she's ready to use her gifts in new ways. She wants to be able to do more with her music—for children and for adults—and that means developing a public persona as big as her talent.

During the Valentine's Day performance, Sara finally does introduce herself as the leader of the band. She lets herself fill the spotlight. Then during a break, when someone praises her ability to sing and play keyboard at the same time, she starts to explain it away with an "aw-shucks" statement. "The chords are easy. . . ." But then she stops herself. She's realizing how remarkable it is that she can do what she does. She smiles mid-sentence, nods her head, and says, "Thank you."

Learning to Take Credit

For Sara, singing talent has carried unexpected gifts, some more welcome than others. The most enjoyable part for her is having a life enlivened by music and song; as many who enjoy singing will agree, music enriches life, both intrinsically and because of the special communication that happens with others when singing together. The kind of ability Sara has—to pick up and carry perfectly pitched tunes as well as intricate harmonies and rhythms—is likely an enviable one to anyone who loves to sing.

But it's not always easy to figure out how to have talent in a society where many women are raised to sidestep credit and shun attention. Sara can point to many life circumstances that limited her from developing her talent to its full potential. She often felt that people or situations were holding her back from pursuing her creativity. But then she came to a place in her life where she realized that most of the constraints were self-imposed.

Sara's story demonstrates some of the self-esteem issues that society is beginning to recognize as factors in the development of many girls who experience crises of confidence. For various reasons, Sara allowed herself to be pushed and pulled by the desires of others, starting with peer pressure in her girlhood and leading to relationships in adulthood where she abdicated control. At the same time, her experiences demonstrate how creativity can set the spirit free even in the most confining circumstances. Because of singing, she maintained a sense of herself through an assortment of living conditions, some rougher than others, and eventually found a unique mode of expression—her own harmonic style, which she developed intuitively.

The contrast between the size of her talent and the size of her ego has created a schism that many women experience if they're raised to be modest. Sara probably would have gone on ducking credit, or letting other people take it, if her illness had not helped her see the importance of using all the time she can for music. She sees that some self-promotion is necessary to carve out opportunities to use her talent. Now she knows it's not conceit but practicality that demands she claim credit for her work. Like many women who don't like to take up more than their share of space on the planet, Sara is finding it a little awkward to stretch her arms wide and gather the kudos she deserves. But she's learning.

Sara's Path

Little Star

*When I was two or three, I started playing tunes on our old
upright piano. I could play by ear, "Twinkle Twinkle, Little
Star." I still have my nursery school report card that says
I always led the class in rhythm and marching. I was in the
church choir starting when I was eleven or twelve. Music, to
me, is one of those things I felt was always there, but I didn't
appreciate it as a talent. I took some music theory classes later,
but I didn't realize until I got my own band that my ability
to sing harmonies and feel it out by ear was kind of special.
I guess I thought everyone could do that.*

Sara remembers her childhood in Vero Beach, Florida, as filled
with music. Her mom played classical music at the piano. Her parents listened to opera, which drove her nuts. "Every Sunday, my
mom and dad would listen to an opera for hour after excruciating
hour." The third child of five, she liked music on the radio and her
older sisters' jazz and folk music.
Sara took piano lessons, but they backfired:

*My piano teacher was very disgusted with me because
I wasn't learning the notes. She'd play it and I'd listen to it
and play it. But when she wanted me to go on to complicated
stuff, I just couldn't see the sense in learning to read the
music because I could copy what she was doing. Looking back,
I don't think she knew how to nurture the natural part of my
talent and still teach me the reading music part. Instead of
getting creative, she got frustrated.*

Singing was something Sara's family did for fun—around the
piano while her mom played or in the car during long drives. There
was never a lot of fuss made about Sara's innate talent. Later, family
members would say that, of course, they recognized Sara's talent. But
understatement was a family value, along with egalitarianism and
community effort. "Nobody ever made any big deal about what I
could do. It wasn't like, 'Wow, you can sing really well.' I always felt
maybe that was why I was so unimpressed by it." In the church choir,
though, she was recognized. "I was singled out as a good singer. I
was in a special trio. We performed pop music. That was probably
the first time I felt recognized as being special for music."
She got her first guitar at thirteen:

*I remember sitting there and moving my fingers around
to find notes to play chords. I just played around with the
strings. I was able to teach myself chords without learning
music. I remember people showing me different fingering for
different chords. I went a pretty long way, learning the basic
chords enough so I could sing. I never set out to be an
instrumentalist. I was always singing. That was the goal.
I wanted to learn how to play so I didn't have to rely on
other people to accompany me. I'd make up songs, endlessly,
with the chords I knew. I eventually learned how to play in
every key. I learned a lot of music theory by osmosis and
trial and error.*

Self-Esteem Crash

Confidence problems unfolded in the classic teenage girl syndrome:

*I was shy but I didn't come off as being shy. Sometime
around age fourteen, I went through a big change. I became a
bit rebellious, flouting convention. And I began experimenting
with boys and alcohol. That's the time my self-esteem took a
huge dive.*

A cheerleader and student government leader, she suddenly started
gravitating toward the "wrong crowd." Her older sisters started telling her that she was getting a bad reputation, but she didn't care.
Looking back, she feels she made poor choices.

*I didn't go on a path that helped me build my self-esteem.
I put myself down and put myself in situations where
I wasn't going to get the respect and acknowledgment for
things I was doing that were creative or part of my heart
and soul. I felt, "At least if guys think I'm sexy, then I'll
be popular." I abandoned the parts of me that could have
led me to some self-esteem and security.*

She moved away from her music. Looking back, she wonders
what might have happened if she had received more encouragement
from her family for her music. Would music have given her a more
positive focus at that time in her life? But she saw her family as valuing the cerebral. Music was not regarded as a serious career choice.
And her family's definition of success didn't seem to include Sara's
creative, not-by-the-books approach to music. "The only way to get
approval from my father was good grades," she reflects. "I wish I'd

had the confidence to say 'Hey, I'm really good at singing,' but at that time I wasn't even considering music as a career."

Her older sisters had gone to universities, but Sara chose to go to a junior college. She had learned the lessons of her family so well, she didn't even sign up for music classes. Sara found herself in a hectic house with friends and a man with whom she became involved. She got pregnant and she married, not really ready for commitment but making the best of it, moving to Alabama where her husband went to college and Sara worked in the library.

During this time, Sara didn't play music at all. She was consumed by the pressures of marriage and new motherhood. She adored her baby girl but felt scared and overwhelmed. The marriage didn't work out; she and her husband separated and Sara moved to California with her daughter, Jennifer, and Sara went back to school. There she lived in a house with eight other students, taking Jennifer to campus daycare on a bike. Within two quarters of getting her degree in social science, she dropped out of school, joined a band, and started drifting.

Her music allowed her to fit right in with the other free spirits around her.

> We'd build a campfire under a full moon and have cheap wine parties. I was just one of the people out there banging on my guitar. But little by little, I became aware of people saying, "You're really good." That's when I started considering the possibility that music should take a little more space in my life. I became more involved in playing, learning songs, and jamming with people.

To take care of herself and her daughter, she went on welfare. Looking back, she thinks that was a disaster: "At the time, I thought it was a great idea. In a way it was the worst thing I ever did. Instead of thinking of limitless horizons, my whole lifestyle became very poor— concerned with making do."

She found a group living situation and enjoyed her young daughter and her freedom, but she lacked direction. She didn't often take the initiative, but she occasionally found herself plunged into musically rich environments. She flourished in the company of other musicians: "I went for a week-long fiddler convention in Idaho several times. We camped out, swam in a swimming hole, and all day and all night people would play music. Guitars and banjos, all kinds of instruments." But Sara still had trouble making good choices, and she went through a series of dead-end relationships, including briefly living in the same house as a drug addict. "It was a low point of my life."

Back in Harmony

Eventually Sara and a friend moved to the central California town of Santa Cruz, a place known at the time as a gathering place for musicians. Sara vowed to become serious about music and went out scouting for bands, finding several she liked. She began singing backup vocals for different kinds of bands: folk trios, country rock, and jam bands. She felt revived. Music didn't quite pay the rent, but Sara found a job that was compatible. She got a job at the public library in Santa Cruz cataloguing sheet music. By now she knew how to read music, and it was a kick to go through boxes of old music by day and sing live music at night.

Every singing experience brought rewards and new lessons, but she had a sense that there was more. She kept looking for the right band but always felt something was missing.

> *I wanted to sing harmonies. I wanted to be very good, to*
> *be superb, to be singing the best harmonies possible. I'd look*
> *longingly at bands that seemed to have their own niche.*
> *It didn't occur to me for a long time that I could get out*
> *there and play as well as sing, with my own band. It didn't*
> *seem real to me that I could do that. I didn't think that*
> *I should dare to presume to start my own band.*

The catalyst came when she was in her early thirties. She heard a song called "Undecided" and got a friend to teach it to her. Something about that song just felt right. "It had a swing feel to it. I thought it would be neat to sing in harmony." It inspired her to seek out more music from the thirties and forties.

> *I'd found a style I wanted to pursue. . . . All of a sudden,*
> *people began giving me material. I heard the Boswell Sisters*
> *for the first time, a group I really like from the thirties and*
> *forties. They remain an inspiration to me. They had a very*
> *unique vocal style. They played with the Dorsey brothers, all*
> *the hot instrumentalists. They had these really unique, trippy*
> *vocal arrangements where they said things fast and would*
> *speed up the tempo. It was like scat singing before scat was*
> *popular.*

She became obsessed with the old songs. Unable to find sheet music, she listened to the records to learn the music and hear the harmonies. "It took me a long time dissecting songs and figuring out how to play them. It was very tedious and time consuming." But she was engrossed. "I'd sit and listen to them over and over and over, figuring out chords and trying to hear where the harmonies were."

Now Sara felt more than just a desire, she felt the need to create a band. There weren't any bands out there doing the kind of music she had fallen in love with. "It dawned on me, I could find some people to sing harmony with me, who hopefully could help arrange things." She didn't think it would be too difficult to find women to sing harmony, but she spent months looking. "I was beginning to realize that singing harmony was a gift. Before, I didn't think it was all that unusual." Finally she found a woman named Sher who could sing alto and do simple percussion and who would end up staying with her. Then she found a singer and keyboard player. Miraculously, the three voices blended together, and the women were all willing to put in the time to develop their own brand of musical magic.

What would they call themselves? One day a friend was reading the back of a Boswell Sisters album. The jacket copy mentioned their "high standards." This friend knew Sara well, and understood her quest for the perfect harmony. "You could call yourselves High Standards." And they did. They began practicing several times a week. "We worked out enough material for one set. We decided to audition at a club, and we got the job."

It was a small nightclub, but unbeknownst to them, the owner of one of the area's most popular oceanfront restaurant clubs happened to be in the audience. "It was amazing, we were recruited right away to play Saturday nights at the "Crow's Nest." We played there for four years." But in the beginning, High Standards had only one set and no time to polish more songs. So they did the same exotic harmonies over and over again and padded their program with some popular standards.

Sara had finally come into her strength as a musician and singer. The promise of her youth flowered in her maturity. "People really liked us, we became popular and started living a late-night party life. There were always drinks waiting for us at every break and after performances people who wanted to party—offering pot and cocaine."

The performing life was heady and wild, but musicwise it stopped being fulfilling. Sara came to see that her creativity was most alive in the formative stages, during the development of the music and vocal arrangements. The creative zip dissipated for Sara after singing the songs over and over again. Her library job had ended and she wanted to continue developing her music, so she worked at low-wage service jobs to make some money.

Sara decided to take up haircutting and went back to school to get a license in cosmetology—a job she could schedule around her music. Then one day her keyboard player moved to southern California and, despite searching and numerous auditions, Sara could find no one to fill that spot. So the trio dissolved and the first incarnation of High Standards began to fade to a memory.

A New Life

Her band defunct, Sara took the opportunity to step back from the partying life. She met a man who, like herself, was moving away from the fast track; Turhan was working on his teaching credential. Sara wanted to continue with music but didn't want to be part of the nightclub scene. This time she was ready for marriage. And when she got pregnant again, nineteen years after the birth of her daughter, she was ready for motherhood, too. "I finally found some respect for myself. My husband was a very good influence. I got grants and went back to school to finish my degree in sociology. I really got creative and inspired about writing music." Her daughter was off to college by then, but close enough to home to visit often, enjoying her new baby brother.

Sara's baby boy, Jay, motivated her to explore a new direction in her musical career. As her son grew, she found herself drawn to children's music. It fit her new stable family life.

> I really couldn't tolerate the bar, the night life again. It was incompatible with raising an infant. I was glad I could find a place to play music and have it be part of my life. I performed concerts, benefits, lots of things involving children and education.

Sara wrote and arranged most of the music she performed, and often musician friends would sit in to add musical texture to the performances. Then a teaching opportunity materialized.

> My teaching job started when I realized that my son's kindergarten class had no live music. I thought I'd go to the classroom and play. Then the kids started asking me to come back. Pretty soon it was more than a volunteer thing. Other teachers hired me, with contributions from parents, to come to their classrooms. I also volunteered in Spanish-speaking classrooms. I began working with the public schools to create a more equitable program, available not just to the classes where the parents can afford to pay for my services.

The job evolved over the next five years, until she was teaching in eight classrooms a day at three different schools. She spent a day at each school and led an after-school chorus at one of them.

As her work with her son's kindergarten class got under way, Sara became engrossed in writing songs for children. A tune or a phrase would pop into her mind while she was playing with her child. "Let's go for a walk outside, you and me and the doggy-o. I'd rather take a walk than go for a ride, you and me and the doggy-o."

Children would sway and rock to the music. She wrote songs for preschool fund-raisers and watched whole groups of kids bobbing up and down to the tunes. She came up with the name Tot Rock. "For the first time, I was writing songs intensively. And I got the idea, 'Hey I'm going to record.' I knew it was going to be time consuming and expensive. It took nine months to record *Tot Rock*. It was all original."

"It was incredibly complex, getting people together, editing and editing again. I heard that music so many times. I did all the lyrics and even made the cover and tape insert on the computer." For *Tot Rock* she wrote music of many different styles—country, rap, rock, jazz, reggae—each song with a lively set of lyrics. But there was one underlying theme to the songs, a theme that has been central to Sara's growth. It's even the title of one of the songs: "You Can Do It."

While passing on empowering ideas to children about how to make life fun every day and feel good about themselves, Sara was simultaneously following her own message—asserting her talent and getting an outpouring of support. Making the tape was a happy collaborative effort. Sara's husband, son, and sister performed on the tape; her dog even contributed a bark. Professional musician friends volunteered their talent to support Sara, and the recording studio facilitated the effort by charging as little as possible.

> *I sold a bunch of copies, for a while enlisting the help of family and friends and leaving them on consignment and at kid's stores. I sent copies to record companies, but I found the business end of things to be tedious and uncomfortable. One recording company returned my tape but later came out with its own product called "Tot Rock." I was furious. But I wasn't able to do the promotion my tape needed. I realized the main place to sell them easily was at family concerts.*

That began a period of frequent performances for children, something that she continues to do today. Her success in the concert world led her to do a second tape. This in turn led to her current job of teaching music and forming choirs.

As her son got older, Sara began hearing those forties harmonies in her head again. She was still friends with Sher, her original High Standards band member. They decided to start up again. Sara had been singing children's music with another woman, Vicki, and Sara and Sher invited her to join them. A fourth woman, Gail, came to hear them practice, then started visiting regularly, and one night asked if she could sit in with a bass. High Standards was reincarnated just at a time when swing music was being rediscovered. The new group began practicing weekly, and Sara arranged new songs. They were asked to play at weddings and festivals. Between teaching music to kids, performing children's music, and doing the forties gigs, Sara was making a modest living from her music.

Illness

At first she ignored the nagging abdominal pain, a growing annoyance she attributed to nerves or some minor intestinal problem. Over the months, it worsened, and she began to experience nausea, occasional excruciating pain, and loss of energy. Her doctor couldn't figure out what it was, diagnosing it as a psychological ailment—though Sara knew the pain was real. Sara thought she should be able to control it, to get rid of it, if it was a "pseudo" condition. The conflict between what she knew and what she was being told was enough to cause her to wonder if she was going a little crazy. Then one night she went to the emergency room because the pain was so bad. It turned out to be colon cancer. The surgeons removed a tumor and infected mass the size of a small cantaloupe. "I was very angry at the doctor who told me it was a figment of my imagination. I should have had treatment sooner. It grew while he ignored my complaints."

"It was so scary and painful, trying to figure out how to deal with it." While investigating traditional medical therapies, she also started reading everything she could get her hands on about diet and attitude. "I went to see a healer, who felt my illness was a signal about needing to claim my power." The idea resonated with her. She realized she had given the power of her illness to the doctor by believing his diagnosis, even when her body was telling her there was a real problem, something she vowed not to do again. Also, for so long in her musical life, she had been shrinking from recognition while at the same time longing for credit for her music: "I began to realize how, when everyone was clapping, I would have this tendency to contract into nothingness." She felt she had been giving away the power in her music, too.

Through the illness, she came to see herself more clearly, recognizing all the influences that had led to an overdeveloped sense of modesty and underdeveloped sense of pride in her talent. She began practicing the words "thank you" and saying publicly that High Standards began with her long-ago concept. She took a journey through her own creative history, recalling what it was like to have the harmony idea and then shape that into reality: "It's important for me to claim the creative spark, to realize what happened each time I had a vision and manifested it. I felt powerful. Sure, the women in the band had important roles to play in the realization of my vision, but the vision, and the will to see it made real, is mine."

Sara's Life Today

During her illness, Sara has been reflecting not only about her health, but also about her music. She's fine tuning what she does with both kids and adults. She's learning what it means to bring her spirit along with her talent to the stage.

When I was in high school, I hung on to music because it was something that, even though I didn't appreciate it fully, I had a really special talent for. I did have a sense there was something about me that was good, that not everybody else had. It gave me something to like about myself. It gave me an identity. Then I gave that up for a fairly long time.

For most of my life I have allowed other people to define my identity. Now though when I hear the kids say, "Here's the music lady," with such excitement, I like it because I realize I have created this identity. I like feeling that's my thing in life, to be the one who brings live music to their lives. And now I'm trying to be more spiritual in how that comes across, through joyfulness. I want to make that joy contagious.

Sara wants to have each child feel that they are unique, but that talent in singing is not everything.

You can think you are not a good singer but still be involved in the music. . . . I'm very noncritical. I try to encourage experimentation and to have children think of their voice as an instrument, so they can be a little more dispassionate about experimenting with it. I say encouraging things. I compliment them. I never make anybody do anything by themselves if they don't want to. Sometimes it's incredible to see that by the end of a session, everyone in the classroom is getting up, singing, and sometimes dancing. In one song, "We All Can Sing," I have actions, steps, moves, and claps in places. Kids naturally want to participate. It allows them to have fun and feel successful.

Part of what I feel now is that I don't want to sing songs that are downers or portray people as victims. I want to put out positive, healing, messages. I don't want to send any energy to the universe that is disempowering or encourages people to feel like they don't have options or choices. I don't like to promote violence and negativity. For example, in a couple of songs I changed the words. In one, the lyrics originally said, "Nobody wants you when you're old and gray." I changed them to "I'm in the mood to throw my blues away."

*The point is, your attitude makes a big difference.
Now when I work with kids, I tell them there are ways to
be creative with music that they won't know until they try.
Kids are often so inhibited and afraid to try something new,
afraid it won't come out okay. I teach them it's okay to
experiment. The voice is just an instrument. It's just like
learning to play a saxophone. You have times when you'll
hit weird notes and times when it won't always come out
the way you want it to.*

Sara isn't quite so tolerant with herself when it comes to performing. She still has high standards for her band. But she's trying to
be gentle with the part of herself that's still a little girl learning to step
out in front of the crowd and take a bow. Her band has landed a
regular Saturday night gig at an upscale country club, and Sara is
becoming more assertive.

*I finally realized that I want my name in the headlines.
I want credit for my creativity. I want to be empowered by the
music that my band creates. Now I sense a greater urgency
about using the talent I have and being responsible for it.*

Conversations and Reflections:
Using Your Voice

Too Good

Sara's story offers a glimpse into two voices that everyone could
benefit by claiming: the singing voice and the metaphorical "voice" of
confidence. The singing voice is a gift everyone has—talented or
not—and using it feels good and enlivens the spirit. The voice of confidence is what's needed for a creative person to say confidently to
others, "This is who I am and what I've done, and I own that."

Learning to proudly claim credit for creativity is a challenge for
many women raised to be modest. Sara demonstrates how hard it can
be to change the self-defeating habit of putting yourself last. Many
women have similar issues with their forms of creative expression.
Isn't part of creativity having the chutzpah to declare your work
good enough to pursue? Can't that sometimes be the hardest part? By
proudly claiming your creativity, you are challenging the conventions
of what it means to be "ladylike": Never brag. Be humble. Don't set
yourself apart. But the point is not to be a lady, it's to be yourself.
Because of her illness, Sara has faced head on the issues that have

held her back. By reading and reflecting about the symbolic meaning of her cancer, she has put herself in a healing frame of mind, ready to cure her body and her creative self from "dis-ease."

Everyone who knows Sara has chimed in with a chorus of "that's not fair" over the difficulty she's had getting her work into the public eye. Sara's sister Deborah, having grown up in the same family, has grappled with many of the same ingrained beliefs that make her recoil over self-promotion. Deborah says:

> I've seen it in my own life, with regard to working with others on architecture projects, or more recently in my work with the college faculty Union both in negotiation and general organizational chores. I tend to give others credit for what I've been the major responsible party for. It's only recently that I've come to see that's not necessary." She laughs. "Well actually I got an award last year from the Academic Senate for all the work I do, much of it behind the scenes. It's called the "Unsung Hero" award. I've taken that as a sign that I don't have to brag about it, but that I should accept credit for work I've done well.

Sara has discovered a new kind of allegiance that comes clear with creative maturity: What do I owe to my talent and passion? Loyalty to the self means getting over the modesty syndrome. In their book *Too Good for Her Own Good,* Claudia Bepko and Jo-Ann Krestan talked about how social expectations can smother talented women.

> The suppression of our creative power is a serious effect of the rules of unselfishness and service. As a composer friend says, "To be an artist is not compatible with being a woman by definition." The whole point of creative work is to let yourself go enough to pick up whatever falls out of our right brain before it disappears. If you're always paying attention to everybody else, that's hard to do. . . . A woman's not supposed to blow her own horn, and if you're an artist, in this country anyway, you have to do it. You have to write your own bio and market yourself. Women aren't supposed to do those things.

Freedom begins with acknowledging that pressure is real: Society may not approve of you proudly claiming your creativity. A safe beginning is with yourself. Try writing or saying aloud to yourself what you value about your creative expression, your gifts and discipline. Then, as Sara has done, begin honestly telling trusted friends and family members who will support you in moving your confidence to a public forum.

Creativity and Growth

It's a radical move for Sara, and for many women, to say the words "I have talent," and then begin taking the steps that follow from that statement. Linda Firestone said in *Awakening Minerva* that her studies have found that both internal and external movement happens when women take pride in their accomplishments: "There is value in looking at a woman's personal creative process in relation to creating a specific product, or it can be viewed more broadly, as in shaping the internal life and vision of a woman." As Sara found, personal growth happens when you stretch to discover your limits—in her case, as a musician and proud performer.

Beyond the singing and music itself, performers invoke another kind of creativity when they learn how to fill the stage. It's communication as much as talent. Sara has been practicing ways to expand herself and project into the audience the same spirit that fills her music. She is developing a relationship with her audience now, just as over the years she has developed a relationship with her music and the women in her band.

It's the same kind of issue that many writers I know face when they have to give talks for the first time. All those years behind a computer, and then suddenly it's them and not their words that everyone is watching. Performing is a skill enhanced by the desire to connect with the audience. Singer/guitarist/songwriter Bonnie Raitt was quoted in the book *Creators on Creating*:

> This incredible exchange of energy goes on onstage, where you're almost transported. For me, the spark comes, very emotional, from the shared experience of what I'm singing about. It's the band when we really lock in and the audience knows you're locking in. I wish I could lose myself more when I play by myself. It's easy to do with an audience, but I tend to be too self-conscious and judgmental when I'm alone. The audience is more unconditional, as if the channel is more open.

One lesson that comes from Sara's story is the value of connecting with people who share your passion. Even in her floundering years, she would rise up and sing when she found herself in an environment that supported that. As the years went by, she became more assertive about seeking people out for musical collaboration, a long way from the days when she waited for a friend to invite her to a music camp. She has been networking with people who can support each other to get their music out into the world in different ways.

Sara has come to value the exchange with an audience, the performing for others, as a peak experience in her life. But her story is still in progress. She is not yet a household word in the larger community, and she is still grappling with those old power issues and showing others how illness can be a metaphor for other life issues. Deborah said she was inspired by Sara's ability to turn a devastating situation into a lesson for herself and others.

> *I think her creativity is a part of how she is dealing with her illness, too. She is taking alternative approaches to healing and looking at the psychological aspects. On Sara's advice, I read* Why People Don't Heal and How They Can *and* Anatomy of the Spirit—the Seven Stages of Power and Healing, *both by Caroline Myss. The books identify the need to grapple with the issues of your life in order to heal. For Sara, that's meant identifying her tendency to give away the power in her life as a central issue to be resolved. The illness has made Sara realize that she HAS to be the one in charge— she has to take responsibility for working towards her health. She can't give that power to anyone else.*

In *The Mozart Effect—Tapping the Power of Music to Heal the Body, Strengthen the Mind, and Unlock the Creative Spirit* by Don Campbell, he talks about how people are using their voices through toning and humming to remove cancer cells and dissolve tumors. "There is some evidence to suggest that toning and humming can have amazing effects for everyone, acting as a 'tune-up' for the body. I've started doing and enjoying some of the toning and humming exercises myself," Deborah says.

Whatever the situation with her health, Sara sees herself immersed in music.

> *Maybe I will consider a redirection of some of my time and energy into music therapy. I've become intrigued with the healing aspects of sound. For example, one doctor suggested that perhaps I could sing at hospitals in the pediatric wards. Singing to sick children—I like that idea. It's one of the things I might do. I want my music to be something that is healing.*

Music for the Sake of It

You have to feel free to sing and be openhearted to sing with others. Sara's story speaks to what most people know if they have any singing experience in their lives, whether it's from church choir, school chorus, cross-country family trips, or simply singing along with the radio. With or without talent, singing can make you feel good and it's a great way to bond with others.

I grew up in a household of singers. I thought everyone sang all the time. A music teacher told me once that anyone can sing, with just a little practice and training, if they can get past their anxiety about it. I still like to sing in the car, invite friends to a sing-along, or just sit down with my husband, the banjo or guitar, and handwritten lyrics to our old favorite songs; but I hardly ever do any of these things. Months go by and my singing voice is croaky from dormancy. Other people I talk with say the same thing, "Why don't we get together and sing?" Meg was remembering when she was a girl and was called "Little Lark" because she had perfect pitch. I've known her for fifteen years and had no idea that she could sing. It makes me wish we were like the Welsh coal miners, singing while we worked. Singing is free and you can do it anywhere.

Although Sara is more talented than people who sing just for fun, she has some of the same lessons to learn as the rest of us. You don't have to do it perfectly for yourself and other people to enjoy it. As much as she loves the process, Sara is still suffering from the sense that it's never good enough. Seeing the music as something beyond herself—with joy to be shared with others—is helping her inspire children and smooth her artistic collaboration with the women in her band. By claiming her creativity, she is freeing the others to do the same. As it turned out, each is aware of her strengths and willing to work to support the others in theirs. All together, the personal growth can be healing.

In your own life, think about if there is anything that seems to be holding you back. If you blame others because you are feeling slighted, is it possible that you may be slighting yourself? Are your standards too high and, if so, can you be proud of getting close to them? What would it look like if you stood up, shining with glory over your accomplishments? Close your eyes and picture the moment. If it makes you too embarrassed to consider, you may have some of the same issues as Sara. She's working them out, and you can do the same if you desire.

Onward

Sara isn't sure what's next for her. She is still battling her cancer and not sure what's ahead. "I've already made some major changes in how I live, and I'm willing to try whatever feels right to me. Taking care of myself requires a lot of time and energy, but I won't let it define my life."

Sara plans to continue performing children's music and teaching music to children. "I love awakening the creative potential in children—if they learn to love music early, it is something they will have all their life."

Sara intends to keep working with High Standards too, as she has been since her surgery. "This new group is finally jelling. It's hard work, but great fun, to do the forties music. In addition to our club appearances and special performances, I think we need to make a CD," she said. "People ask us for one when they hear us perform. I'd like to do that, and maybe get into the distribution of it better this time than I did with *Tot Rock*. Then we might be 'discovered.'" She laughs, saying, "I think I might be able to handle that now."

9

Cultivating a Magic Garden: Nurturing Your Vision

Gardening, to me, is similar to painting. It's a matter of having a canvas that's alive. It's a matter of moving your plants around until they look like you see them. My artistry will never come from a paint tube. I can create my painting right here and live in it.

—Donna Freeman, gardener

Meet Donna in the Garden

An unobtrusive sign on the iron gate says COMPASS ROSE GARDENS. First-time visitors coming for weddings, fund-raisers, or parties have no idea what to expect behind the gate. "Compass Rose" is the term for the directional symbol on maps, the center of the compass. This place is near the sea, the air is salt fresh, and a collection of beached boats nearby are rusty with age. But when the gate opens, the astonishment begins. Hanging fuchsias, tea plants, lilacs, lavender, and cineraria decorate the pathway—separate clusters of plants that together create an amalgam of color and texture.

There is a pond that's surrounded by a sway of fox glove and eight-feet-tall gunnera elephant ear plants. Lily pads grace the surface of the water, and the pond has an elfin bridge. The seaside winds may be bellowing outside the gate, but benevolent trees safeguard the garden. A shady spot inside a grove of adolescent redwoods serves as a place apart from parties and celebrations, a sanctuary for quiet meditation, waiting to be discovered during a stolen moment away from the crowd or on a solitary return visit. A tiny cottage invites a look inside, and through the curtained window you can faintly discern wicker furniture and a bed, all covered with the same floral pattern.

Donna stands inside the cottage, looking out. From her window, she can gaze out over a gathering. At some point, she'll emerge, like a radiant blonde-haired pixie, blue eyes reflecting a glint of the sun. If it's a wedding, the bride and groom will walk up and greet her as though she were a proud and generous aunt. If it's a political event, she is lauded like a head of state. If it's a community gathering, grown-ups treat her like the unofficial mayor and children compete for her attention as though she were a latter day combination of Mrs. Santa Claus and Mary Poppins.

When you meet her for the first time, Donna appears to be the queen of the garden. She extends a hand. Look closely. These are the hands of a working woman. Not too many hours ago, Donna was digging in the dirt, moving a plant here, pulling weeds there. Not too many years ago, she was standing in this same place, surrounded by nothing but thick scrub brush and tree branches as far as she could see. During those days, you could see her with a scythe in one hand to clear a path and a sketchpad in her other hand to record the vision in her mind. She loves to tell the story.

I would come down the path to the future garden and just sit and look, absorb all I could, and it evolved. To get to where the deck is now, I literally had to crawl on my hands and knees to get through the underbrush. I almost died from poison oak, but we were on our way to paradise.

Finding the Seeds of Creativity in Your Own Backyard

Earthy and unpretentious, Donna defies society's stereotypes about how artists look and act. She personifies the new definition of creativity, which includes everyone with a creative vision and the courage to bring it into realization. Donna couldn't care less about developing a sophisticated image, proudly clinging to her Arkansas heritage and drawl; yet she is refined in the greatest sense of the word, far beyond social affectations. Her creativity started with a sudden and powerful vision, and she rendered it into reality—right in her own backyard.

Donna's experiences exemplify ideas that are applicable to any self-expressive endeavor: It is possible to have a creative life even as lists are falling out of your jammed calendar and address book. Tending the garden became a way of tending to herself. She was responding to an inner longing when she started her garden, and the work demanded solitude. Yet the resulting garden is a place of connection—where community members come together, political careers are launched, and major life events are celebrated. In Donna's brand of creativity, the inner and outer lives can become compatible. Intuition plays a big role: trusting your vision even when it may seem impossible to *have it* materialize.

To people who hold back from their dreams because of practical considerations, Donna tells how she didn't have enough time or money to accomplish her goal, nor did she have the requisite horticultural training when she started her task; but intuition carried her vision forward. Her garden is a blossoming monument to possibilities: "To anyone who has a vision, I say follow your heart. I know from personal experience that anyone can make their vision reality. Sometimes I look around this garden and I can't believe this is real. If I could make my dream happen, honey, so can you."

Donna's Path

Scenes from a Childhood

Donna's childhood offered little artistic "culture" in the classic sense. Growing up poor in rural Arkansas, there were no trips to the art museum for her and her sister; a big outing was running out to the railroad tracks and watching the guy on the handcar pumping the handle up and down to move himself along. The images from her childhood remain framed in her memory.

> *We raised hogs and cattle. We lived on a hillside covered with pine trees and a green called "poke salit." One of my favorite things to do as a little girl was race the garter snakes along the path to the ridge. We had huckleberries, lots of dogwood in the bottom land, hickory trees for the nuts, an odd apple tree here and there, sweet gum trees to harvest for tooth-brushes and to chew the resin. Inside, we used oil lamps and cooked on a wood stove.*
>
> *When bathing in the summertime, we would have to draw the water from the well and put it in the washtub out behind the house, and as soon as the sun warmed it up, we got in it. We made our own lye soap, rendered the pork fat, made cracklin bread and fried okra. We thought that we were as rich as anyone. Well, actually, I thought that. My parents were aware how bad it was. There were many years when the price of cattle would drop over the winter and you would sell those cows for less than you paid for them.*

In a childhood of poverty, Donna created her own sense of bounty. A tea party: Go dig in the yard for some sassafras. A swim: head for the creek. A tasty snack: chew on some sugar cane or pick some huckleberries. A thrilling brush with danger: lean over the rickety sides of the well and peek over close enough to see the water. A favorite Christmas present: a sack full of pecans. In addition, there were books from the library, gatherings with family, and lots of singing.

The Baptist church was their social center. Her mom was a schoolteacher, the descendent of prominent old line southern families who had come to America in the 1600s. She was a natural musician who, despite their poverty, made sure her two daughters had music lessons by professional teachers. Donna remembers her mother's industrious creativity.

> *My mom did wonderful needlework. She never just sat but always had a project going: crocheted tablecloths, bedspreads, knitted sweaters, capes, and slippers by the dozens. She also*

did tatting, now a lost art, where you use a bone or wooden shuttle with a thread wound on it; it's the art of tying knots with this shuttle and very fine thread to make decorations for fine fabrics. Her fingers went so fast, her hands were a blur.

Her mom taught Donna how to transform simple objects into something useful or entertaining, like turning a patterned feedsack into a dress and transforming orange crates into dressing tables with blue silk organza. Donna's family didn't have the wealth of their ancestors, but they had the stories and would make treks to places where their great-grandparents and uncles and aunts lived, places that the government turned into monuments. Through the stories of her ancestors, Donna developed a personal view of politics that later would influence her work in the world. And her mother's garden would be the other influence: "My mom loved to garden, and flowers were her favorites."

Dark Influences

The idyllic scenes from her childhood, however, were interrupted by torrents of pain that could flood over everything with no notice.

My father was an alcoholic, who never drank away from home, unfortunately. He was a very jealous man, verbally abusive and violent at times. I was his "buddy" and he would take me squirrel hunting. That was the good dad. Then he'd turn mean. When I was small, I was confused. Then I was mad. The threats to my mom were the hardest to take. He was great when he was sober, but he was also a victim of circumstances, losing both his own parents when he was thirteen with three younger siblings he was responsible for.

Donna's mother didn't feel she could leave and raise two daughters on her own, and often would fall into periods where she felt "blue." Looking back, Donna recognizes that her mother suffered from depression. Some of those "blue" times would last for days, maybe even weeks.

Later on in life, once Donna had discovered the meditation of gardening and began reflecting on her past, she would remember the delightful things from girlhood, such as the taste of huckleberry cobbler. Looking at the violent images from the past was like looking down that deep scary well when she was a girl. Still, as she allowed her memories to flow, she began to feel cleansed. She started to see with clarity why she made certain life decisions.

Her father's rages prompted her to marry young to escape. Her family had moved to the northern California valley town of Tracy, where her mom taught first grade, her father worked for a creamery, and she and her sister delved into a new social life. Donna became absorbed in theater. But her father's drinking got worse and worse. "I couldn't have anyone to the house. He was usually unpresentable." Her aspirations took form by the time she was sixteen, and they had nothing to do with the stage or screen. "I had to get out of the house. I could not stand living with alcoholism."

She wanted to marry her high school sweetheart—and did so, finishing high school as a married woman. Their first baby came three years later, then shortly afterwards another. Her husband's desire to become a fisherman took them north to the little town of Bodega Bay. She had two babies when they moved. Three more would come soon.

> I thought I was miles from anywhere. I was so missing my friends, and they all thought I had come up here to die . . . of boredom and loneliness. I had no telephone, and all those babies. For the first year, with two toddlers and then a newborn son, I cried a lot. We were so poor we couldn't afford a telephone. My dad bought half of the boat for us but I tried to hide the state of our finances from my parents. Commercial fishing was so bad for us that if it hadn't been for the store owners here, we would have had to move. They let us charge groceries, sometimes all winter, then we'd pay them during the salmon season. But after the first year, I never cried over being alone again. I became very active in the community.

Donna whipped up adventures for her kids that didn't cost a penny, going camping and traveling with home-cooked food instead of going to restaurants. Other mothers looked to her for inspiration. She organized them. When the children wanted to take a school field trip to Disneyland, she put together a fund-raiser and gathered sleeping bags, arranging for a sleepover at a school in Orange County. Soon school officials were turning to her when a need arose. Need money for a building or park or field trip? Ask Donna, they'd say, she can gather the political support and money and get it done. Donna was heady with the excitement of making things happen, moving and shaking and watching others pick up the rhythm. She thrived on all the conversations and parties and gatherings of people.

Finding Time for Herself

Amid all the activity, she felt a longing for something. "Be still, now," a voice inside seemed to say. "Be quiet." She discovered she could find the quiet through gardening, concentrating on the movements of digging and planting and pruning and watering. A fledgling sort of meditation grew.

> *When all five of my children were young, I wanted my garden to be nice for them to play in.... There was very little time for solitude. Most of that would come at night when everyone was asleep and I was able to daydream and read about gardening and flowers, shrubs and trees. I was a voracious reader in those days and craved the knowledge that would allow me to accomplish my dreams. I always regarded beauty—natural beauty—as one of the most important elements in my life, no matter what the medium.*

It was during a rare flush fishing season, when the crab pots miraculously filled and the wholesalers were benevolent, that Donna, with her little-used but hard-earned real estate license, made what would turn out to be a pivotal life investment. She bought a little cottage on coastal Highway One. Behind it was the steep drop of a hillside that appeared useless to all eyes but her own. She kept looking at it and wondering what might be there. For eleven years, the cottage was a rental home, bringing in some income during the lean times. The hillside began collecting brush brought in from a nearby creek; weed seeds flew around and sprouted a formidable briar patch.

During that time, her small front-yard gardening projects provided refuge. Time would disappear as she started in full light: suddenly the fog would roll in, dusk would be upon her, and she would have to work by porchlight. But opportunities for such meditative stretches were rare. There weren't enough hours in the day to meet her responsibilities, which multiplied as people recognized her competence at getting things done. Her reputation for whipping up support for worthy causes had leaked into the political arena. Now political candidates were coming to her for support, seeking her inexplicable technique for getting the political machinery working.

A Painful Passing

As her outer life hummed with activity, though, Donna was drawn into a bleak shadow world for which nothing in her life had prepared her. Her mother, a lifelong source of love and inspiration, had Alzheimer's disease and began the slow descent into disorientation and erosion of personality that comes with the brain disorder: "It was the most excruciating experience I have ever had to endure. I still cry when I think of the injustice of that."

She had been close to her mother since birth, being the proud daughter who went with her mother, the teacher, to school. She spent her childhood trying to learn the tricks of her mom's handiwork and uncover all the stories about their family's history. When Donna had a family of her own, her mom would visit. "She would come up here and would love to work in the yard. She loved my fuchsias and would always take cuttings home."

Watching her lifelong role model drift into Alzheimer's was the most painful experience of her life, helpless as her mother became more confused each day:

> She used to cry and ask me, "Honey, what in the world is wrong with me?" and we would both cry. I took her to several physicians, and it was obvious she was suffering from some sort of dementia. That began the nightmare of my life. We built her a house in Bodega Bay, but she could never stay there alone. As her mind deteriorated, we sold the house and tried to keep her at home. It was devastating: She could stay awake for twenty-four hours at a time, and I couldn't.
>
> She could unfasten any lock and climb to get the doors open to wander. She was brought back a few times before I realized she was gone. Once she fell in a ditch a couple blocks away. The next six years were a living hell for her and for me. I found four different nursing homes ... my mom ran away from all of them, always wanting to go "home." Home was Arkansas. She lost all her dignity and slowly she herself was gone. She weighed fifty-two pounds when she died. The worst times by far were when her mind would be lucid for a couple of minutes and then she would know there was something terribly, terribly wrong.

Donna brought her mother to live with her, to die at home. Even in her last stages, her mom still responded to the beauty of a new blossom. "The trauma of my mom's last years with Alzheimer's was such that I was able to escape only into my dreams of a paradise that I would create for her." On the property behind the rental cottage, willows and brambles had clogged the earth and swept through the gulch to sprout there via rains and floods. It was a mess. But Donna began to see in her mind a terrace and a pathway and a vast living flower arrangement that could blanket the brambled acreage:

> It was about the time that my mother died when I started designing the garden in my head. We moved into the house near the acreage and I would come down the path to the future garden and just sit and look, absorb all I could. When I would walk into this tangled overgrown thicket of berry vines, poison oak, and old willows, I would just find a place to sit and meditate about what was to be.

Filling the Void

The void Donna felt after her mother's death was palpable. She began suffering from her own depression, feeling melancholy. Sometimes she was unable to get out of bed. It was the vision for the garden that brought meaning into the void. Donna felt guided as she moved through the brambles, a sketchpad in her hand.

I crawled back to where the summer house is now. I knew that was the spot. As I sat in the different areas in meditation, the overall design came. I dragged a few of my friends around down there, again, crawling to get to the places I wanted them to see. I am sure they were all humoring me when they agreed this would be a beautiful place for a garden. I am sure that most of them thought me certifiable.

She had a small inheritance from her mom that she decided to use to start her project.

In order to design the gardens, I had to learn about plants, so I would read and read and read. I would sleep with books on horticulture. Eventually I learned enough to do what I wanted to do. I am still learning, but that will go on forever. My husband Clarence gave me support and long hours of hard labor.

Due to her past accomplishments, those around Donna allowed her a little eccentricity. As much as some protested, no one stood in her way. Or if they did, she didn't notice. Her husband humored her and did what he could between his own jobs to help with the work. Her children pitched in. Slowly the garden began to take shape.

The garden became a spiritual place for me almost from the beginning. I come from very religious families: Baptists, Southern Baptists, Methodists, and Assembly of God. I am a very spiritual person but not a very religious person. I have found my spiritual center right here in the garden. I have leanings toward Buddhism and a sort of a hodgepodge of beliefs that I have gathered from all religions. I certainly believe that God is right here in the garden.

Donna let nature guide her decisions about where to put the plants.

When designing Compass Rose, it was very important to me to leave all the natural parts that were here when I started. The calla lilies and large sword ferns are right where they were found. I think that by not having a "landscaped" look to the gardens, they are much more spiritual. I love putting in little benches that are tucked away out of sight, pruning the brush so that people must bend down to walk through the path into the shade garden. There are many little areas like this. It would be hard to make a judgment whether the gardens are more spiritual or romantic. To me it is both in equal portions.

The creek was cleaned. The tiny redwoods planted in a fairy circle. And the flowers grew. Donna transformed three acres of weeds into a complex meander of floral compositions, and one day it was finished—the garden was perfectly arranged, materialized exactly as she had seen it in her mind fourteen years earlier.

Donna's Life Today

In the solitary moments, dawn, maybe, or dusk, Donna breathes in the aroma of blossoms and earth and salty sea air and feels at one with all of it. During these moments sometimes comes a flash of insight about what—or who—belongs in the garden. It may be a new plant. One day she decided she wanted the irises that her grandmother had raised in Arkansas, so she got them, planted them, and grew them big, purple, and healthy in Compass Rose. Especially in certain areas of the garden, she says, there is "a special kind of energy." And the plants, she says, all have "a place where they belong." She will be walking down a particular path when suddenly she sees a Japanese maple that belongs elsewhere. She'll dig it up and move it. She knows when it looks "right."

She sees the garden as a place to grow possibilities for others. The most unlikely candidates for romance have found one another and fallen in love during garden events. Children going through grammar school graduation ceremonies under the canopy of willows feel celebrated and part of something grand. Environmental and political activists meet and trade strategies as Donna plays hostess to the powerbrokers. She does not take her political influence lightly, but tries to let that aspect of her life reflect the values that her garden is about. "I try to choose politicians with integrity to support. Sometimes you slip up and are mistaken, but most of the time I have felt so secure that they wanted the world to be a place that we would all want to live in."

During political events, there's all the jockeying and maneuvering that goes with the business. Donna can speak in her sweet Arkansas drawl and look like the belle of the ball who isn't bothering her pretty little head with big ideas, but she's keeping a careful watch for the genuine versus the fraudulent. She glows with good-spiritedness and has a joke or story ready for any lull in the conversation.

Then the gates close, and she tunes into the mysteries. She continues to move deeper into the spiritual places within herself and the garden, sometimes in quiet conversations with other women, many of whom have told her about experiencing a presence in the hidden places of the garden. During her time in the garden, one woman discovered she was a healer and changed her life to pursue her gift: "There is a palpable energy in the garden. I do believe that something that powerful can make magic. Most everyone who comes here feels the magic and mentions it to me."

Donna rents the garden for weddings, scheduled in between the events she hosts for friends, family, the local school, and politicians she supports. This is also the place where people gather for memorial services.

> I have had many friends who have "gone to the other side,"
> and the garden is a memorial to them. We have planted trees,
> rhododendrons and a variety of plants for each of them. . . .
> This really is a memory garden.

She sees herself as a caretaker of her community, while simultaneously tending to the development of each sprout and blossom in the garden.

> It is paradise for me. I love it. I have friends who come and
> meditate, others who will call and say, "I need to walk in the
> garden." Almost everyone who comes here tells me the garden
> is magic. I do believe it is.

Conversations and Reflections: Growing Through Solitude and Connection

Tending Your Root, Sharing the Fruit of Creativity

Donna's inner beauty and spiritual life, along with her flowers, have blossomed over the years, demonstrating the transformational power of creativity. Compass Rose Garden is a living monument to the kind of magic that happens with the daily tending to a passion. Her story can be particularly inspiring to busy women inundated with commitments. She became creative in spite of her obligations to others, and as a result of pursuing her creative vision she has enjoyed her relationships more.

Yet there was a time in her life when Donna operated under the oppressive belief that dampens many creative spirits: that taking time to pursue a passion means taking your focus away from your responsibilities to others, and that doing so is selfish. Her story is incentive for pulling the cover off that myth. Here is a woman as close as you can get to an "earth mother," because she gives so much to others, with genuine affection. Yet she made a one-hundred percent commitment to creating Compass Rose Gardens—a pursuit that, at its heart, was a solitary one—because it was something she needed to do for herself. In the process, she discovered a freeing truth that lay beneath the old shroud of guilt: solitude and connection, as Donna found, are equally essential parts of the self.

One analogy is found in the root and the fruit of the tree: Tending the deep parts of the self, invisible to others, lays the groundwork for the fruits of creativity, which can also be seen and appreciated by others. Seeing those aspects together happens through exercise. Sufi poet Rumi urges: "Let yourself be silently drawn by the pull of what you really love." Donna let herself be drawn into the garden and into a creative life. As a result, she ended up with more of both physical and emotional space for the people in her life—including herself.

Creative self-nurturing can happen through day-to-day devotion to a task. A simple repetitive act can slowly turn into a miracle of consciousness. During periods in my life when I've written religiously in a journal, at roughly the same time every day, my awareness shifts. I'm more tuned into nuance, and my days unfold with more perception. In the back of my mind, asleep or awake, is the knowledge that I will be soon recording what is important, and thus, I find myself more attentive to what actually is important and less likely to waste energy on what is not.

Does this mean I do this every day? Unfortunately not. As with singing and dancing and other activities I know will enhance my creativity; it's so easy to think of the daily writing as superfluous, something to do after the laundry gets done. I know intellectually— and the women in this book demonstrate over and over again—that the activities that put you in touch with your real self help all the mundane chores fall into place.

What keeps me from acting on that knowledge? It would be so much fun to do that free kind of non-goal-oriented writing every day, sing more often, and regularly kick up my heels. But all that potential for aliveness tends to get squashed by the dead weight of the combined daily minutiae. Like saying to a child, "I'll play with you later," it's so easy to put off creative activities. Most of us are motivated by a certain amount of guilt (the kind that comes up when the laundry is spilling over). Why not transfer a little of that to the creative self? "Oh dear, I've neglected myself again. I'd better go play a little." Think about the activities that seem to set your spirit free. Schedule them into your calendar and expect people to respect your time.

Seeing the Lotus

The benefits to the spirit of creative exercise are as clear and life changing as the benefits to the body of physical exercise. The challenge is to do it. Sun Bu-er, the twelfth-century teacher of Taoism who raised three children and at the age of fifty-one began her full-time practice of "the Way," wrote:

> Cut brambles long enough,
> Sprout after sprout,
> And the lotus will bloom
> Of its own accord:
> Already waiting in the clearing,
> The single image of light.
> The day you see this,
> That day you will become it.

Sun Bu-er's garden image captures the way Donna's self-awareness deepened and her sense of purpose crystallized through the regular work in the soil, but the metaphor could apply to many activities. It could be finally getting around to writing the novel you've been playing with in your head, tuning up the neglected piano, or sketching the midnight visions for a painting. Or maybe it could be just listening to the playful child's soul inside you that protests against the daily grind, imploring, "Isn't there a way to make life more fun?"

In *The Woman's Book of Creativity*, C. Diane Ealy urges us not to get too caught up in choosing the perfect creative activity, but instead to practice with whatever tool is available.

> Like the genie who has to be released from the bottle in order
> to do what she's here to do—grant wishes—passions have to
> have an outlet. Once we find one way to express a passion, we
> will find other ways. Or other passions will want to be heard.
> Like the creative process in general, the more attention and
> nurturing we give to our passions, the more they will respond.

Most of us recognize what gives us pleasure, often because it's the last thing on our list of things to do.

What's Handy?

For women schooled in taking care of themselves last, creative urges are quickly followed by admonishments: "Don't be foolish."

"You can't change at this age." "It's too late to start something new." "You'll never make a living at it." Keep in mind that "Perhaps later, when I have more time" can translate into never. Women like Donna who manage to accomplish great feats of creativity do so by allowing themselves to follow their vision and dedicate a significant amount of energy to their pursuits. Donna's children were grown and the responsibility for her ailing mother had ended, but she still had dozens of other people and commitments she had to put aside. From time to time as she worked on the garden, she lessened the amount of energy given to others so she could support her vision. And no one fell apart. In fact, her sons and daughters showed up with backhoes, garden tools, books, and lunches for her, ready to support her as she always supported them.

Taking a small step to engage in an activity that fulfills you can be as life altering as making a dramatic change. It may be as simple as finding a half hour a day. It can seem like a huge feat to find even the smallest amount of regular time. Sometimes it's best to just do what you can, with whatever you can find, in whatever time you can carve out. For some women, the predawn hours before the family wakes up or the midnight hour after everyone goes to bed hold the promise of solitude. Others use their lunch hours at work as quiet time, sneaking off to a restaurant or park bench with sketchpad, journal, or book. One woman I know goes to the beach alone with her notebook once a week. She's committed to keeping some link to her creative roots at a time in her life when daily time seems impossible to find.

Most women don't have the luxury of long expanses of time for their artistic pursuits, so their creative work may get done in stolen moments here and there. One friend who is a single mother, painter, and lawyer said she can't imagine dragging out her easel and canvas and paints because that would take longer than doing the actual painting. She finds that she has to improvise something to exercise her extraordinary gift, so that it doesn't disappear into the framework of the day. The logistics of her daily life have grown so complex, she has to admit, that even pulling a small sketchpad out of her pocket seems like a difficult task: But it's a starting place.

The challenge is more than the physical act of creating something; it is finding enough time to get into the state of mind for creativity to happen. Working on this book has provided a mini-laboratory for my co-authors and me to look at our own creative process. Just finding time was a huge challenge for Meg, a wife and full-time working mom who also is caring for her own mother. "I never get much 'spare' time to indulge my writing, or any other creative pursuit, outside the workplace. If I'm going to do it, it has to be time seized from sleep, sometime between bedtime and breakfast. My favorite time is the quiet hours before dawn, after I've had at least some sleep and some distance from yesterday's pressures."

Even if we grab for the closest tools at our disposal—the pen for the professional writer, the hoe for the backyard gardener, the pencil for the artist—the creative act is not casual. It's not just going through motions, but digging inside for a part of the self that becomes manifested in something outside of the self. That requires you to be present and open. It helps some women to have a symbol that helps them find their creative "zone" more quickly. Sarah Andrews bows to a Hindu statue before she starts writing. Nancy likes nesting with the stacks of material all around her house so she can dig into her creative work and have everything in view and at hand.

Intuition

In talking with creative women over the years, I've been struck by how many of them bow to unconscious forces that seem to guide their work. Trusting intuition was the beginning of Donna's garden. She was working from a sweeping vision of what "belonged" on that weed-strewn acreage, with no context other than a mental image. Unknowingly speaking the language of artists, Donna described the garden as having a direction of its own, leaving her with the job of allowing it to be. It is the classic act of creativity to "see" something that does not exist and proceed to materialize the vision. Scholars have been fascinated for centuries by that initial insight, the life-giving seed of creativity.

In her book *Drawing On the Artist Within*, Betty Edwards examines the vital element of intuition. She found that the word intuition is related to the Latin verb "intueri," which is defined as "the power or faculty of attaining direct knowledge or cognition without rational thought and interference . . . seeing something directly, or, in other words, 'getting the picture,' without having to 'figure it out.'" Donna didn't know Latin, nor did she recognize that when the "big picture" flashed in her mind she was experiencing an ultimate creative moment—seeing the garden that was to be. It didn't need to make sense to her, and it certainly made no sense to others. But she dug in.

Studies of the creative process historically have involved male artists and were facilitated by men, so they have tended to produce a step-by-step analysis in which the "aha" moment was seen as one phase along a continuum. It's different for women, more recent analyses have shown. As C. Diane Ealy found in her studies, women tend to create more holistically. Until recently there were thought to be four steps in the creative process: preparation, incubation, illumination, and verification. But women might start anywhere in the process and go from there. In her book *The Woman's Book of Creativity*, Ealy says:

*We see the whole first, then break out the details. Men tend
to do the opposite. They use linear thinking, seeing the details
first, then fitting those together to form the whole. . . . In
contrast, the holistic process enables you to see the whole
picture at once, then sort out the details.*

In Donna's case, if she had sorted out the details first, she probably
would never have pulled that first weed. In the beginning, she simply
surrendered to the mental picture of the garden asking for life. In retrospect, she sees the confluence of mysterious forces that led to her
living masterpiece.

Crisis and Inspiration

What does it take to get to a place in life where you're ready to
access the deeper parts of the self? Being open—temporarily stripped
of the layers of distraction that protect our vulnerability—can allow
impulses as strong as the one that moved Donna to design her garden. Routine can leave us with calluses that keep us from feeling too
much that's new or different. Sometimes it takes a crisis to open up,
as Donna did after the death of her mother, but she had been working hard toward it for years. Although creativity is not necessarily
associated with suffering (and this is a welcome notion to some
women we talked to, who felt they couldn't be in the creative "club"
unless they were in a constant state of discomfort) it is clear that
sometimes personal pain can broaden perspective. Reaching for a
creative tool can be like an emotional lifeline, grabbing something to
fill the void left by loss.

That deep feelings and profound opportunity should often be
inextricably linked is one of the confounding connections with which
artists struggle. Pain peels away the extraneous and demands attention for the real. In *Creators on Creating,* edited by Frank Barron et al.,
Austrian poet Rainer Maria Rilke discusses how he believes that it is
the emotionally brave, who allow themselves vulnerability, who earn
a connection with the "Angel" of creativity:

*This sudden shifting of all one's forces, these about-faces of the
soul, never occur without many a crisis; the majority of artists
avoid them by means of distraction, but that is why they never
manage to return to the center of their productivity, whence
they started out at the moment of their purest impulse. At the
onset of every work, you must recreate that primal innocence,
you must return to that ingenuous place where the Angel
found you.*

Pure creativity seems to flow from an innocent place. Think of the times you have felt most vulnerable and childlike, perhaps due to a major shake-up in your life. Transitions can be times of great creative movement, because you're forced to give up some habitual ways of thinking and go back to a more open state of mind. Are there any transitions happening in your life now or in the near future? Are there ways to take creative advantage of being unsettled?

Creative Spirit and Compost

Teachers of creativity often encourage their students to look for clues to their innate creativity by remembering the details of childhood events. Natalie Goldberg, in her book *Writing Down the Bones*, offers some perspective on the rich gift of memory. While Goldberg's observations are about writing, they aptly apply to other creative endeavors that grow out of self-reflection and personal experience.

> *Our senses by themselves are dumb. They take in experience, but they need the richness of sifting for a while through our consciousness and through our whole bodies. I call this "composting." Our bodies are garbage heaps: We collect experience, and from the decomposition of the thrown-out eggshells, spinach leaves, coffee grinds and old steak bones of our minds come nitrogen, heat and very fertile soil. . . . Continue to turn over and over the organic details of your life until some of them fall through the garbage of discursive thoughts to the solid ground of black soil.*

Donna was inspired by her memories to make her garden fertile ground for recreating many of her symbols of childhood joy. Her creation includes not just the plants themselves but the various accouterments of life: the big wooden table in the kitchen, the familiar prints she chooses for tablecloths, and even a bathroom that's separate from the house (it has flush toilets, but the cold walk out in the night is reminiscent of an outhouse). She can surround herself with her favorite symbols from childhood and banish what was bad. As a teenager, she was fearful about having people over to her house because of her dad's alcoholism, but today she can invite hundreds of people over for gatherings. She can be fully herself, not feeling she needs to hide anything.

The Genie in the Garden

Donna's garden is a magical place, and I wanted to explore why. But of course the elements that make for magical feelings originate in a realm that defies ordinary language. At times like this, I like to look deeper at words for clues. Sure enough, there is one that helped me see that there is a link between what we recognize as creative genius—like Donna's work in her garden—and reverence for the mystical. As Willis Harman and Howard Rheingold said in their book *Higher Creativity*:

> *The most important clue to the puzzle of human creative potential might be staring us all in the face. Our language itself is the encoding mechanism par excellence for preserving certain kinds of meaning in the face of changing cultural values. The newer word "genius," for example, contains a significant resonance with the much older term "genie." A genie is a magic spirit, sometimes benevolent, now considered to be mythical, who is able to grant miraculous favors to mortals on special occasions. In a sense that has lived on in our language for generations, people have believed that certain specially talented individuals must possess the aid of a genie.*

You probably won't go so far as to imagine a literal genie hovering around your life, but what if you tuned into more of the images that pop into your head and don't seem to "make sense"? Often the best ideas can present themselves as dream symbols or recurring thoughts, and giving yourself time to translate these symbols can lead to a deeper self-awareness and creativity.

For the Sake of Gardening Alone

Donna's garden is her creative expression, but even for women whose primary creative outlet is something else, the garden can be a place to get in touch with our "genie." Associated with beauty and safety, the garden has long been a symbol for life-changing experiences. In many religions, gardens were where the revelations come to the prophets. As garden writer Katherine Grace Endicott wrote:

> *Gardening is not about improving the house or getting a bit of exercise. That is only what we tell one another when embarrassed by the deeper truth. Gardening is the principal way in which we come to understand that we belong on this earth and are part of it. It is the way in which we care for what is home to our species and to all earthly life forms.*

Gardening can replenish the spirit. Alice Walker said in Lilith Roger's book *Raising Bread and Roses*:

I get energy from the earth itself, and I get optimism from the earth itself. I feel that as long as the earth can make a spring every year, I can. As long as the earth can flower and produce nurturing fruit, I can, because I am the earth. I won't give up until the earth gives up.

Onward: Following the Cycle of Nature

Donna strives to live in a way that allows for the full range of experience. Through gardening, Donna was able to let both her joyous and her painful memories come to the surface, and all of her memories are contained in the magical world she has created in her garden. Inviting people to Compass Rose Gardens for funerals is essential, as are the celebrations of weddings and graduations. It's all part of the cycle of life, and she's determined to be attentive to all of it. As Donna talks of the sad passings that she has marked within the leafy framework of Compass Rose, a flame-haired grandchild is prancing about, playing and laughing under the trees, near Donna's grandmother's irises, which her mother helped tend before her death.

Of course, my biggest regret is that my mom did not live to see "our" garden. Her spirit is here, but I wish we could have spoken about the beauty and the magic of Compass Rose. I hope that her eyes are seeing through mine the solitude and the specialness of this garden. It was truly for her that I went forward with it.

10

Celebrating Eccentricity: Freeing Your Creative Spirit

Creativity to me is the original essential whim that each person has. If you pay attention, it's an urgency, something you must do. Who could ever judge another's creativity? We all have it. It's like breathing. But to own it sometimes your life has to change.

—Helen Lordsmith,
psychic, free spirit

Meet Helen in the Moment

Helen Lordsmith is a sparkler. Her earthy laughter lights up a room, as does her usually golden, occasionally flaming red, hair. She has a gift for bringing herself fully into the moment and for making the moment her own. She decorates herself and her environment in her own flamboyant way, as though honoring the muse who has blessed her with a capacity for fun and eccentricity and a psychic sixth sense.

Helen feels connected to the divine, but stays connected to her physical environment by bringing bits of herself, evidence of her whimsy, into her dress and her environment. In her living room there are always fresh flowers because, she says, "I need fragrance." She arranges dozens of votive candles on fanciful tiers around the house. Year round, she has tiny white Christmas lights: "I wrap them around plants, across glass and mirrors. I want them up all year." Such touches are her trademark.

Helen dresses for her own pleasure: "If my first question is 'How will this look to others, how am I coming off?' then I know it's not based on me. Sometimes I want to wear something just to please my eye." You could never find Helen's outfits in a store window or a fashion catalog. Friends don't recall seeing her in a designer suit or, for that matter, a T-shirt and jeans. Her clothes are always chic but somehow her own style. Looking at Helen—even if you don't know that she is also a painter and a pianist who spent a few years singing light opera—you suspect there is a creative soul underneath.

Long before secondhand clothes were a trend and long after she needed it to stretch her budget, Helen was the queen of thrift shops. Ask her about any city she's ever been in, from Los Angeles to Memphis, and she can critique the offerings of their Goodwill and Symphony League racks. Helen is like those actresses you read about who take their favorite scarves and pictures with them on location to dress up an impersonal hotel room. Helen does that even when she's housesitting for friends, and she's known to leave mementos nestled in flower petals on their dining room table, welcoming them home. She laughs:

> I think a lot of my creativity is based on the idea of making a
> silk purse out of a sow's ear. I take something that is limping

around and give it horsepower. I ask, "Where is the beauty here? What's inside?"

Helen can't remember ever buying clothing or furniture that was complete before she did something to fix it up and make it hers. But what Helen adorns herself with is just the tip of her creativity. Much of her life, her art, and her work are as eclectic and magical as the Indian blouse with tiny mirrors, the antique opera cape, or the bone necklaces and bangles that she uses to decorate herself. Her external whimsy signifies something much deeper.

Helen has an open channel for absorbing information unused by most people. For more than twenty years, she has made her living as a psychic advisor. People come to her hoping she can tell them things they don't know about themselves. Her discipline is setting aside her own ego so she can tune in fully to what she sees and feels. The mechanism that delivers information to her is surprisingly accurate— so much so that she has a growing list of clients, including a mixture of New Age and regular folks plus a sprinkling of the rich and almost famous—who rely on her readings.

In her work and in her life, she is committed to being fully absorbed in the present. Because of her philosophy, Helen lives a nomadic and adventuresome life. Along the way, she's been married to a fisherman and a journalist, and she's the mother of two sons, and she's a grandmother. She's lived in a condo on the Pacific, a resort town in Mexico, a cabin under the redwoods, and in Berkeley. Eight years is the longest period she's lived in one place as an adult, and that was when she was caring for her ill mother.

Helen has moved back and forth across the country and up and down the Pacific Coast. She was fifty before she ever considered buying a house, and she still doesn't have credit cards. One day she'll be driving a red sports car and the next she'll be in an old blue Cadillac. She believes in fate. She could be the originator of the concepts of "the universe will provide" and "follow your bliss," just by example.

Helen appears to be the ultimate free spirit, but she has had to work for it. Although she grew up in an environment that offered the seeds of creativity, Helen lived under the influence of a mother who strained under the weight of others' expectations—giving up her own creative life to try and conform to social expectations that didn't suit her. Helen grew up determined not to make the same mistakes, and that meant making up her own way of doing her life. She strives not to impose her will or order on others, but responds to what is actually happening, accepting each moment as a surprise and a blessing.

Learning to Be Fully Present and Tap into the Divine

Helen has redefined wealth and security in a way that doesn't depend on money. She lives her definition of luxury: Unencumbered, she decides her own work hours and can come and go as she pleases. Her profession as a psychic advisor is a little offbeat and her bank account fluctuates, but Helen has attained a quality of life that the financially flush might envy: She has freedom. She leaves her mark, whether she's just walking into a room or moving in.

Helen's lifestyle is not a coincidence. It is an intentional direction that Helen chose at a young age. She decided that no person, no thing, no job would be responsible for her happiness—except herself. Her story is a reminder that ultimately it's up to each individual what kind of physical and emotional environment she creates for herself. You can surround yourself with beauty even if you don't have money. You can feel a magical connection to the universe even if your childhood memories aren't perfectly rosy. It's up to you.

Helen's Path

Rags to Gowns

Helen grew up in southern California, the only sister of three brothers. She played dress up as a little girl, going through her grandmother's closet and putting on performances. She remembers going on forays with her grandmother and mother up to Palos Verdes on the morning the garbage trucks came: "Before they got there, we'd grab old lamps and furniture from the trash. My mother would refinish and remodel the most amazing things. I think that's where a lot of my creativity came from."

Her mother had a flair for design and showed Helen how to create her own treasures, but her mother's attitude was not something Helen wanted to emulate. Helen's mom was disappointed with her life, and that unhappiness was troubling to Helen as far back as she can remember. Growing up, she knew the story of how her mother had wanted to be an artist, but, because of marriage and children, could not follow her dreams. A strong memory from Helen's childhood is the day that her mother opened a drawer, took out all the old drawings she'd done as a young woman, and burned them in the incinerator. Helen recognized the significance: "She had always wanted to go to New York to study art. This was the end of her dream. I knew that would come to haunt her."

Her mother felt burdened by her family and job: "She blamed her misery on her family ... that she had to bring home a paycheck." But Helen saw other sides of her mother too, glimmers of the girl her mother was. When Helen was a young woman, she and her mother took a bus trip together and her mother started to reminisce about a long-ago bus trip when she was the same age and moving to California to be an artist. Helen watched her mom's eyes brighten with memories of life before her burdens. The lesson was not lost on Helen. She decided that she would never let herself become entrapped the way her mother had. "She never had time for herself."

In her teens, Helen began to recognize a gift that was developing—a gift of particular sensitivity to what was going on with other people: "I was always telling people what they were feeling. Always the mediator. Always the big sister." That awareness crystallized when she was nineteen and her friend came over to Helen's house with a tarot deck—a deck of cards used to examine the past, present, and future. Helen started reading everything she could on the subject, studying the higher learnings of the tarot. The tarot appealed to her because the pictures were a way of communicating information she picked up about people: "The tarot pictures validated my sensitivity." People began coming to her to "read" the cards and then reporting back that her observations had made a difference in their lives.

By then she was married and had her first son, and was living in Berkeley. It was the mid-1960s, and you didn't have to have much to get by. She did odd jobs, like cutting hair and doing house cleaning. Her fulfillment came from creative endeavors, and she had an array of talents. She painted regularly for many years, recording both her inner feelings and the landscapes and places she discovered during her travels. She played piano, accompanying herself as she sang for the joy of it, and she occasionally sang in light opera productions.

In part reacting to her mother's unhappiness in life, Helen made an effort to make life entertaining and interesting for her children. She took them different places—on long trips as well as day excursions to see curiosities close to home. She was careful not to impose her expectations on them but let their natural abilities develop. Without making much of it, she'd give them materials they needed for an endeavor that seemed of interest to them, and she'd save money for trips to see places that they discovered through their readings. Games were part of daily life, there was a lot of laughter, and there was no big fuss over money or, as was the case sometimes, the lack thereof. The lesson she had learned and wanted to teach her kids was that material things were incidental to the real stuff of life.

Officially Psychic

Steadily since childhood people had been coming to Helen for advice, and it became clear she had a gift. She decided to develop it. To become a psychic reader she studied in Berkeley with a woman named Helen Palmer, being trained to contact her own intuitional channeling. That took her beyond tarot: "Reading the tarot for people gave me feedback. My ego got a lot, but for a long time I didn't feel like I had a special gift."

She met Palmer when she went to her for a reading, and then in turn Palmer asked Helen to read the tarot for her. Helen says she once confessed to Palmer during her psychic training that she was worried that she didn't know if she could trust the information because it seemed "like I would pull it out of the blue." Palmer told her, "It may be that pulling it out of the blue is how it works for you." Palmer convinced Helen she did have a special gift, although Helen practiced it for years before finally charging clients.

Helen describes the psychic feeling she experiences as a combination of an active imagination and deep visualization, where she finds herself connected with a group of spiritual advisors who can help her answer questions.

> The whole back side of my head is opened up. Things come to me. I've learned to count on it, internally. . . . [But] this work is a butt kicker. It's not like a magical mystery tour. It's a complete observation, like being in a dream. You move out of your right brain into your left, and the way you make the move is that you let yourself imagine that you're dropping down into the earth. That's one visualization tool. Then you see a house. The answers are inside the door. It's all imagination. That's the psychic tool.

Relationships

Being a free spirit is one thing. Finding someone equally free was not so easy, especially in a culture and generation that puts such an emphasis on career and money building. Helen says wistfully about one relationship: "I kept wanting him to jump into his highly creative nature. He said he had to stay in the highly practical world. I think when I suggested he quit his job and we get a van and just drive around and follow our hearts was when things started to fall apart."

Helen has had some lonely times, but she never seriously considered changing her lifestyle—she would not go for an unfulfilling job or relationship just to be part of the mainstream. Without knowing it, though, for years she spent much of her energy supporting and advocating for others in her life, neglecting to give as much attention as she might have to her own painting and music.

That awareness dawned on Helen during the last years of her mother's life. Because she has kept herself free of encumbrances, Helen was able to set aside everything else when her mother became ill. Her mom had been pressured by external expectations when Helen was growing up, but Helen could demonstrate a kind of complete emotional presence for her mother—something she had attained by rejecting those same pressures. It seemed important for Helen to use all of her creativity and energy and love to be present for her mother, helping her mother attain a sense of peace and comfort in the world during her last years. Helen's adapted her mother's trick of being able to subsume her ego to the max: It didn't seem to be the time for any extroverted creative work, but rather Helen felt the need for going inward and being there with her mother.

During this time, Helen went through a dormant period in her creativity, as she poured her energy into her mother.

> I spent that time being invisible. I didn't dress. I didn't
> paint. I just focused on her. I stopped being social. But
> I like to think that I was still working on my creative self.

That was a time of grief and regrouping. Helen came to understand that her mother's unhappiness did not have to do with circumstances as much as it did with emotions. All those years Helen had been thinking her mother had a particularly difficult life, but it became clear to Helen that her mother's attitude was part of that. And Helen could see a little of her mother's martyrdom in her own life. She had given up a lot of herself to look after others over the years. The configuration may have been different than her mother's—Helen being a free spirit compared to the tightly wound soldier her mom was in life—but still Helen had put aside some of her dreams for others.

She realized she had given up some of her own interests in art and painting, particularly in relationships when others in her life needed support for their own creativity. Being with her mom for years at the end of her life was at once the ultimate martyrdom and a way out of it: "This was the time I was going to drop it. It may sound funny to go into martyrdom to kill it, but it worked. It was creative, but it wasn't pretty."

After her mother died, Helen fell in love with a man whom she first met when his dog bit Helen and they all went to the emergency room together. Together they moved into a suburban neighborhood, adding strictly "Helen" unsuburban touches. She hung a four-foot-tall giant Balinese head on the wall that anyone could see walking down the quiet, middle-class street. One day she felt the need to start painting again, announcing: "I'm ready to get out the oils and the canvas. It's an urgency."

Helen's Life These Days

Helen talks about the relationship between the creative and the intuitive:

> It's the magic. It's where you see the pictures, hear the sounds. The dimension that's watery. Where you do the cloud readings. . . . We've all got it. We've all had lifetimes where we saw. But it takes a willingness to drop the head. You think if you're in your head you're in control, but it gets in the way of being wide open. You can create, even if you're unpracticed, if you're wide open.

Helen exemplifies the definition of creativity that includes "insightful" and "visionary." Nurturing her own creativity, she says, means staying in the present and listening to herself. She celebrates every day like a special occasion. She doesn't just "get dressed" in the morning, she puts on a costume. She doesn't just occupy a room, she decorates it as though it were a special occasion. And she can do most of it on a shoestring. She is free to pay close attention to what's happening around her, listening to what the breezes tell her, deciding if she wants to follow.

She cautions, however, not to romanticize what she does: "I spend a good part of every day wrestling with my ego. When I become free from my ego, I become relaxed, laid back, and floating. Sometimes I may get a full hour of float."

While many may miss the present entirely, busily stressing themselves out to get to the future as quickly as possible, Helen seeks to capture the moment long enough to read it for messages. She's called a psychic because she comprehends what people are feeling, sees aspects of them they can't see themselves and can even, many will attest, accurately tell you what will happen in the future. Her clients range from New York artists to Beverly Hills business women. Even though psychics now advertise in the back of *The New Yorker* and advise First Ladies, Helen knows the notion of pulling counsel from another dimension still raises some eyebrows: "My brother told me to call myself a personal counselor when I was applying for a house loan." While her brother may worry about her credibility in society's eyes, he depends on her psychic counseling himself. Helen doesn't worry about validating herself in the mainstream.

Outer Appearances, Inner Truths

Getting dressed is not a casual business for Helen. She believes that how she decorates herself is a form of self-expression.

It's not that I reject the conventional, but I like to think of having my own uniform. When I get dressed I'm putting on my uniform, trying not to think of an audience, but what is warm, and comfortable, and feels good to me.

One of Helen's favorite definitions of creativity is one she read on a Zen tarot card: "It said that creativity is an entry into the mysterious, that expertise and technique are just tools. But the key is to abandon oneself to the energy that fuels the birth of all things, to be open to what wants to be expressed through you."

Psychic Knowledge

Helen's nine-to-five friends sometimes look at her with envy: She's not tied down with debt or corporate bosses, and she's seemingly footloose, in charge of her own time and choosing her own company. In some ways, she seems to live in another world.

A lot of breakdowns in a person's life come from not being inner-connected. Being inner-connected brings peace. And creativity comes out of incredible peace. There's an energy that comes from that silence. It has nothing to do with the end result or survival or success. You get there by responding to that place inside, not what's going on outside. People may not believe it's in there. But it's in everyone.

Still, as it is with many creative types, the person she does the most work on is herself. Helen's friends, who envy her free-spiritedness, might be surprised to know that sometimes she loses confidence: "There are times when I feel like I don't fit."

Helen suggests that this is a common vulnerability in eccentrics: "I think that in some ways wacky, artistic people are not sure of the real world and often avoid it. Either because they don't think it's very interesting or maybe that they can't make it there." Helen has lost lovers and friends because she just couldn't make the leap into the "real world." Interestingly, one of them still calls her seeking psychic input on career and relationship choices: "Same with my son, who wanted me to do past life readings of his babies. But we do that in a cloistered place. He would never admit that to the forestry friends he drinks beer with."

Helen considers her children creative people, although they dress more like Paul Bunyan than Peter Pan: "I think my sons are magical human beings. They are childlike, in that they believe in life. There is nothing in life that has taken such a toll on them that they don't still shine."

Forget the Outcome

Helen emphasizes the necessity of detaching from the fear of criticism in order to keep her source open. She keeps watching the moment, trusting in the process instead of looking for results: "My creativity demands that I stay out of the way of my ego. If the ego gets involved, it gets obsessed over an outcome. It's the same whether I'm doing my work or painting a picture or being in a relationship. I cannot be focused on how it's going to turn out."

Obsessing on the end results of creativity gets in the way of seeing the present: "I try to stay wide open, absolutely objective and the quintessential observer. . . . I never know what I am going to paint. I never know what I am going to put on when I get up in the morning. When I work with someone, I never know ahead what we're going to be looking for. It comes out of the void."

Conversations and Reflections: Keeping the Creative Channel Open

Sensitive or Psychic?

Helen's bright-eyed, high-energy presence is contagious. Susan says: "Helen makes me believe in magic and that we are all witches— most of us good ones." Helen talks about how she feels connected to God and divine messages. Seeing her overall glow makes it easy to believe her words.

How does a person manage such a daily feat of vitality? There are some techniques that others can learn from Helen. She stays away from anything confining—whether it's a suffocating relationship or a loan that carries encumbrance. She disciplines herself to pay attention to what is happening now, pushing herself to shake off what happened yesterday and not worry about the future. Her small acts of daily grace are something that most anyone could adapt to their own life.

What is gained from making regular gestures of reverence in our everyday lives? Helen will tell you it's a reminder that we can control our attitude toward life. "The whole experience of living is divine. Life is a dance even if it looks like a crisis." For Helen, the payoff for attentiveness is serenity and an open channel for capturing messages from something beyond the self. Living in the moment, to her, is like "clearing all the chalkboards inside myself." This enables her to handle what comes along with minimum judgment and maximum attention, although she says she is always working on both. For her, the result is a sixth sense about what is happening with others. But even people without psychic abilities can gain a rich understanding of life if they incorporate Helen's trick of listening to "what comes through the silence."

Through my various interviews for this book, it became clear to me that life's "mysteries" are very much part of the creative process for many women.

When women tap into their creative selves, we move into the intuitive, wordless realm—the "watery places" as Helen likes to say—where we find inspiration and make connections that seem inexplicable. Many women have claimed their creativity by honoring the mysteries. When Annie had otherworldly experiences with dream images of her dead mother, she decided not to ask "why," but instead learned from what her subconscious was trying to teach her. When doing the scientific work of geology, mystery writer Sarah trusted information she learned through her holistic, nonrational thought processes, as well as the more conventional scientific methods, even though her colleagues didn't want to rely on her intuition. Donna recognizes a mystical force at work in her garden, which she believes was part of the source of her landscape design vision. All of these women were open to the inexplicable messages that seemed to guide them. Women who are actively creative seem to accept the unexplainable with grace. Sometimes stuff happens that's amazing, and you won't always know why. Helen says we're all psychics, we just need to practice at it. How women interpret their mysteries is different, but even mainstream researchers are acknowledging the relevance of the psychic and paranormal arenas.

Paranormal events don't make logical sense, are easy to dismiss, and create anxiety for people who prefer that reality follow a few simple rules. But scientific theory is expanding to include ideas that previously seemed impossible; for example, quantum physics has found seemingly unrelated particles, at distances apart, mimicking one another for no apparent reason. Many researchers of creativity have bowed to the likelihood that psychic events do indeed occur. All in all, as happens so often, the research is catching up to what intuition tells us: Things are not always as they seem, and we can know a lot more than we can explain.

In the book *Higher Creativity,* Stanford Research Institute social scientist Willis Harman and science writer Howard Rheingold write about recent research on "remote viewing." This is the ability to know what is happening at a place one has never visited, through telepathic communication. They have also investigated the phenomenon known as psychokinesis, which is the movement of objects through thought.

> *Surprisingly enough, this exploration of paranormal phenomena brings us back squarely within the spectrum of creativity. For research on remote viewing suggests that the creative/intuitive mind could be getting information in other ways than from the lifelong learning of the person. Research on telepathic communication suggests that we are all joined at a deep level, thus emphasizing that we should not be too hasty to assume limits to the creative unconscious. Research on psychokinesis indicates a connection between mind and the external environment, which opens up the possibility of some kinds of miracles. In the end, it is not clear that there are any limits to the creative/intuitive mind other than those stemming from the individual's belief system.*

This is not to say that we should believe every telephone psychic ad, but clearly there is reason to pay attention to strong intuitive messages we get. We know when something rings true, and if we're open we may learn more. Helen is someone who has devoted a lifetime to taking in the full spectrum of information available to her and expressing herself through the creative life. From her, we learn that creativity doesn't need to explode, it can come out in little sparkles throughout one's life. She shows us how a commitment to one's intuitive urges can define a life, bringing style you'll never find in a store and riches that money can't buy.

Deborah remembers feeling a psychic connection with her best friend from high school:

> *I would always know when she was going to call—and she me. I still get twinges when I realize I need to talk with her. Usually it turns out we have been thinking of each other. Once we both bought the same outfit, down to the shoes and purse. And I know of stories from my former husband's family, who credit surviving World War II to psychic intuition. I believe that the collective unconsciousness is there to be tapped into. I don't have the skills to consciously do that, but I respect those who do. Perhaps at a basic level, all creativity is a form of slipping into that stream and being connected to everything else.*

For the Sake of Doing It

A primary theme threading through the stories of actively creative women is the value of their creative work as an end in itself, rather than for kudos from others. Each of us may ask ourselves about our own creativity: Who am I doing this for? Susan says:

> Helen told me when she first started doing psychic work that she was enjoying being the helper, being seen as special or needed — "being thought of as amazing," in Helen's words. Helen said she had to take all that away and see how much of her work she was doing "just for the sheer pleasure of doing it." That led me to pay attention to my own motivations.
> As a writer, there is always the ego lurking. Am I sounding clever and smart? Does this make sense to someone else? Will they get it? But there is the occasional moment when I have written something down, smiled at it, decided it was just for me, zapped it from the screen, and felt perfectly satisfied.

Symbols

It's intriguing how people find ways to symbolize their uniqueness. Not everybody can figure out how to live as independently from convention as Helen has, but it's possible to maintain pockets of independence and reminders that you're taking your cues from the inside instead of the outside. There's that old phrase about what constitutes good art: "I can't define it, but I know it when I see it." The same can be said about many creative people, and Helen is one of them. Seeing her casually over the years, I've noticed that she never looks the same twice. Her clothes change, her looks change, she's constantly evolving. The formula is fairly straightforward: The way you live your life every day can express your individuality.

Helen helps us remember that it is possible to make up our own rules about fashion, environment, work, and success. Using some of Helen's strategies can lift the spirits and free up energy that may be drained by imaginary burdens.

During a time when I was in a creative slump, I carried a huge purse in which I placed a favorite book, a Walkman with a musical tape, a small video game that reminded me of vacation, a journal where I could do freewriting, and various rocks and keepsakes that friends had given me. They made me feel more lively, even when I didn't open the bag. It was symbolic of the "real me."

There's something soothing and empowering about surrounding ourselves with reminders of who we are and what we care about. It's childlike in the best way. When Volkswagen came out with its new Beetle, people went wild over the little flower vase, a detail that was a whimsical reminder of freer times. People respond to symbols. It's a way of staying connected. Waitress Sherry Jean likes aprons, so travelers bring them back to her. Gardener Donna likes birdhouses for her trees, so visitors bring them to her.

Choosing a symbol is making a personal statement. Helen does so every day in different ways, generously sharing herself with others and at the same time honoring her own sense of self.

What are some little ways, forms of outward expression, that you could use to symbolize reverence for your creative, intuitive self? I think the recent angel craze—people wearing pins, sending cards, and buying books that depict angels as "with us" every day—is one indication that people in general are looking for reminders of the spiritual life. Mainstream symbols work for some people, while others prefer Helen's technique of finding a personal eclectic mix. When did you last wear something just for your own delight, maybe stepping out of your usual style just for fun? Maybe it's wearing rainbow bold colors or silver shoes. Or maybe it's borrowing artist Georgia O'Keefe's clothing statement and dressing in all black. You don't have to always be a retro or gothic type to occasionally don a "costume." Clothes do make a statement, even if to say, "I'm entertaining myself today." Likewise, gathering little symbols around your desk or bedroom can make aesthetic arrangements meaningful to you and interesting to others. What ways can you put some of your self out there into the world, experimenting with a little eccentricity?

Honoring your "self" in obvious tangible ways, as Helen found, can be part of an ongoing discipline of honoring the self in the more mysterious, intangible ways. Try paying attention to those inexplicable "coincidences" that happen, odd ways in which you sometimes seem to "just know" something. Instead of startling over the strangeness of a mysterious episode, try to remember your frame of mind when it happened. Is there a way to re-create that situation, welcoming your subconscious to assert itself on a more regular basis? Often all your inner creative self needs is an invitation to speak to you in the strange, wordless language of intuition, and you can decide to accept the messages even if you don't understand them. Writing, drawing, or talking about the images can be a way of making them less abstract, upon reflection. But there's joy in the initial intuitive phase, when you get inspiration and the only words that come to mind are "thank you."

Onward in the Watery Dimension

Helen's challenge is the same as mine and perhaps yours as well: how to differentiate between the outer world and the inner sense in making decisions about creativity and life. For all her access to inner senses, she still considers herself a natural people-pleasing type: "I am a master at knowing how to step into someone else's world and make them the center of attention." The struggle, then, is to please herself first. For example, a recent weight gain has challenged her to figure out what she wants as opposed to what others want.

> *My demons are judgment, criticism, and comparison. So I look at these extra pounds and compare myself to others and feel unfit. But that's a comparison that is based on something that is outside of me. External rules again. If I worked on achieving the right-sized body and then maybe got a face lift, which is what a lot of women I know do, I would take energy from the moment. I would stop being observant while I worked on the technical parts.*
>
> *What I understand about me is that this trait of comparison won't go away even if I have the body, the ideal 130 pounds, the beauty, the money, the man, my paintings in an art gallery. Those feelings won't go away. I'm clear on that. They are a part of me. My challenge is not to feed them—judgment, self-deprecation. When I feed that, the other part of me goes to sleep. What's left when I'm not feeding the monster is love.*

Helen continues to live for the moment—most especially "the moment of exaltation when you are telling the truth." She caresses her newly zaftig self, laughs, and says, "I may be going through my Buddha stage."

11

Taking Center Stage: Laughing with Your Demons

As soon as you choose creative expression, your worst demons arise.

—Pauline Pfandler, actor,
director, and teacher

Meet Pauline and Her Divas

In the basement of an old Mission-style church, as a chamber choir practices in another room, Pauline gathers with a group of women in loose clothes and stocking feet, alternately letting out belly laughs and uttering words that are spontaneous and true. The women are oblivious to the squeak of violins next door, tuned in to one another's movements and words, poised for instant response. They are here for themselves rather than for an audience. They are their own audience, witnesses to one another. Pauline believes in witnessing. By witnessing, she means unspoken encouragement, no right or wrong, no judgment, no critic. In a safe place, she says, women can go deep into themselves: "If you have a witness, you can go further. You know you won't get lost."

For two and a half hours, she will bray and coo at her students. "Bravo, my divas," she will say. She will love and goad them into words and actions they never expected to say or perform. She puts them in scenes that will have them going home amazed at themselves. During an improvisational game called "emotional chairs," the women move from place to place, changing feelings each time—from fear to joy to apathy.

Staying in the present is a trick that she practices while she advises her students. "I don't tell people to focus, because that's like screaming at someone to relax or be happy. What I say is to do something as fully as you can. If the task is to walk on the stage and pick up a chair—pay attention to that chair and put your all into it. It's that whole thing about being in that moment."

The shy accountant will be making up opera and assuming the power and attitude—if not the voice—of Jessye Norman. A woman who normally wears Gucci and real gold will become a homeless person. What comes out in the room comes from each player's interior. "Dance with your demons," Pauline urges. "Go there. Just do it. Just try."

Pauline Pfandler says she teaches improvisational theater because she needed to learn it herself. She wants for her students what she is constantly working on personally: "I want to get women to tell their own truth." She's spent a lifetime in an ongoing struggle to accept all of herself—including the "demons" that plagued her childhood and the voices that tried to shout her down over the years.

Now she shows others a way to freedom. She will make them laugh, at her and at themselves, so hard that when they leave they will have sore cheeks from grinning. And they will know themselves just a little bit better than they did when they walked in the room.

As one class is winding up, Pauline asks Michele, a usually effervescent student who has been hanging back, "What's going on with you?" Michele explains how that day she'd felt intimidated on the street by a group of teenage boys and that it bothered her that she didn't know how to react. Pauline turns it into a class exercise, and pretty soon Michele is not scurrying into a store to get away and feeling small, like she did that afternoon. She is looking them in the eye and walking confidently to her car. "It's the old 'Act as if,'" says Pauline.

"Sometimes if you think yourself strong and powerful, you become it." Acting out an upsetting experience—redoing it your own way—can help women tap into past traumas. It's a tool she's used in her own life, creating the person she needed to be to assert herself while protecting herself. As a child, it was dealing with abusive parents. Later, it was being overweight in a skinny world, then being a lesbian in a straight world.

With short, streaked blonde hair, often dressed in sandals, tights, a big sweater, and artfully mismatched earrings, these days Pauline is comfortable being herself in a life she has chosen. Transformation is her thing. She has taken it to a larger stage and now works with others on community productions and in the classroom, where she teaches others to play with what's inside.

Pauline is a guide, but only because in her own life she has traveled through self-doubt and yet has emerged as "herself"—a woman who has come out with her sexuality, her insecurity, and her scarred childhood. It was with theater that Pauline stitched together some of her early demons and created the strong and solid woman she is today. She helps empower others through her theater and improv classes: "Bette Midler sums up my life. She said, 'If only I'd known that one day my differences would be an asset.'"

Putting Your Demons to Good Work

Pauline's story is about the risk and the reward that come from reaching deep inside to find what's most honest and individual about the self—and then sharing that with others. Exercising creativity can be like a personal archeological dig, scratching below the surface to find the treasures preserved in the rubble of experience. Pauline went to the core of her being, facing hellish memories and feelings.

Pauline likens her journey to the Sumerian myth about Inanna, who went to the underworld to gain wisdom. What Pauline likes best about the myth is that "Inanna chooses to face what she fears most." Now when she works with her students on improvisational acting, she urges them to produce unfiltered reactions, expressing the parts of themselves they usually keep hidden. "Whatever arises is perfect. Whatever emotion, movement, and sound is perfect. Be in the moment. Give in to yourself!" she entreats. She tells students to get their ego out of the way and look for the self: "This is a place to go out of your mind."

For creative people, the question Pauline poses is intriguing: If you don't edit what comes up, can you use it? Through improv, she shows others how letting it all out can help you find the good stuff. She quotes Bertolt Brecht, "Performance is everything you don't throw out after rehearsal."

Pauline demonstrates how you can toss out the demons who aren't pulling their weight creatively. If you don't control your demons they may control you. Even Pauline, who has faced and overcome so much, still struggles with self-esteem. In her story, we can see the alternative to addictions and self-criticism—confronting those demons and laughing in their faces. Pauline says: "Bobby Earl, he's a recovery guy, says, 'If anyone talked to me the way I talk to me, I'd have to kill them.'"

Pauline teaches a lesson that can apply to any discipline: Get to know what's inside you, all the way down. In her one-woman play, *Born Guilty*, she brought her demons to life, gave them names, and let them play out their parts on stage: "I learned about me. The power of a woman's growth is to name her truth."

Pauline's Path

Laugh or Die

Pauline was the middle child of six in a San Franciscan, Irish Catholic family, in which violence and sexual abuse intruded early.

> *During the beatings I'd leave my body, and that was the beginning of creating another world. I also got pegged the clown. When you live in a brutal, alcoholic, incestuous atmosphere, you discover that if you keep them laughing, maybe they won't go after you. . . . My cousins and I would put on shows for the adults at family parties. You know, chenille bedspread productions. The adults would laugh and laugh. Of course, they were all pretty drunk, too. We're Irish.*

You laugh or you die.

My father would beat me with a belt. He called it the lady maker. My mother was an alcoholic, a very sick woman back then. She would sic my father on me. Tell him I'd been bad and he had to beat me. She was trapped with all us kids. I have a lot more compassion for her now. They thought brutality was a way to raise a kid, and I was wild. I would spend hours out in the woods making up safe worlds.

Looking back, she reflects, "There weren't enough parents to go around." She and her siblings had to fend for themselves emotionally. Pauline was left alone to cope with sexual abuse. She was molested when she was ten. She tried to escape attention by putting on weight, and by eleven, she was overweight: "Only in later years did I realize that the weight was creating boundaries."

Amid the horrors, though, Pauline caught glimpses of what looked like freedom. There was one aunt who would let her come over and "hide out" when there was trouble at home. She always made Pauline laugh. "My aunt was a stitch." Survival and humor became linked in Pauline's mind.

After high school, she began attending a junior college. She had no clear career goals, but found herself hovering around the periphery of the stage, doing backstage work for community productions: "I was too fat to play the ingenue." During this same time in her life she was having a few adventures, and on one of them she found her calling.

When I was twenty, my sister and I hopped freight trains and went to Alaska. It was rugged, wide-open country, and I had this what I guess you would call an epiphany of what I wanted to do. What I had to do. It's that deeper knowledge that we're able to call up from time to time. I just knew I had to do theater. I had never been encouraged to be an actor, even though I was passionate about theater. I did mostly set design, but then I got a speaking part. I was playing a comic character. Suddenly all this laughter came up. It felt like a wave of love coming at me. I was hooked. I knew I wanted to make theater my life.

She decided to go to the University of California at Los Angeles to finish out her degree in theater arts. Along with her typewriter and suitcases, she took a lousy self-image. Bingeing and purging became a way of life, and she was drinking. She recalls the pressure she felt. There were three hundred theater students competing for each good role. She wanted to be good enough to get one of them, and she ended up getting a few.

After graduating, she looked, as is fairly common, to a relationship for self-fulfillment. She chose someone who gave her safety but was her polar opposite: "He wanted to go in the army, and the day he left for boot camp I went to the movies to see *Ghandi*." They split up and Pauline moved to Minnesota. There she joined a woman's theater company, got sober, and came out as a lesbian. Coming out as a lesbian she said was no big deal. "I didn't wrestle with my sexuality." For Pauline, it was more like coming home than coming out.

Living Free

She had to look at what alcohol was doing to her. In a voice as strong as the one that spoke to her about being an actor, she got the message to give up drinking: "One day I said to myself, 'You can either deal with this at twenty-eight or at fifty-eight like your mother.'" She entered a twelve-step program and got sober.

Also, she says, "Out of my fog of booze I began my political awareness." Pauline maintains that the primary reason she does theater is to express her politics and explore her spirituality. Pauline wanted to write and develop plays from a feminine and political perspective: "This is my political work. Some people join the Green Party. I do theater within a context." After she got her degree in theater, she was disappointed with what she found: "Nowhere did I hear my voice or women's voices. You could play a virgin or a whore, either way you were a victim." She envisioned other roles for women.

One of the first plays she produced was called *The Story of a Mother*. It was based on conversations between mothers and daughters, and in the middle of the play the actors would stop and lead the audience in a meditation on their mothers. When she did *Inanna*, she invited women to be like the goddess and go down and face their shadow sides. "In facing our shadows we integrate," she says. "I try to ask myself, why should an audience spend ten bucks to see this if it doesn't relate to their life?"

Without the anesthesia of alcohol, her childhood fears and pain began rising to the surface. Memories disturbed her sleep. She'd wake up in the night, hearing the words of characters whom she recognized as voices from her past, voices from herself. She'd be tired the next day: "One day my walking buddy suggested, 'Why don't you write it down?' I decided to do that because I wanted to get some sleep." She ended up creating the four characters who would later become her first one-woman play, *Born Guilty*.

By this time, Pauline was living in the San Francisco Bay Area, where there is a larger audience for avant-garde theater. She performed the play at various places throughout the Bay Area and in Seattle.

Borrowing Audre Lord's term, she called it "a mytho-biography" and said, "I wrote that piece in a year, but I lived it for twenty."

But Pauline insists she wasn't doing her own therapy on stage. The point was not to heal her ailing soul, she said, but to speak to others. And it worked:

> One of my characters popular with women was Peggy, a codependent approval junkie. Peggy kept saying "everything's fine" and running around asking if people were okay, because if she stopped, she would start to feel things. After the play, women came up to me and said, "That's me." I still have people repeat lines from Born Guilty that they say made a difference in their lives.

Pauline put herself in the drama alongside her four characters: "I had identified the personae that were keeping me from real joy and real creativity." There was the thug, telling her, "You're a fat, ugly impostor," and needy, insecure Camille, imploring the world to feel sorry for her. These characters, Pauline's demons, needed to be exorcised. By writing them into her play she was able to put them in their place: "It's extremely empowering for women to realize there are demonic forces that are not reality. They're just our voices of fear and insecurity."

Even though her reasons for going on stage were more artistic than personal, theater has also helped Pauline make peace with her family. "I decided if I was going to win in my life, I had to forgive." With one of those deep laughs, she reflects, "I don't want all these people having free rent in my head by hating them."

Freeing Others

Despite the theme of self-acceptance in Born Guilty, it still amazes her that she had trouble accepting the praise that came her way, that she still felt insecure and mired in performance doubts. She immediately picked up on the irony: "Here I did a play about self-hatred, and then I couldn't stand the compliments." Seeking real approval from others is still a work in progress. "I'm still working on that, to stand with an open heart and take in the compliments. When someone tells me I've done well, I want to hide."

Learning to accept her own success is part of a metamorphosis still underway for Pauline, "from who I thought I was to who I am becoming." While others may see Pauline as bold and experimental in a way they want to be, she doesn't see it that way: "I keep myself in a very small box in terms of what I can do. I have to grow a bigger template."

"Fear of rejection is a big one for everyone," says Pauline. *Born Guilty* got mixed reviews—more good ones than bad—but she went into a deep funk over the bad.

> *I wrote a play, toured it, and it had a good run. I told my truth in front of hundreds of people. I even changed some people's lives. But I decided I was a loser and the play was shit.*

She can scoff at this now, but only after suffering what she says was "a year of profound self-hatred." She finally came out of it after working on herself and being with friends, like the one who gently cupped her face one day and said, "Stop whining."

What Pauline has learned is that being on stage is not a lot different than being out there in real life, especially, she thinks, for women. "We are constantly having to prove ourselves. Running that 'I'm not worthy' tape." After ten years of directing and teaching, she wants to do more acting. "You have to keep re-creating yourself as an artist. Not just stick with one safe mode, but try something new. Bust yourself open every five years and redefine yourself."

Pauline is giving that advice to herself as much as to others. In the past eleven years, she has produced and directed twenty-two shows, ranging from Dr. Seuss to Shakespeare. Her latest creative effort is the creation of a theater company, in which she seeks to meld her roles as educator, theater professional, and political activist. She once told an interviewer, "You will never see a *Cats* here, babe. I want the audience to leave riled up."

Pauline's Life These Days

Pauline gets a lot of energy from helping others find their voice and their laughter: "I want my theater to be healing. To be more than pretty costumes and words." When she teaches improvisational acting, she emphasizes honest responses and leaves no time to edit. "If there's lying going on, I can't stand it. In improv, I tell my students you have to face what you fear. It's liberating. Here I am."

Besides doing her own plays and leading improv, Pauline also teaches children's theater. "Kid theater is a powerful self-esteem builder." She's watched it work in her own life and grins like a proud parent when she sees kids walk a little taller after a good job.

Approval Seeking

Pauline isn't blind to the expectations and judgments of others. To the contrary, being an actor as an adult and having lived in an abusive home as a child, she knows how to read people. But instead of allowing their opinions to rule her, she assesses them, figuring out who they are and what they want.

> *As a violent home survivor, you figure out the exits. You're forced to become an energy reader. In my twenties and thirties I was an approval junkie. I was told I was a terrible flirt. That's how I validated myself. Now I catch myself when I'm doing something just to seek another's approval. I finally have boundaries. And if someone is threatened by my honesty, my largeness, or my lesbianism, that's their problem. My biggest challenge on a regular basis is looking inward for validation.*

Inspiration and Hard Work

When she begins to design a play, Pauline takes long walks to recharge herself and allow new ideas to flow.

> *I go for a three-mile walk and put on my Walkman and walk through the orchards to this magnificent ridge. Tom Waites, Randy Newman, Kronos Quartet, Rickie Lee Jones—they give me inspiration. I use music to quiet the monkey mind. I go into an altered state and an "overhead" kicks in and I howl and scream. I wait for one central image to come to me. One potent theater image.*

Pauline has learned about her own limits and what she needs to go through to do a production: "Before a play, everything falls away and my life supports it." So does her life partner, whom Pauline married in a formal ceremony. Pauline says, "I'm putting myself out there. I'm not hiding. I not only deal in a world of male privilege, but heterosexual privilege. I don't collude in that anymore. I don't apologize for being a woman or a lesbian."

They have a mutual agreement to support each other's creative works and not resent the time they take from the relationship. "Two weeks before I open a show I'm absolutely psychotic," Pauline laughs. "I give myself up to projects. You have to. To be good you have to work really, really hard. And that immersion is joyful."

Artistic versus Financial Survival

The decision to pursue theater meant giving up the security of a regular job. It was a choice between comforts—the deep kind of comfort that comes with living with integrity versus financial comfort that comes from a steady paycheck. Acting has become life-sustaining for Pauline, and she feels it is a calling to share the benefits with others. But that has meant doing without.

"I've chosen to live outside the norm. For one thing, I don't have financial security." Pauline says this is common with people in theater. But she grew up in a blue-collar household, and says:

> *I had to learn that being poor isn't equal to being a loser. I do a daily meditation that I am not my money. Sometimes I wake up clawing at the life boat, freaking out, in a state of panic because I'm overdrawn on my checking account and I'm forty-four. Then I talk to the fearful one inside of me and make a list of my gratitudes, sometimes through clenched teeth: "I have a house. I have food. I'm healthy. I have a car that runs."*

Conversations and Reflections: Using Creativity as a Safe Shelter for Meeting the Self

Acting Out

Pauline has provided fresh air for many women who are ready to turn their troubles into creative fuel. Just sitting in on her improv class and watching caused little shots of adrenaline to pump through my body, only from thinking about doing some of the wild exercises the women were doing. Susan has been taking Pauline's improv class for more than a year. Susan says that delving all the way into a situation where you're so exposed can cause major changes and forays into wild behavior.

> *I still get nervous before class, and I still feel exhilarated afterward. I think I get close to the real "me" in improv, because there is no time to edit, look around, put on my persona. Sometimes I am snaggle-toothed and ugly and I am loud and I am cocky or I am pitiful, all things I wouldn't let show in real life. I can go into all these people with ease and without worrying how I will look or if I'll be clever enough. I've been able to use it in my writing. Sometimes I will write a line and laugh out loud and think "I can't say that!" and then I end up going with it. Sometimes it works and sometimes it doesn't—just like improv. But I feel so high having pushed it.*

The message is this: Get over yourself by acting up and acting out. Pauline does it on stage, but you can do it on paper, on canvas, in a wild frenzied dance. You can make a deal with yourself the way Pauline makes a deal with her students: Don't edit, express the first thing that comes to your mind, face the unattractive as well as attractive aspects of yourself, give up control, let it out.

Deep expression involves letting out the thoughts, memories, and feelings that in daily life you usually work hard to keep tucked away, out of sight. Those hidden parts are what Pauline calls the "demons"—the old memories, unwanted thoughts, and self-doubts that live inside. They sap energy that could be creative fuel.

Pauline took a wildly dramatic approach by writing a play that made a caricature of her inner voices—the scared one, the one with bravado, the critical one, the one lost in denial. Once she had extracted these characters from within herself, they lost their power over her. She talked back to the inner voice that was always ragging on her, dressed that voice up in a trench coat and gave her a slimy cigar. Once trotted out on stage, that voice became just another costume that Pauline controlled.

Although there are times when emotions and problems are overwhelming enough to warrant professional counseling, there are ways to put those problems to work in the creative arena. When we look at the contorted faces in Picasso's paintings or read about family madness in Jane Smiley's fiction, we probably are seeing some variations on the demons these artists have encountered in their lives. Their subjects don't necessarily correspond to actual people or circumstances, but reflect a part of their reality.

Believing in the Self

What makes it possible for some people to perceive and believe in their inner vision enough to take action? Sometimes it's compulsion, but beyond that is often a feeling of trust that something larger than the self is at work, that you are a vessel for creativity. It's the same thing news photographer Annie feels when she is behind the camera.

Interestingly, both Annie and Pauline use the same Martha Graham quote as inspiration. A friend of Pauline's gave it to her once when she was struggling over a play, feeling it wasn't working. The quote resonated with her.

I liked the part that says, "I don't even have to believe." That is the green light for women to keep going even when someone says "no" or you have the doubts. I try this: When I start to say "I can't," I realize what I'm really saying is "I won't."

Little tricks like that can help you in your creative endeavors. Try keeping a quote—like Pauline and Annie keep Martha Graham's—taped some place where you can see it, repeat it, and hope to one day let the wisdom all the way into your life. Whatever it takes to look a little differently at your habitual way of seeing the world.

What Pauline demonstrates is that perception of experience is more important than content. You can put your own spin on events. Try on a new attitude, a new voice. Pretend like you're in an improv class. Talk to the boss with confidence, flirt a new way with your sweetie, laugh in a situation that used to make you cringe, just breathe deeply and don't respond in the same old way when someone pushes your buttons. It's possible to try out new ways of being: Tell yourself, "Oh, this is just an act," but see if the real you likes it better.

Permission

Performing artists have long delighted in the freedom that comes when they can say to the world, "I'm on stage now. The rules are different here." It's an invitation for honesty, permission to be irreverent. Performance artist Karen Finley talked about the day she discovered the protective qualities of the artist's refuge. She was arrested while doing a one-woman show that was a parody on the woman as sex symbol, part of a commissioned art series, in the window of a JC Penney store in downtown San Francisco. In an interview in *Creators on Creating*, edited by Frank Barron, Alfonso Monturoi, and Anthea Brown, Finley tells how she was being dragged off by police when the curator of the show walked up and explained she was acting as part of a performance series. Finley recalled the satisfied sense of amusement she felt at first. But then she felt sad, thinking:

> *What if I was a person who didn't go to art school and wasn't given that educational privilege? I would have been arrested, if I was just a person expressing myself that way, and didn't have a curator. I thought what about if I was on drugs or insane? It made me start thinking of things in a different way: that art is a shelter.*

In a sense, Pauline has become a curator for the students in her improv class. She gives the women permission to act as they please, safe and protected and surrounded by the context she has woven in which "there are no mistakes." Women who come to her class once a week get to play with parts of themselves they wouldn't dare let out elsewhere. Pauline has created this shelter, into which she has invited other women, teaching them, "It wasn't about killing your demons, but transforming them."

How can each one of us detach from our demons, examine them, laugh at them? Taking classes is one way, but stepping back from habitual behaviors is another: Being tolerant of friends when they act out. Laughing at ourselves. Not taking everything so seriously. As with most transformational prospects, the first step is recognition. Where did we get the habits that make us recoil or hide or whisper when we want to step out and be visible and shout? Listening, as Pauline did, to those wretched old voices, we can start to talk back to them. To do this requires solitude, time out from the routines of the day.

Receiving Creative Time and Space

Pauline's comments about the respectful working relationship she has with her life partner delighted and intrigued my collaborators and me. Those of us who are married with families still have the instinct to leap up and take care of others before we take care of ourselves. Susan tells about one night when she was writing a column at her computer, in that private world when the words are coming together, when she heard her husband starting to unload the dishwasher. She had to stop herself from jumping up and saying, "I'll do that." As Susan and I kept noting during our talks for our book *Goodbye Good Girl*: "We tend to think everything's our responsibility, but whose voice is saying that? Often as not, it's us, not someone else."

Belly Laughs

In the classroom, Pauline's students turn themselves inside out in front of others and get to laugh in the process. Laughter is letting go, making room for new ideas. C. Diane Ealy wrote in the *Woman's Book of Creativity*:

> *Laughing makes us lose our inhibitions, at least temporarily. This loosening breaks us out of routine thinking and helps us see an issue from a new perspective. Humor warms up our mental flexibility for making creative leaps. In other words, ha-ha leads us to aha!*

In Pauline's life, laughter springs from a deep place that might have otherwise been filled with pain. There were times when she tried to fill it with food, drown it with alcohol. But she made a conscious choice to follow her creative self. At one time she worked as an account executive for a public relations firm in San Francisco. She made money, but she also drank too much and was bulimic, always telling people "I'm fine." By contrast, being in theater in her various roles as an actor, teacher, and director feels honest to Pauline.

She uses her actor's ability to get into another character to get her through panicky times. "I take a breath. And I act as if I'm walking in a beneficent universe that really wants to support me." This is not the universe she knew growing up. The sharp edge of humor has helped Pauline cut through personal trauma that had congealed over the years into self-doubt. Her childhood experiences could have presented a permanent block to creativity. Instead, she dissected it and came up with a laugh-until-you-cry approach to theater, and that laughter breaks up old pain so that creativity can flow.

Power

Seeing the self as a vessel for creativity often leads to a spiritual journey, and as with Donna and the divine presence she senses in her garden, the source of that power often can't be defined by an existing religion. Pauline sees herself being inspired by something beyond her. She doesn't call it a "higher power" but a "deeper power." And for her, it's decidedly female: "I had to fire the punitive white guy in the clouds from my Catholic youth, but I couldn't do this if I didn't believe in a magnificent being, the Universe, the Goddess."

In *Awakening Minerva*, writer Linda A. Firestone likens this creative approach to the power of Gaia, Mother Earth.

> *Risk-taking, a tolerance for chaos, an openness for the unknown, disregard for certain rules, patience and goal-directedness all comprise Gaia's volcanic power. Creative people cannot hold within their physical and psychological beings that which must be expressed. To do so means to suffer great pains and trauma at the energy turned inward. Its destructive force can be unrelenting until the energy is finally exhausted and the next eruption occurs.*

The volcano analogy seems to apply to people like Pauline, who've held a lot in until they're ready to explode. Her booming "Be Gone!" brought a scurrying parade of characters, ideas, feelings, and convictions from deep inside her. Her demons might have been happy feeding on ice cream and sucking up alcohol, but Pauline grew tired of being a nice hostess.

Taking center stage is one way to trot out experience where it can be seen in the light, examined, and illuminated—or tossed aside. Pauline's is a dramatic version but similar to what, for example, some painters do on canvas and writers do with pen and paper.

The process is what makes therapy, peer counseling, and friendships so healing—sharing what's inside in a safe environment. It becomes art when the deconstruction is followed by a reconstruction into something that can entertain or illuminate others. When we find something inside ourselves that contains a grain of universal truth, the next step is to develop the idea into something tangible. The internal volcano can lead to a work that creates mini-eruptions in the terrain of other people's lives or society in general.

Waking Up

Why do creative ideas often come during sleepless nights, from dreams, or in other moments when we're caught off guard—such as an improv class? Most of us have spent years creating our guard, the collection of internal censors that protect us from pain or confusion. Our deepest feelings, buried memories, and strongest desires wait for the guard to be distracted or fall asleep, and then they begin to slip out. Then we have a choice: set them free or find some way to ignore them.

Alcohol, drugs, food, and other dulling substances can help temporarily, helping us to anesthetize, swallow, or destroy what's disturbing us. They also stand in the way of our own happiness. Julia Cameron calls these substances blocks. In *The Artist's Way*, she writes:

> *Rather than paint, write, dance, audition, and see where it takes us, we pick up a block. Blocked, we know who and what we are: unhappy people. Unblocked, we may be something much more threatening—happy. For most of us, happy is terrifying, unfamiliar, out of control, too risky!*

Numbing out is generally far more acceptable to society than allowing what's real inside us to erupt. Anne Wilson Schaef says in *Meditations for Women Who Do Too Much*:

> *All addictions are built on illusion. Why is it that we find self-deception and illusions so much more attractive than honesty? It could possibly be because we are surrounded by a society where illusion is the name of the game. Denial runs rampant at every level of society, and there is not much support for "truth speakers."*

Pauline's demons got their exercise on the stage, but you don't need to have a big audience to recycle difficult experiences into something that may be both artistically and personally productive. All that's necessary is some forum for "letting it all out"—releasing your unedited feelings and memories. Stream-of-consciousness writing, throwing paint on canvas, or even putting on a one-act play for yourself while driving alone in the car—giving a voice to all those unexpressed thoughts—gives you a chance to toss out what's inside you.

Improvisation can work through many forms of expression. It's fun to try something new, as writer Susan discovered by taking Pauline's class. But you can choose any form of self-expression. The lesson of improv is to let yourself go through the awkward stages— letting your thoughts and feelings come out unedited, so you can pick and choose what you may want to develop and maybe even share with others at some point. Choose whatever activity you can do that lets you "see" yourself, and see if you might be able to play with some of those old demons.

Onward: Leaving Trouble Behind

Ask Pauline where she'd like to be in ten years and she says living in Paris studying theater while her partner studies French literature. But it's only one of the many possibilities she has. She's pretty confident about being able to materialize her vision. She's still changing, but has come a long way from being the people-pleaser, largely due to the insistence of her own creative urges, calling out to her in the night. She loves the idea that she's altering the current landscape of theater in the process. She quotes Paul Robeson: "All theater is politics." She is comfortable with the role of social challenger—takes pride in it, saying: "My friends are all kind of weird, eccentric. I like to get away from status quo thinking."

Pauline urges others to find their own way, trusting that real support will follow and leaving behind the illusory approval from others. "I say you should fire everyone in your life who says to you, 'No, you can't do that.'"

12

Picturing Success: Putting Yourself Out There

Creativity is dissolving parameters and exchanging the voice of fear for passion. As artists, our job isn't to put our name on the map, it's to explore all the mountains, valleys, and rivers. We are the terrain of our expression.

—Carole Rae Watanabe, artist, teacher, founding member of "The Danger Rangers"

Meet Carole in the Studio

Carole Rae Watanabe, with close-cropped black curls and big colorful glasses, sits quietly in a wooden chair with a cup of coffee in her hands. She is calm and relaxed, as though nothing is on her mind but what is right here in the studio. Sunshine is reflecting on the bright white walls, illuminating paintings of surprising movement and color. A Bach cantata floats out of speakers. This space of gentle music and stark light contains dozens of paintings—hung on the walls, resting on easels. There are paintings of flowers, cafe tables and chairs, women with dream-struck eyes.

This dimension of Carole's world exists apart from practicalities, making a living, negotiating, and having to explain herself. This studio is a sanctuary for the wordless flow of pure creativity, which is a mystical and blissful experience for Carole. It is easy to forget that the work done in this studio is supported by an office in Carole's nearby home that accommodates the full technological fanfare of "reality": phone, fax machine, computer, e-mail, account books.

Carole is a woman determined to make a living from her art. She is an entrepreneurial and marketing whiz. Her soul may be fed by the contemplative work in her studio, but once outside she gets jazzed by finding new ways to make a living from the work she loves. By putting creativity into the business end of art, she created a teaching forum in the idyllic setting of the French countryside.

She acquired her gallery résumé in a traditional way during her years as a paper sculptor, but when it came to painting—the medium closest to her heart, which she rediscovered in midlife—she began to conjure up her own innovative gigs. For example, when an eighty-five-room hotel was under construction in the small northern California town where she lives, Carole thought it would be sacrilege to decorate with the predictable framed prints that show up on motel walls. She convinced the owner to draw on the talents of the local artistic community and embarked on a collaborative effort with other painters to come up with original works for the new hotel. No one had heard of such a project before. Carole smiles and explains, "It just made sense."

"Marketing is the bottom line if you're going to follow your bliss," Carole says. She says she's kind of shy but has always had to make a living at her art, so she got over her fears about putting herself out there. She's very clear about when she's wearing her artist's beret and when she's wearing her entrepreneurial hat. Both require imagination. Her goal is to find ways to perpetuate richness in providing new artistic opportunities for herself and others. Such as her house in France.

In the countryside of Soreze, Carole has a house that is a shrine to art and the summer home for annual creativity workshops. She invites women to live and do art in her home—many who have never painted before. These "playshops" demonstrate her theory that everyone has artistic ability, which grows with exercise and practice. She takes her students to fields of sunflowers, old castles, "Impressionist" dinner parties, and, ultimately, back to themselves.

> We have candles and a fire in the fireplace. We talk about accessing our creative souls. Then they begin to paint, write, dance, or cook. Every day they gain more and more confidence and pretty soon they are ecstatic. They are becoming new creative beings. It's not about learning technique. It's about finding your path and voice in paint.

At home she is Carole, the working artist, wife, friend, and business woman. In France, she is the personification of the muse. The studio she rents a few blocks away from her California home is sort of a halfway house, not as removed from regular life as France, but still a place where her creative self can breathe.

Carole has an abundance of creative magic in her life today. She even had a miniature castle built in her California backyard as a fanciful place for visitors to stay. But her bounty was earned through real world lessons. She knows from firsthand experience about danger, retreat, and triumph. Carole's desire and ability to put her art into the world—and to guide fledgling artists—was born of her own struggle to express her artistry. In her early twenties, her artistic expression was partially paralyzed by thoughtless criticism. It took a life crisis to free her. Now she is part of an informal group of women who call themselves the Danger Rangers, artists who venture bravely into the uncharted creative territories of their lives.

Taking Risks in Art and Business

Underlying Carole's story is the power of confidence and persistence. She also offers strategies for keeping the creative pump primed and sharing the results—even if the world isn't immediately receptive: "You have to keep picking yourself up and remembering the

Buddhist concept of Beginner's Mind," which is a state of grace—being open to learning without shame over not knowing everything all at once.

Carole demonstrates how creativity and commerce can blend. The two aspects of life exist in different realms for many people. Creativity involves deep individual expression, going to that wordless place apart from the rest of the world. Commerce often thrives on surface social interactions, making chitchat and convincing people that a product is hip. Mixing it all up can be crazy-making for some. But Carole shows how it's possible to promote something that comes from your soul. Just because there's a price tag doesn't mean that the personal aspects of art must feel compromised. Carole believes there's an important reason for women to learn salesmanship: If you can find a way to make money from your creativity, you can spend more time doing it.

There are great benefits for women who allow themselves the no-pressure exploration of piano, quilting, watercolors, writing, or any creative endeavor taken on just for the sake of personal pleasure and growth. But for those who dream of making a living from their creativity, a few good tricks can help.

To be an income-producing artist, Carole says you have to know the work is good enough to sell—and then find the specific niche for the level you are on. That has to do in part with the objective quality of the art, of course, but Carole says it also has to do with subjective factors like how comfortable you are with selling something you have made yourself. It helps to have had a lemonade stand or sold Girl Scout cookies when you were a kid, she says. "Remember those childhood experiences of feeling proud enough about what you were offering that you expected the neighbors to pay your asking price. That's the practical challenge of being your own agent."

On another level, Carole's story demonstrates how much integrity is involved in living the artist's life. She is continually tracking her own artistic development, writing about it and sharing it with others. She has had some mystical experiences with synchronistic events that make her feel part of some larger creative spirit. Perhaps it's easier to put your art out there when the work seems driven by forces outside the self rather than solely by the ego.

Whether or not you're willing to take the risk of marketing your art has a lot to do with circumstances. For Carole, as with other women in this book, a life crisis delivered the demanding evidence that life is short and the "old way" of living wasn't working. Carole decided, "Life deserves to be fully met with all the creative juice that you can muster." It was time to drop all barriers to the creative life and go for it.

Carole's Path

Interrupting the Flow of the Artist's Wellspring

Carole Rae Watanabe enjoyed one of those blessed childhoods where creativity could thrive. As far back as she could remember, she was painting pictures that gave her the thrill that comes from pure, joyful expression. There was never any need to explain why she painted what she did or to analyze how her pictures stacked up against other artists' work. She was an artist all her life, eliciting happy and proud responses from family and teachers—until after she graduated from high school and enrolled in an arts college.

As a college freshman, she took her first painting class with a professor who squinted his eyes at one of her paintings and asked her to explain symbolically what her art meant. She had no idea what to say, she was tongue-tied, and that was unacceptable to her teacher. "You have to know what your symbols are," he scolded her.

> *I went home and looked in magazines and tried to figure out what my symbols were. I could not, at age eighteen, talk about symbolism. I painted what moved me. I showed my paintings to people and they said, "Oh, that's wonderful." This was much different.*

Carole was faced with a sudden block, unsure how to describe with the analytical side of her brain what she had created from the intuitive side of her brain. The creative spirit that once had moved through her freely now was stopped with demands for logic: "I stopped painting. I was so humiliated." She decided to change her art focus to sculpture.

Then she found a friend in another professor at the college, a woman who taught weaving. At first Carole scoffed at this applied form of art. "Just teach me what I need to know to incorporate the concepts of weaving into sculpture," she entreated the teacher. The teacher responded gently, "To weave, you need to know everything about it." Because of Carole's respect for the teacher, she settled into learning all the details, histories, and possibilities of weaving. During the ensuing years at the college, she would delve into the mechanics and details of other art forms as well, including sculpture, ceramics, and papermaking. She didn't paint again. She did, however, marry a painter.

Marketable Art

The couple moved to a rural area of Mendocino County to be free spirits and artists, living off the land, building their own home, and exploring the beauty in an area that would become a haven for artists. They needed an income, though, and Carole's weaving skills offered more hope than her husband's painting. Needing to make money from her craft for survival was scary but ultimately a blessing. "That was my boot camp. That was my basic training for life," Carole reflects now.

She had a couple of neighbors, older gentlemen who had retired from businesses, who decided to become mentors to Carole. "One of them said, 'First you need business cards' and he took me to a business services store." Carole sold her crafts and was so successful she taught her husband to weave, and they began making hats and shawls and blankets, beautiful things they sold at craft fairs.

One day a woman stopped by who owned a gallery in a nearby city, and she was interested in carrying the work of Carole and her husband. With an upscale new outlet, prices and demand went up. Pretty soon, Carole was teaching her neighbors to weave and developing a thriving crafts business. But marital problems led to a separation. Carole's husband stayed in the community with the business they had developed, and Carole moved to San Francisco with her toddler son.

> My son was two and I had to make a living. I remembered what my teachers had told me, that 85 percent of art students did not end up making their living doing their art. I decided to focus and immerse myself in entrepreneurial activity — creating my own marketplace rather than asking for acceptance in galleries.

Carole contacted the best tapestry weavers in the Bay Area and began the first gallery in the U.S. to sell tapestries as fine art. It was called the Carole Rae Fiber Center and was housed in the San Francisco Galleria Design Center. Through learning the gallery business and also designing and weaving a line of limited edition tapestries that were marketed through interior design showrooms throughout the U.S., Carole was able to buy her own house and begin considering taking some new risks in the art work. Still no painting, but she moved back to sculpture. She developed her own medium, using papermaking for three-dimensional art.

In retrospect, Carole chuckles at the practical way she went about developing a new form of art. She knew she wanted to do papermaking, but she had all those weavings around. She couldn't just throw them away. She made paper and enclosed the weaving in the paper, into sort of a sandwich. Then she sliced the whole thing and marveled at what she saw in the cross section: a delicate and interesting layered effect. She arranged the pieces on canvas and framed them. The art-buying public responded. She liked the idea of incorporating what she found in her environment into the art itself.

"Papermaking was liberating, it was like being in kindergarten again. It was play." One day she was creating a huge piece on the sidewalk in front of her studio, "A kid came by and rode his bike right through it. At first I was horrified, but when it dried you could see this tire tread and it added to the piece." The more she relaxed and allowed the art to unfold seemingly on its own, the more successful she became.

Mystical Flames

Carole remarried and returned to the country, building a home with her new husband, staying within commuting distance of her studio in San Francisco. She rented out her city house to a group of art students. In the quieter countryside, she began experiencing a new depth to her work, feeling inexplicable emotions as she was creating. A mystical element began to emerge in her work. One day, she was working on a new sculpture, incorporating a pair of three-dimensional hands on a canvas with flames. Included was one of her personal symbols—an "X" in a circle, signifying centeredness—and other images that arrived in intuitive bursts for no apparent reason. "I was playing around with all these symbols and arranging them like collages. My husband asked me what it was about. I said, 'I have no idea.'"

She had the sense of the hands being in pain, and it made her uncomfortable that the muse was guiding her personal symbol into the flames in this perplexing collage. Six weeks later, all the symbols made sense.

> My house in the city burned down. The renters left their paints and art supplies by the heater. They exploded and blew the roof off. That house had been my anchor when my son was little. The house was a symbol of stability for me. Now I had to rebuild it. I thought of my collage. There were the hands. There was the fire. There was the symbol of myself going into the fire. I was in touch with something when I did that collage. It's bizarre, on the day of the fire I awoke early and drove to the city and found upon arrival that my house was burning. It was like I had a precognition.

Carole says that she began to see more and more such "coincidences"—inexplicable links between her art work and life.

> It's synchronism. When you're on an open channel with life, a lot of synchronistic things happen. You're getting information all the time and when you do art all the time, you become much more sensitive to everything. Art teaches you more in-depth ways of seeing.

Reaching for Life, Finding a Paintbrush

The life-changing experience that led her back to painting came after she turned forty and was diagnosed with Lyme disease, a debilitating nerve disease caused by a tick bite. She was drained of energy and experienced periodic difficulty with speaking, sight, and motor movements.

> Suddenly I found myself with limited time, limited energy. That made me look at what's essential to me, how I really wanted to spend my life. I decided to start painting again. That was the incredible gift of my disease.

For the first time in twenty-two years, Carole was holding a paintbrush in her hand and looking at a blank canvas. All her insecurities flooded forth, along with memories of that shattering discussion with her first art professor so long ago. Each day she would get up, paint for an hour, sleep for three hours, and then paint for another hour. It was the labor of love and survival.

> I made so many bad paintings. It was so hard getting back. But I knew I had to reconnect with that part of my creative soul, and this was the way. I'm an artist. I had to do this. I felt like painting was the only thread connected to my inner aliveness and well-being.

This time, it was the internal critic with whom she had to contend. If the years had taught her anything, it was that no one outside herself could pull her off center unless she allowed it. Now, though, the contest was with herself, and the only way for her artistic spirit to prevail was if she could keep her hand dipping the brush into the paint and putting the paint onto the canvas. She had the feeling that the work was "coming out of somewhere else," something beyond her. She didn't stop to analyze, but just continued painting.

> It's the persistence that creates confidence. If you're persistent enough, then when you have confidence, people perceive it and

want to participate. But at first you have to give yourself the
support. You just have to do it.

Inspired to Inspire

On her palette, Carole created pictures of the life around her—
rooms, faces, birds—images she'd seen, images she'd dreamed. It felt
right, and the paintings began to look more like what she had seen in
her mind's eye. The act of painting felt exhilarating, and she wanted
to find some way to share her thoughts. She began getting together
with other women artists, and together they developed a language for
discussing the intuitive ideas that led to their work. To each other,
they acknowledged the feelings, fears, and excitement that came up
as they worked.

She and the other Danger Rangers embarked on collective artistic play. They had a dinner party where Carole was camouflaged as a
table covered with hors d'oeuvres, popping up at the end to reveal
herself. A feeling of freedom emerged from the play, with one person's muse touching another.

Carole wanted to share this freedom with others, including
women who had not yet found such opportunity in their lives. She
began holding workshops for women who also wanted to paint, providing a safe refuge for creativity. She developed exercises for begin-
ners. One was to have a woman lie down on a piece of butcher paper
and have another student draw an outline of her body. On that large
space, inside the outline of her shape, the woman would then write
down everything she could about her own identity. The drawing,
along with the writing about the self, would guide the new artist into
ideas to be explored through painting or writing. At the end of the
session, the student would roll it up and take it back with her to her
daily life with advice from Carole to continue expressing herself
every day.

"Make each encounter you have with anybody a complete experience," Carole advises her students in a voice she also uses on herself. "Don't leave out the hard parts of the conversation. Be totally
honest, no ambiguity and no manipulation. You'll begin feeling the
power of a clean, self-trusting self."

Carole's experiences as an artist and a teacher began working
together to move her beyond her familiar environment. She went to
the countryside of France to paint, where she breathed in the air that
seemed especially pure because it was so far away from distractions
of "regular life": phones, computers, bills. She could go further with
her work, concentrating longer, without feeling constrained by the
opinions of others. She found the residents of southern France

pleased at the sight of someone sitting in front of a landscape, painting plain air: "If you go into a village and begin to paint, people come up to look and comment. There is a respect for artists." Carole didn't mind the language barrier, feeling that it was rather pleasant not to get engaged in conversations beyond simple greetings.

When she returned home, struck by the contrast between the art-friendly French countryside and the distracting nature of the day-to-day U.S. experience, her entrepreneurial streak flared up, and she began thinking of ways to take other artists—and people who wanted to become artists—with her to France. Out of that came the decision to buy a home in Soreze.

Carole's Life These Days

Turtle Mode

Each summer now, Carole hosts a group of women who want to engage in expanding their creative forces and capabilities. "Kindergarten is the only prerequisite," she says. She gentles them into what she calls "turtle mode"—a slowing of pace, lots of naps, sitting around the fire and talking about ways to invite in the creative spirit. Time and again she is amazed by what they create.

> I watch these people painting, some of whom have never
> painted before. Every day, they get more and more confidence.
> By the time they leave, they are new, creative, blooming
> human beings. They have accessed it.

When she closes up the house in France and returns to her home in northern California, she strives to bring back with her a little of the "turtle mode" that enables her own and others' art to thrive. She knows what it feels like to have the sensation slip away: "Suddenly there are bills to pay, letters to write. There's the computer again."

She decided to get a small studio near her home, so that she could make regular voyages away from her workaday life. Inside the studio, where her richly colored paintings hang against the stark white walls, she can drift into her own sense of time and space. She uses the metaphor of moving from "inside the box," the strictures of everyday life and its responsibilities, to her own place "outside the box," where she is free to engage her creative spirit on her own terms. She has learned to protect her solitude and clear her mind. She usually does her entrepreneurial, domestic, and business duties on different days than she does her painting: "When I'm not here in my studio enough, I start losing it—the ability to be open. Creativity is something that you have to nurture and take care of."

These days, Carole is producing so many new ideas that one envisions in her mind not the proverbial lightbulb going on, but something more like Fourth of July fireworks. Painting is only one way she has of materializing her visions. She's also involved in new creative projects, which play lightly with serious issues. Her illness brought her close to the subject of death. Instead of turning away from that after she regained her health, she began looking for ways to express her awareness of the fleeting nature of life. Thus was born the "coffin project," in which she and other women design their own coffins while writing about life and death.

At the same time, Carole is paying homage to her childlike, fairy-tale urges through her castle-building project. She's working with women in an "empowerment with power tools" workshop to build a miniature castle in her own yard, a refuge for ritual and magical moments. "You'll have a castle because you are a princess!" a friend declares. Carole smiles, "Yes."

Ordinary to Extraordinary

Carole's life is extraordinary today. A beginning artist might look at her work, her confidence, her financial success, and think, "I'll never get there." But her challenges were similar to those experienced by many beginning artists. Carole's response was a series of willful acts, coupled with persistence, that allowed her to meet those challenges and succeed on her own terms. Once she learned, she wanted to help other women gain confidence. She didn't teach them her way, but how to find their own. She's convinced everyone has artistic ability.

Carole did have some advantages: She made it through her formative years before she received the discouraging messages from the world that many receive earlier in life. She was a young adult when the professor inadvertently plugged up what previously had been a free flow of creative juice. "I am sure most people can remember when they crumbled. I'm lucky it didn't happen in grade school. That's when most people experience it."

Carole believes it's freeing for women to remember when they first heard gratuitous criticism that made them "stop and think" before stepping outside the box or coloring outside the lines: "Often it's just a thoughtless comment by someone perceived as an authority that puts a cap on the creative wellspring. Go back in time," she suggests, "and argue with the nay-saying voice." There is something to be learned by identifying your creative setbacks, and doing this may manufacture fuel for the creative fires within.

The Artist as Entrepreneur

Carole is happier pursuing her favorite form of art—painting— than the papermaking and weaving that was leading her down the fame-and-fortune path. She encourages women to choose their form of art based on what feels right rather than what will sell. While ultimately valuing process over product, Carole says there's an essential feedback loop that occurs when women put their work out into the world. "Overcoming fear of expression is the first step, sharing the expression with others is the next."

Carole makes the argument: "Displaying one's work leads to being 'seen' by others, and that's what feeds the muse." For her, self-imposed deadlines, making sales, and hanging her art work in shows are ways of keeping herself going in the studio, grist for the creative mill. Instead of relying on the big city gallery circuit, she is selling her work in local venues. She knows the gallery owners and that makes for folksy interactions instead of cold business deals. She works closely with other women, believing that women need each other to become confident about their art.

Carole believes that the historic pressure men have felt, and the opportunities they've had, to make a living from their art is one reason why they have dominated the art scene.

> I know so many women artists who are great but because they don't have to market their work, they don't. Without the feedback, they begin to languish and lose their momentum. . . . In a way, women not taking themselves seriously is a detriment to their work.

Although promotion isn't necessary for art—and sometimes keeping it private can strengthen the work—for many there is a time when going public is right both artistically and personally. Commercial success has been one of Carole's goals, but she says what keeps her creative juices flowing are the intangibles of self-expression and connection with others.

> I think fame is like water in a basket. But I like to sell my work. I like people to call me up and say "I love it." I like to meet the people who buy my work. I used to be into being successful in the way that everyone wants to buy your work, so the price tags go up and more people want to buy your work. I did that for many years, but that was just a big ego thing. Now I have more perspective.

Conversations and Reflections:
Persistently Pursuing a Vision

Carole is someone whose life is testimony to the emerging definition of creativity that includes everyone. When I first walked into Carole's studio, my eyes pooled up. The vibrancy of the artwork resonated with me, but I was also moved to tears by the potency of the environment—those stark white walls, the soothing music, and how much her studio seemed to be away from it all.

I was familiar with the concept of "sacred space," but had never felt someone else's so powerfully. We hadn't met before, but here I was, this stranger choking back tears. Carole didn't seem in the slightest daunted by my emotional response to her space. She has had a lot of experience watching other women become moved by her art and her commitment to it. What she said was, "Welcome!" And before too long we were talking and laughing. A couple of hours with Carole left me with a visceral sense of the dual nature of artistic success: You have to struggle hard to get the world—and yourself—to take your art seriously. Then, to keep it going, you need to remember to let go and have fun.

The prospect of declaring oneself an artist, deserving of a studio, seemed dizzying. At what point do you say, "This is who I am"? Carole claimed her creativity as a child, but allowed a clumsy professor to rob her of her first dream of becoming a painter as a young woman. That experience caused her to put down her paintbrush for two decades, but she had a resilient spirit and reached out for other tools—looms and paper and cloth. Creativity seems as much an act of will as talent, though it helps to have both. Even if you're not doing what you feel is your "real" art, exercising creativity in other ways can keep you in shape. One day, like Carole, you might be ready to go for the big risk.

Try a Bigger Brush

Carole teaches chutzpah. She gentles her workshop students through performance fears that come up. "I tell people our Danger Ranger motto, which is 'exchange passion for the voice of fear.'" If someone feels nervous about putting brush to canvas, saying something like, "I can't do this because I'm not creative," Carole encourages them to pick up a bigger brush. Whether or not the final result is something that has meaning to others, conquering the fear of expression influences other aspects of life.

Overcoming fear is an integral part of creativity for some women, because new energy is set free. Linda Firestone wrote in *Awakening Minerva,* "Nurturing fears that no longer reflect the present reality demands a good deal of creativity energy." It may be unrealistic to instantly banish the face of fear from one's creative space, but many women have developed tricks. Carole's is to get a bigger brush.

For writer Natalie Goldberg, author of *Writing Down the Bones,* what works is to let the nagging critic, whom she calls the "editor or internal censor," have its way for a moment.

> *If the editor is absolutely annoying and you have trouble differentiating it from your creative voice, sit down whenever you need to and write what the editor is saying. . . . The more clearly you know the editor, the better you can ignore it. After a while, like the jabbering of an old drunk fool, it becomes just prattle in the background.*

In order to heal our creative wounds, should we consider rewinding the tape of our lives and pausing on those excruciating moments? Julia Cameron says in *The Artist's Way* that she believes it's healthy to go back and remember the wounds.

> *As mental health experts are quick to point out, in order to move through loss and beyond it, we must acknowledge it and share it. Because artistic losses are seldom openly acknowledged or mourned, they become artistic scar tissues that block artistic growth. Deemed too painful, too silly, too humiliating to share and so to heal, they become instead, secret losses.*

Remembering the long-ago snipes received at school is one of those wincing exercises that may help us recognize that the problem was with the teachers and not us.

I remember one time in grade school when I was coloring a person. When it came to the socks, I imitated a weave with crisscrossed lines, quite clever I thought. The teacher was annoyed, pointing out that one should always color with lines in the same direction and that the crisscross was sloppy. Our family often colored and painted at home, and there were no such strict rules. Remembering that helped me track the slow evolution of a subconscious and thwarting belief that my creativity was something private and apart from "work in the real world." Slowly I've been relieved of that cloud layer in my life, seeing my way clear to be myself.

Meg remembers doing a folk dance in grade school when everyone was to hold hands and move in a circle. She went in the other direction from everyone else. "You're going the wrong way!" the teacher told her. "No," she replied, "everyone else is." Meg would like to hang on to that confident spirit from her childhood.

Who hasn't experienced unconstructive criticism from a controlling person misusing authority? Going back into those memories may ultimately prove liberating, as they were for Carole when she finally realized and reclaimed the creative vision she blithely gave away at the age of eighteen to a critical professor.

Getting It Out into the World

Sharing your creative spirit and helping others claim their creative selves are bounteous gifts. Many women in this book have managed to carry their work into a public forum. For some, displaying the work was incidental to the creative process. For others, including Pauline with her theater and Vera with her dancing, the work gained meaning from the sharing. That's certainly the case for Carole, with her social nature and desire for feedback. She encourages women to share their ideas with each other, bonding together in groups like her Danger Rangers where they can trade stories, laughter, and encouragement.

Women can get braver through hearing the tales of other women's chutzpah. A classic example of this bravery is artist/composer Laurie Anderson's march into a publishing house after she completed her bachelor's degree in art in 1969. She had designed a mystery story in drawings and chose Bobbs-Merrill because it was only a bus fare away. The receptionist told her no one was available to see her, so Laurie said she'd wait awhile and did so, plopping herself in a lobby chair and staring straight ahead for five hours.

Finally an editor came out and said he couldn't stand seeing her sitting there any longer. She showed him her drawings and they signed a contract immediately. In the book *Women Music Makers* by Janet Nichols, Laurie recalled: "It was satisfying to think that maybe the rules weren't quite as strict as I had thought, that you could just try something." Among writers, there's a long tradition of collecting rejection slips as badges of honor. It's an accomplishment just to have sent something out.

I remember one fledging novelist in a writing workshop who told me that she had trouble getting her family to take her writing seriously until she got an agent. That seemed to impress them as something "serious." Another way to put some muscle behind your claim to creativity is to have some language for explaining it to others. So many women, including several in this book, have stumbled when others challenged their methods or initial products. That's what knocked the young Carole off her path.

Today, Carole urges other women to claim their creativity as a birthright, not waiting for someone else to give permission. Susan talks about how she has caught some of that brave feeling from Carole: "When I first met Carole, I thought that maybe I could paint if I didn't worry about the fact that I didn't have lessons and didn't have any obvious talent. But I might be able to throw some color down and not worry about the form. Her freedom is infectious."

Saying "I'm an artist" can become a self-fulfilling prophecy. It helps to find words to describe your own creative process, in addition to following your creative spirit, proving to others that it's real.

Your Own Way

More and more women seem to be enjoying the freedom that comes from admitting that their creativity works in a way that is intuitive and nonlinear. Annie's accomplishments with a camera came from her self-awareness of her own process. Sarah's mystery novels—and her work as a geologist—grew from her holistic approach to gathering information.

Carole has been ahead of her time, too. For years, she has proudly explained that for her, expression comes first, her understanding later. She doesn't need to know why she's embarking on a certain painting. It's enough to have a strong image in her mind—a flower, a shadow, a certain light. Later though, she's apt to see something beyond or inside the painting she has created. The meaning emerges from the image, even if the image does not necessarily begin with a raison d'etre. It's like Donna being able to "see" her whole garden while it was still weeds, or like Deborah, Meg, Susan, and I knowing that we could look around at women in our own lives and find the essential nature of creativity.

It takes practice, but confidence comes from finding words or taking actions to express one's reality, even if it means saying and doing things before we have any clue why. Grand women have been doing this throughout history. Alice B. Toklas once said of Gertrude Stein, after a dinner party, "This has been a most wonderful evening. Gertrude has said things tonight it'll take her ten years to understand."

I've been able to breathe easier as I hear other women admitting what I know about myself. Sometimes I know an image or an idea or a story is just right long before I understand the concepts behind it. It's anecdotal learning. This is the same reason some of us know more about history from what we read in biographies than from textbooks. It has been so freeing to be able to say to editors, "I know this is a good story, but I can't tell you the angle yet." I started trusting my intuition and it's proven accurate enough times that others are beginning to trust it, too. Carole says she has seen it over and over again:

In the beginning, you have to keep your own vision alive, and your confidence and persistence ultimately will bring others along.

Putting a Price Tag on It

The big leap of confidence often comes the first time you ask for financial return for your creative work. Carole thinks a lot of women recoil from selling their work because they were programmed at an early age that it's somehow immodest or not ladylike to do so. She believes our ideas about money are fashioned before we're ten, depending on how much luck we had with those Girl Scout cookies and lemonade stands.

As my collaborators and I worked on this book, we talked a lot about the relationship between creativity and money. You can't ignore the cold breath of fiscal reality. Meg worried that we might be misleading women if we made it sound as though you can simply trust the universe, as Helen has with her work as a psychic. Having a strong inner vision and a lot of chutzpah aren't always enough to make a go of it. But, as Carole demonstrates, you can tip the scales in your favor by being willing to take work out into the world.

Susan pointed out how encouraging it is to hear Carole talk as casually about selling her art as about her childhood lemonade stand. Shouldn't we all be able to proudly ask for compensation for our work? Susan says:

> It appeals to me that she claims her right to make money at something she loves. For too many people, the idea that you could do something you love and charge a sweet price for it is self-canceling. Like that notion that women can either do good or make money, but that we can't do both. You can do both.

Birgitta, the baker, is another role model for this. She derives utmost satisfaction from her artistry in the kitchen, but says she also likes working on the books and counting her financial returns. Carole suggests the importance of developing both the inner creative self and the inner business self—maybe on different days, maybe in different spaces, but she believes they're equally necessary if your goal is to make a living.

Onward: In the Creative Club

Before she developed words to explain what and why she was doing what she does with a paintbrush, Carole had trouble translating the mystical element of her work for the access of others. Now that she has the words, she delights in using them—along with her paintings—to express her wisdom. There is one sentence she carries with her like a talisman. It helps her remember how much of her good self goes into her work. And that it's her job to be able to do more. Look closely, and it appears in feathery script in the background of many of her paintings: "Whatever the question, love is the answer."

Carole invites everyone to become honorary members of the Danger Rangers:

> *The aim of being a Danger Ranger is to get over being*
> *someone and begin being yourself. Being yourself is terrifying.*
> *There are no rules, there are no rights or wrongs, there is no*
> *perfect or imperfect. There is only acceptance of whatever is*
> *happening on a real, instinctive, subconscious basis. You are*
> *the only guide to your pure and honest self.*

13

Daring to Change the World: Believing in Your Dream

It is creative, working with the elements of human relationships. I don't think about it, but I know when it happens and I recognize the power and feeling.

—Dyan Foster, organizer of
programs for troubled teens

Meet Dyan in the Teen Theater

The teenagers are wearing various symbols of what is cool, some declaring their independence with falling-down baggy pants, piercings in obvious and unlikely places, shaved heads, or even a few tattoos. What most aren't wearing is the teenage "mask": that self-protective veneer that people in this no-longer-children, not-quite-adults age group often acquire. These teens are interacting comfortably on stage, performing stories from their lives—stories that sometimes help them work through their troubles and express their visions.

Dyan Foster is the director and nurturer of what's happening in this room, but she's usually off to the side with watchful encouragement. Her presence is one of the universal mother, but with a hip kind of charm that comes from her immersion in a youthful, multicultural environment. She is perfecting a stance that seems to work with teens: She's a solid presence without being intrusive, tolerant but clear in her expectations, loving but not controlling. She's a touchstone with soft edges.

Around Dyan, teenagers tend to be relaxed and direct. Unlike many situations in which teens feel alienated, here they are inclined to meet the eyes of a visiting adult instead of look downward, smiling gently instead of holding their jaws rigid. This is a place where they know they belong.

Dyan's brainchild, Roots for Youth, serves and is staffed by teenagers. Together they oversee several social service programs aimed at reducing juvenile crime and substance abuse while allowing teens to discover their potential. The teens tell her this place is like family. Some have been coming here regularly for six to seven years, participating in the educational theater group known as Teens Teaching Through Theater.

Some are newcomers, brought in via a troubled road. One of the programs in Roots for Youth is teen court, an alternative to Juvenile Court, where kids can go to be tried and sentenced for misdemeanor offenses, like graffiti and theft, by a jury, literally, of their peers. Dyan says:

> It allows young people to create their own media. It's educational and its empowering. I see teen court as a form of media. There's something cleansing about it. They come clean. It's

*open to the public. They're held accountable, and they get over
their shame.*

One of her recent inspirations was the "victim's roundtable." After youths go through teen court, one of the consequences is participation in a session where offenders meet with a panel of people who have been victims of crime and tell the kids face-to-face how it feels. The setting is formal, and most of the talk is serious. But occasionally there are light moments. Dyan smiles when one of the kids makes a slightly irreverent joke; she's tolerant of teenage humor, as long as it doesn't involve putdowns. Her affection is as obvious as her insistence that these kids start taking responsibility for their actions. The combination has won her credibility among the teens. They know she's fair. So when Dyan calls one of them on his attempt to duck responsibility for a crime, the others listen.

*"It was my friend who stole. It wasn't my idea. It's just that
my friend gave me some of the money," the youth protests.*

*"But you chose to be there. And you spent some of the stolen
money!"*

"Well . . ."

There's no blaming hard stare when Dyan speaks. She is more inclined to describe than to judge. Her face is kind. Surrounded by other youths who get the logic of what Dyan is saying, the offending youth begins to get the idea that he has to change his attitude. There is a slow shift in this young offender's assessment of his own situation. He moves from "It wasn't my fault," to "It was more my friend's fault than mine," and eventually to "Okay, okay, I shouldn't have done it. I'm sorry."

The youths receive sentences that represent logical consequences for their offense, often some combination of community service and restitution. But the more profound measure of the program's success—and the triumph of Dyan's work—is when a youth gets a light of recognition on his face, reflecting self-awareness and a decision to accept personal responsibility, which often leads to positive change.

Although she is twenty years older than these teens, Dyan does not feel separate from them. She remembers her own youth clearly—how the "bad" kids often seemed the most interesting, but how sad it was that, unlike herself, her friends in high school were often neglected and poor, with little hope for the future. Since childhood, Dyan has played the dual role of participant and caregiver in the lives of troubled kids. Now, a pioneer of new programs that are working to help juveniles, she is bringing those roles together and changing lives.

Becoming a Vessel for Social Justice

Dyan demonstrates a kind of creativity that is often overlooked but weaves the fabric of our society. She has a vision of what would make the world a better place, combined with the ability and drive to materialize it. Instead of feeling powerless as many people do when they consider the magnitude of social problems, Dyan's mind generates systems for making a difference.

The phrase "Think globally, act locally" isn't just a bumper-sticker platitude, but a concept that gives life meaning to many social activists. People who are behind the scenes all around us, often unrecognized, usually underfunded, and self-motivated by the desire to make their communities and world a more humane place. Few are cut out for this kind of work, but those who can manage it have a particular brand of creativity that requires an ability to visualize the future, tolerate the inevitable conflicts of human interaction, and maintain a powerful source of motivation. Dyan is inspired by a strong ethical sense and abiding religious faith that has taken the form of a particular challenge that now defines her life: "I'm trying to make sure that all people, and in my work, particularly young people, have equal access to make it in society."

Through Dyan's story, we see the art of social responsibility. Just as with writing a poem or painting a picture, the creative aspect of her work involves a combination of intuition, skills, and trust. Her "product"—the softened look on the face of a youth who learns to empathize and take responsibility—is as fulfilling and wondrous to her as a prize painting is to an artist. As many creative people do, Dyan sees herself more as a vessel for the work that's getting done than as the creator of it. She's motivated by ideals, but what keeps her going are the moments of divine inspiration when she sees how to make the program work better and then witnesses the results—youths who are better human beings because of her work.

Dyan has been drawn into the world of troubled teens, but her brand of creativity applies to all areas of social justice work, accomplished by people who maintain vision and commitment, even when the surrounding community isn't inclined to offer support. It's an ideal of social justice that many people hold, but Dyan is among those living her conviction. She has had flashes of inspiration about how to penetrate the tough veneer of young criminal offenders, knows how to reach their conscience, and is slowly gathering help from the community to make it happen.

Dyan demonstrates the power of faith—in her case, faith in humanity, the promise of youth, and God—in the quest to materialize solutions to social problems that seem overwhelming to most. The creativity involved in starting and overseeing an organization often does not receive the same recognition that solo endeavors get. But to envision and carry out healthy new forms of human interaction requires all the elements of inspiration, perseverance, and respect for unconscious forces that mark any creative act. Dyan keeps going because she receives fulfillment from the work itself, knowing that the long-term results may not show up for decades.

As an African-American, middle-class woman who spent her teenage years in a predominantly white area, with friends from different socioeconomic and ethnic groups, Dyan developed an ability to move in a variety of different circles. As the daughter of an educator and activist, she has inherited a sense of responsibility for other people. As someone with deep roots in a church, she has been raised on the belief of the inherent goodness of the human spirit. As someone with a passion for theater, she learned to see the drama in life as well as in art. She uses this rich heritage for good. Dyan has always been attuned to the injustices that cause suffering. Since girlhood, she has sought to make a difference in other people's lives. As an adult, her passion for social change has materialized in her unique youth program.

> I don't think there was a plan of action. It was like,
> "Don't lose sight of the potential." Keep holding it, keep
> nurturing it, keep fanning the flames ... I feel I fell into
> this and God made it possible.

Dyan's Path

Dyan was raised by a strong mother who believed in helping others. Dyan's mother took in children in need of a home to live with herself and her own two daughters, all the while working as a teacher and rising through the ranks of education to eventually become a principal. Dyan grew up believing this was standard, that all moms felt responsible for other children besides their own and for as much of the rest of the world as they could handle.

> There was the teacher-caretaker influence. When I was small,
> my mom brought another little girl home, a girl who didn't
> have a family, and raised her. We always had someone living
> with us.

They had a middle-class lifestyle, but Dyan didn't grow up with a lot of material excess. Her privilege came, appropriately enough, in the form of educational opportunities. "Summers I would go to a theater company." She rode the bus for more than an hour each way to San Francisco to study acting. She recalls the experience with much pleasure: "I'm still somewhat amazed that my mom let me do it. The theater was in a rough part of town. But she trusted that everything would be fine, and it was." It was from the success of this teen venture of her own that Dyan realized the transformative power of theater.

As a teen, Dyan experienced the rush of satisfaction that came with self-expression on stage: "I remember those moments of being on stage. It was a natural high. I'd think, 'This is great.'" Those memories would later become pivotal in her creation of a program to help youths find a safe forum for working through their problems.

She also has memories of what—from the point of view of a youth—didn't work.

> I remember a lot of things feeling "not right." I remember one time when three teachers brought together three classes of students on campus to deal with some new policy. I don't remember the exact subject, only that the kids started getting agitated, saying "This is a setup." I remember feeling that what the teachers were saying didn't ring true, that we were being manipulated.

That memory, too, would shape her later work with youths, reminding her that kids know when you're being straight with them and when you're not.

As a teen in a rural-turning-suburban town, Dyan frequently found herself in the company of poor and often neglected people.

> I hung around with the kind of people whose houses were funky and dirty. It was the fringe crowd. They were more fun. They were on the edge and pushing the edges, and I liked that.

She was aware of the discrepancy between their circumstances and her own: "I knew I had opportunities my friends didn't have."

Dyan tried drugs and alcohol, but didn't come close to the serious substance abuse happening among her friends: "I didn't do half of what they did." Her social group included young adults in their twenties in addition to the high school kids. Some of the adult partyers had children, and the way the children were treated disturbed Dyan.

I always did have a sense of feeling hurt because people had children and didn't take care of them. I can remember hanging around one house. There was a five-year-old and everybody used to send her to the store to steal things for them. I felt bad for her. I'd bring her clothes and comb her hair and try to take care of her.

She was modeling the behavior taught to her by her Mom: Take care of the disadvantaged, particularly the children, who have no means of changing their situation.

Dyan hasn't fully analyzed why in her young adulthood she found herself in the company of the fringe crowd. It just happened that way. "I was always hanging out with people who were in trouble." There were a lot of laughs, there was a lot of excitement, but there also was a lot of tragedy: "A fair number of my friends passed away within five years of high school."

Dyan was part of the crowd, but a part of her remained safely separate. "My friends would be getting high, and for some that was their life, but I knew I'd be going to my theater group the next day." She would think about ways that she could help make their lives better. It was clear to her that her access to education and a stable home life made the difference. Life wasn't fair. She wished she could change that. Out of that feeling emerged the beginnings of a commitment. Dyan wanted to equalize the chances for all young people to have a good life. She recognized signs of ability—maybe even of greatness—in some of her friends, but she realized that the outlets for developing their talents were very limited.

Faith

Dyan's mom was a devout member of the local Baptist church, and going to church was just something she and her mother did every Sunday, no excuses. Growing up, God, church, gospel music, and community were givens, not something Dyan dwelled upon. She absorbed the values from a church where people supported one another in life-giving ways, looking after ill members, taking in needy members, offering encouragement in work and domestic projects. Above all, there was the idea that individuals were acting in accordance with the divine: "One of the songs we'd sing in church was 'Use Me.' I grew up believing people have a purpose." In her late teens, she attended church only sporadically, but even while not actively participating in religious activities, she kept her faith and her sense of social responsibility.

Acting Locally

As a young woman, Dyan began to see how her values had been shaped by the opportunities she was given: the intellectual stimulation at home, the theater experience, and her social life. She was convinced one of the differences between her and her troubled friends—the ones who were not making a healthy transition into adulthood—was that she had been raised without television. She felt disturbed and fascinated by the effects of media in people's lives and for a time considered a career in market research and advertising. She wanted to change the messages that were going out to young people.

She enrolled in a nearby university and invented her own major, spanning the philosophy and communications departments, called Ethics and Media Studies. Her focus of study was the role media played in children's development. "I felt then and I feel now that kids don't need all the stuff that television brings to them." After receiving her B.A. degree, she went to the University of California at Berkeley to receive a credential for teaching at the community college level, but an opportunity came up for working in her chosen field of media.

In her hometown, a fledgling public television station was getting off the ground. She went to work for the station, working on the organization and the programming for three years before it went on the air and for four years after. She developed both her organizational and media skills, watching programs carefully and finding herself thinking about new ways to apply what she was learning. One day she tuned in a program on PBS about teens in theater. As she watched the teens on the television, she thought about the youths she saw every day in her own neighborhood. To her, they presented a picture of frustration.

> There are kids who are constantly hanging out. They have
> a portfolio full of drawings. One wants to design clothes.
> Another wants to make films. There's no outlet for their
> creativity. It's a shame. . . . I've always said young people
> do not have a role in our society, they do not have a job—
> a way to count their contributions in a positive way. There
> aren't any expectations. They are incredibly sophisticated
> and talented and smart. You can never have enough for
> them to do. I wanted to give kids an opportunity to harness
> their aspirations.

Dyan observed that identifying goals was particularly difficult for children who came from a different culture than the dominantly white, upwardly-mobile people generally seen on TV. Children who didn't see themselves fitting the media "image" were less inclined to believe they had choices. Dyan remembered how theater made a difference in her life and thought drama might well become a vehicle for change in the lives of other youth. "I wanted them to find something they could be proud of doing." She wanted the kids to discover something they could commit to, something that would speak to their experiences. And she wanted the kids to be involved in creating something for themselves and for the others who would follow.

Individually, it was impossible to meet the needs of all these kids who had no outlet for their creativity—especially those who came from households with substance abusers, kids like those she has a special affinity with from her younger experiences. But as she watched the program on teens in theater, she saw how she might bring some of the troubled and displaced youths in her neighborhood together for a close-to-home creative adventure.

A newlywed, she told her husband about the idea. "He was extremely supportive. He bought me this beautiful desk I wanted. He's always been there with me. His name is Peter and I started calling him 'Peter the Rock.'" Dyan left the television station after the birth of their first child and soon after that started making her dream reality. One day, Dyan invited the kids on the block to her house and together they declared themselves an acting troupe: Teens Teaching Through Theater, or "T4" for short. She'd seen these kids doing elaborate routines just for fun—dance and comedy and acting out. She knew they could bring it to the stage, and she knew just how empowering and inspirational it was to find your voice and validate it through performance.

Starting Small

"They rose to the occasion. They're savvy. They're very concerned with respect, and they got it through this." The kids wrote, directed, and acted in their own plays under Dyan's guidance:

Fifteen to twenty kids came to my living room once or twice a week, a tiny little living room. There was something there for them. It fed them somehow. And I had lots of ideas. It was fun.

The family feeling was there from the beginning. These teens became part of Dyan's life. Within three years, she had her second child. She liked having the neighborhood kids around the house. "I had a lot of potential role models for my kids, and a lot of babysitters," she recalls. Within a few months, T4 was performing at schools, community centers, and churches. The plays were about their lives as teenagers, with scenes about friendships, romance, life at home, and life on the streets.

T4 developed in a way that Dyan characterized as "organic"; one step led to the next, the group got bigger, and the kids became more and more creative. She told herself: "Just keep holding it, keep nurturing it, keep fanning the flames ... what's important is that these young people feel comfortable and safe." Pretty soon, her living room no longer could accommodate all the kids who were interested in participating.

Spilling Over

The success of T4 meant more involvement, and more involvement meant she needed more resources: "It's like a cup of water that fills to the brim, and you need a larger container." Dyan's motivation for working with teens was her delight in their company and satisfaction in helping them shine. "It's transformation, that's what it's about for me. Watching kids mature, stretch, and develop." She had the satisfaction, but her caregiver's spirit and a former party girl's sense of fun were no longer enough to keep T4 going. She needed money for a larger space and the organizational skills to raise it.

She had a mentor who urged her to incorporate as a nonprofit organization, and Dyan made the transition from neighborhood theater director to executive director, while continuing her role as theater leader, too. She named the organization Roots for Youth. "There were a lot of details," she recalls. But what helped her was keeping an awareness of how her interest started in the first place. "I've always been clear about not getting lost in politics." She set up a board of directors and started fund-raising.

Her work was all volunteer for years, but getting a paycheck was a change. She didn't want to alienate any of her students by charging them. And they were providing a service to the community with their performances. So with the new board of directors, Dyan set out to raise donations and grants for the program. She found a space for rehearsals and the organization's office. Money started trickling in. It wasn't enough to pay her a salary, but it was just about enough for rent and some production costs.

Two things kept Dyan going: her relationship with the kids, and her relationship with God. They added up to a strong belief that her theater group would survive.

> There was a very strong faith that this was going to be a reality. I don't think I ever wavered in that. There was no question in my mind. For three-and-a-half years, everything was on faith.... My job was to provide the opportunities for young people to effect changes in their lives and then to get out of the way.

"We had these really close relationships in the group." Kids would encourage each other to choose appropriate outlets for self-expression. "It's using your innate creativity and talent and using it in a positive way." Kids who had angry feelings could act them out on stage.

The program's building space was big enough to accommodate theater groups as well as the offices, and a lot of the work with kids occurred right there. The building also became a social center, where kids would work with one another to brainstorm about finding or creating healthy activities out in the community, such as doing ropes courses, breakdancing, making skateboard clubs, and doing graffiti on walls where it was legal.

> A lot of times I'd hear kids say, "There's nothing to do," and while there are plenty of things to do, you have to know where to find them, and most of them cost money—something this group of teens did not have. It was certainly true there are not a lot of resources, support, or funding for kids to express themselves in individual artistic ways, particularly if you're nonwhite. Maybe there's a low-rider bike club, but there are not a lot of other activities aimed at people who aren't part of the dominant culture. My big thing was to provide opportunities.

Dyan observed with fascination and pleasure how the teens would step forward and come to one another's aid—whether it was to get through a theater scene or stand by a friend in a crisis. The power of peer relationships was being recognized by experts, and Dyan saw how it made sense: Teens would listen to each other in a way they'd rarely listen to adults.

Hitting the Wall

As Dyan listened to the teens supporting each other, through T4, she felt like she'd fulfilled part of her calling. But the funding wasn't coming through. There was rent to pay, materials to buy, equipment needed for the office. The occasional donation wasn't enough. And the big grants were eluding her. Dyan wasn't making a dime herself, but was shelling money out to cover costs. She told herself to keep the faith, but there were limits. The program was in debt and so was she. She needed a job and she needed money. It wasn't working to tell herself, "Hang in there."

She was in Vancouver at a business conference with her husband when she almost decided to quit. Out of town on a rare getaway, Dyan got the distance she needed to be able to see herself more clearly. She was stressed, worried, overworked, and stretched past her limits. "I hit the wall and couldn't go on." That's when the phone call came saying Roots for Youth had won a grant through funds available to deal with teen issues related to substance abuse.

The county had a far-sighted administrator who saw great promise in programs like T4 and agreed to sponsor their activity if T4 would agree to accept youth with substance abuse problems. Not hardened criminals, just kids who needed some focus for their life, some way to discover that they were worthy human beings. Dyan's program fit the bill. "I'd wanted to do it right and now we could. I was so relieved. I started jumping up and down on the bed."

Another inspiration further clarifying Dyan's mission with local teens came once again in the form of a public television program.

> PBS did a series called "Generation at Risk," and they showed a teen court in Odessa, Texas. I saw how that could work here. It allows young people to create their own media. It's educational and empowering.

Seeing Solutions

Dyan now had an answer for all the kids who said to her, "I could do better than my attorney." She'd say, "Go ahead." The idea of teen court was for youths who were first-time misdemeanor offenders to make their case and be judged by their peers. She envisioned teen court as an extension of T4.

"These are usually kids who made a stupid mistake, kids who have problems with the system. Sixty percent have some issue around substance abuse." Maybe they did graffiti tagging at a school, stole something from a store, got in a fight, or got caught with drugs. Dyan's teen court would be for kids from all over the county who got arrested but who appeared to authorities to be lost kids in need of some guidance, rather than bad kids in need of punishment.

The creative process of her work with kids began to reveal itself. Somehow she knew when an idea would work.

> It would just feel right. It's like a moment of clarity when things synthesize. It's very organic, not forced. It's natural, like the next little blossom on a tree. It fits. It's a very different feeling than administrative work, when people get together and say "how can we meet this directive." Those situations can feel forced and false, like trying to fit a round peg in a square hole.... Ideas that are right feel like the natural progression.

When Dyan floated the idea of a teen court by juvenile justice officials, she found that people were ready for a new route for steering adolescent and early teen offenders away from a criminal lifestyle. And there was funding available for identified early offenders. So she agreed to work with that population. Teen court was born with the help of a six-year grant. Dyan was back working with the disadvantaged, the young people on the fringe: "It felt like a calling. I didn't choose the work, it chose me."

Her students in T4 helped Dyan set up teen court in a way that incorporated theater and ethics, the two fields she had blended in her university studies. It worked: At the same time that the drama of the courtroom scene captured the youths' attention, individually they were touching each other's hearts and minds. Over time, teen court would prove to be one of the most effective deterrents to crime the local Juvenile Court had seen. Dyan says it's a pretty simple formula: Kids may make all kinds of excuses for themselves when they get in trouble, but they can usually see right through each others' stories. "It's interesting to have a child who has committed a burglary sit on a jury and talk to a child who has beaten someone up and say, 'You should not have done that.'"

Dyan watched the faces of the children as they let down their guard, listened to their peers, and decided to atone for their small, first crimes. The message Dyan wanted the kids to get was, "When you make a mistake you can learn and move on. You do not need to feel shamed and blamed. Your mistake is not what defines you." They could have another chance. Dyan started tracking the kids who had gone through teen court. An independent evaluation of the program supported her observations: After three years, 98 percent of the youths who had gone through teen court had stayed out of trouble with the law. Teen court, and the concept of peers being accountable to their peer community, proved to be wildly successful.

Sometimes Dyan would witness dramatic turnabouts in a child's attitude and feel part of a profound healing process for the human spirit. She remembers one exchange between a victim and a young offender that left both of them crying, along with everyone else in the room at a victims' roundtable session.

There was a boy who had stolen the purse of an older woman who was at the roundtable. He'd been with two other boys and they had used her ATM card to get money out of the bank, hundreds of dollars. She recognized the boy and told him to stand up. At first he said, "I didn't steal the purse, I just went to the ATM." She said, "Look at me." Then she spoke directly to him, told him how the robbery had affected her, how frightening it was. She told him she was a grandmother.

He ended up apologizing, his eyes were teared up. So were hers. She invited him to come over. She said "I'll be your grandmother, too. If you need something, you can come see me, you can just ask, you don't have to steal from me." She was crying, too, and so were all the rest of us.

Moments like those are what have kept Dyan going. She couldn't always track the thought processes that were guiding her to set up forums such as teen court, scenarios designed to encourage learning and healing and a better world. But she began to see how the forces of creativity were at work through her, even if she couldn't always explain it.

Teen court seemed to belong to the kids, as did the theater group. They volunteered to help with administration and in the court. They called their peers if someone forgot a court date or seemed reluctant to participate: "Is this the first time you've been in trouble? Do you want to avoid problems with the system in the future? What's happening with your family?" There's care and wisdom in the youths' voices as they counsel one another. They're teaching each other, through theater and friendship, and Dyan is there on the sidelines, knowing she has helped alter the course of these teens' lives, creating chances for new beginnings and happy endings.

Dyan's Life These Days

At teen court and Teens Teaching Through Theater, Dyan's busy showing others the steps and then stepping out of the way. Local attorneys, teachers, and law enforcement officials volunteer their time. Surveys show the program is working for the kids and for the community. Money's still tight. The six-year grant that created teen court and saved T4 will soon be up, and Dyan is once again searching for money. It seems that part will never change. She did not get one grant she had hoped for, and now Roots for Youth is considering downsizing, maybe shutting down the theater portion of the program.

She's pregnant with her third child and has watched some of her other children—the ones from the neighborhood—grow from troubled teens into responsible adults. There are still few dividing lines between Dyan's work and her private life. Her life is her work. Sometimes she feels like she's going up against the wall again, but then something happens to revive her spirit and renew her faith, such as the interaction she witnessed between the purse snatcher and the victim, who faced one another and ended up seeing each other for who they were, a troubled boy and a caring grandmother, who became friends—perhaps bringing about a permanent change in the boy—because of Dyan's program.

> It is creative, working with the elements of human relation-ships. I don't think about it, but I know when it happens and I recognize the power and feeling. That's the beauty and the challenge of the work. Those are elements that are hard to quantify and tell people about and put numbers to. You can't put it in a grid and hold it up for people to see. It's hard to convey to someone reading fifty funding applications. That's why you have to look for support in other places. My challenge and my strength is faith. I know that to be true.

Conversations and Reflections: Creating a Better World

Recognizing Creative Social Justice

Watching Dyan in action is a reminder of how much our society depends on this particular brand of creativity—the kind that leads to better lives and relationships for the disadvantaged. History books tell stories of people who have been recognized for their social vision, but in every community there are behind-the-scenes people who are making lives better all around them. Supporting others—particularly the disenfranchised—and seeing the best in them is generally a thankless job in this society.

Acknowledging that working toward a better society is a crea-tive endeavor can bring long-overdue recognition to people like Dyan and others who devote their life to causes. That acknowledgement can also open the door to understanding the source of frustration for many people who see problems in society and suffer over "not being able to do anything." Social action can pave the way to finding anti-dotes to that frustration, freeing up your creative energy.

People have felt similar social frustration in the past, yet some-how the old social machinery is still chugging. Will the planet be destroyed by toxins? Will we destroy one another with guns? Will one country try to decimate the others with nuclear bombs? Those questions rattle around in the backs of many people's minds. It helps to have a tradition that says, "If you're concerned, then do some-thing."

Talking with Dyan and other women in this book, I became aware of how many creative women find unique ways to exercise a sense of social responsibility. And I recognized how each of us influences the other. Annie the photographer says that doing the fundraiser to buy toys for kids at Christmas brought her as much joy as it brought them. Baker Birgitta donates bread to local organizations that feed the needy in her area. And, of course, each of us can find opportunities for "random acts of kindness" that can be accomplished on a whim every day. For Mother's Day, my mom asks us to give to philanthropic organizations in her name. If you believe that each person has special gifts and deserves a chance to exercise them, you may also want to find ways to empower others. Such actions bring to life the belief, summed up in two words, that defines the work *Girls Speak Out* author Andrea Johnston does to inspire girls around the world to find their strength and creativity: "Everybody matters."

Creativity comes into play as each of us finds an expression for what many experience as a natural instinct to help others. For many people, social action means identifying organizations that are doing good work and supporting them. And then there are those like Dyan who have a talent for envisioning a new social choreography that can create major changes in the lives of others.

In her book about feminism and spirituality, *At the Root of This Longing,* Carol Lee Flinders wrote, "What a Gandhi knew, a Mother Teresa, a Dorothy Day, is that when individuals are drawn to a selfless cause—the relief of human suffering, the dissolution of the barriers that separate us from one another—energy and creativity come into play that simply don't under any other circumstances."

There is a particular type of creativity that comes into play when people see how society can be improved. The women in the Rockefeller family worked for generations behind the scenes to spend their husbands' and fathers' oil business earnings for the good of others. It wasn't until Clarice Stasz published a book in 1995, *The Rockefeller Women,* that someone examined the intricate study, commitment, and faith that informed the family's philanthropy; among other things, they worked to create the first juvenile justice system and colleges for poor students. Recognizing such work as creative an invitation to value what you and others put into social service.

Taking the Dare

If you're someone who puts effort into volunteer work or social action, you probably already know the creative interplay that occurs in the process. You receive while you're giving, and you learn while you're teaching. It's a privilege to participate in a process that's making a difference. At a recent gathering of women in Donna's garden on Women's Equality Day, several women stood up to talk about the work they were doing, some through preserving the environment and others through social work. Their eyes shone and there was excitement in their voices. Seeing their vision materialize in a revitalized stream or the elimination of blight in a poor community brought them obvious rewards.

Dyan helps demonstrate the synergy. She's a study in effective goodwill: She's not interested in power, nor does she take a controlling, over-doing approach to trying to take care of everyone. Rather, she is quietly at ease and enjoying herself—it shows in her gentle smile, laughing eyes, and a relaxed enjoyment of the theater that is going on all around her.

Dyan's success in the dicey role of teen organizer rises from her trust—in herself, in the teens, in God, and in other people. She has gotten along by knowing that the money, energy, and support will come, eventually, as long as she does her part. At the same time, she keeps herself open for cues from the universe about new ways to proceed. She is taking risks, but in steps that feel comfortable because she sees what's working before moving forward. She observes others, interacting rather than controlling.

In her book, *Awakening Minerva*, author Linda Firestone invokes the myth of Demeter, Goddess of Grain, in describing the creative talent involved in nurturing others.

> *Demeter's power was reflected in the impact she had on the world around her; it was embedded in her feminine aspect. Demeter acted out of her essential creative nature; nourishing the world fulfilled her need to express herself in her style. She did not need to throw lightning bolts to demonstrate her strength. Her actions were tied to the expression of self, to her inner essence.*

Firestone says that women's creativity in social action often involves taking cues from others and using the interaction to come up with systems, while continually tuning into that place of "inner knowing."

Creativity in Leadership

For many women, the solitary aspect of individual creativity is only part of the picture, and the underlying motivation of creativity has to do with making connections. Creative work that is social in focus is often about love and connection, and it requires a special type of leadership.

In their book *Singing at the Top of Our Lungs*, Claudia Bepko and Jo-Ann Krestan describe the type of woman they call "the leader," who makes a bridge between love and work. Their description fits Dyan and gives affirmation to women whose creativity comes from connection with others.

> *The Leader is a woman who is focused on love but not love for the sake of conformity to female stereotypes. For the Leader, love is expansive, it is generative. It can't be contained within a family or a primary relationship. It is love that values relatedness as a life-enhancing force. . . . She seeks to make bridges between her inner worlds and outer worlds, between her deeper passions and their expression in the external world. Relationship is her medium. Her private experience of caring spills over into an energy for caring on a more public level.*

Honoring this form of social change is yet another way in which the historic "women's work" becomes recognized as creativity. Like sewing, gardening, cooking, and child rearing, providing leadership has been part of women's historic role of tending to the community.

During interviews with Dyan, I was overwhelmed by the logistics of how she pulled off her organizational work, but Deborah was part of those conversations and she helped explain from her experience as founder of a union that represents faculty at her college. In start-up situations, Deborah said, inspiration often comes in response to a need. How do you keep from getting overwhelmed? Deborah said the first step is to investigate what's already out there in similar organizations—which Dyan did with the other teen groups and Deborah did by investigating other campus unions.

The challenge of leadership is getting everyone else to stick with the work: "Keeping a group motivated and focused becomes more difficult as time goes on, especially once the glamour has worn away and you're left with the mundane day-to-day business of keeping an organization going," Deborah said. There's the regular communication with others and constant monitoring of responsibilities, and training as membership and issues change.

There's a consistency of energy necessary for the kind of work Dyan and Deborah do. Both are working in areas rife with politics. "Keeping energy of the organization focused is sometimes difficult when other more sexy political issues surface." For Deborah, at the core of her work is the realization that the local union exists to protect the rights of faculty, and that she and her colleagues are working hard to improve faculty terms and conditions of employment. For Dyan it's the slow, incremental process of watching teens change and grow—and the joy that comes from watching someone find and claim their voice.

Honoring the Creativity in Your Social Interactions

Without even realizing it, you may be exercising the kind of social creativity that Dyan demonstrates. Maybe you're doing your work on a smaller scale. Facilitating relationships and fairness within your family, being a responsible neighbor, or volunteering for schools or community organizations are ways many women exercise their imagination for the greater good. Perhaps you are a voice for team-work and connection in your workplace, unwittingly choreographing situations where people can express themselves more freely and comfortably.

Often women take their social skills and concern for justice for granted. If so, claiming your creative self may involve giving yourself credit for what you're already doing. You might want to make a list of all the ways you use your imagination every day to make the social systems around you function more smoothly. And you may wish to start voicing your recognition of other women who are doing the same. Celebrate the moments when, as Dyan says, "the seeds for change you planted begin to blossom."

Onward: Creating New Definitions of Success

Every time she gets together with teens, Dyan sees signs that her pro-gram is working. Teens are maturing and achieving self-confidence. For example, she watched the progress of one, who had a sullen dis-position and a load of problems as a result of his parents' bitter divorce. When Dyan first met him, he was right on the edge of trou-ble, part of the walking wounded known as "at risk." But in the thea-ter group, he became engaged, smiling and laughing without the self-conscious broodiness that initially characterized his behavior. Dyan watched him gain confidence, writing and acting in his own skits. One of the success stories, this young man graduated with a high enough grade point average to gain admission to one of the schools in the University of California system. He was talented all along, but Dyan believes that the support he got in the theater group made the difference.

Dyan defines success by how the students define theirs. For one student it was becoming a filmmaker, for another it was excelling in debate. For Dyan, it's opening the doors at Roots for Youth another day.

But her vision for the future is shifting. Losing the grant may require a regrouping of effort. Dyan is very interested in starting a school. She wants to call it The Arts and Ethics Academy. Her target student population is that group of high school students who are not succeeding in traditional schools, and the curriculum will be tailored for them. Once again, she is willing to try something new and different—something that will serve to encourage those on the fringe to grow and learn. Right now, she's in the exploration stages: "We're looking at structures, and of course trying to find money or a friendly institution willing to take us on. I'm excited. This is a great project to look forward to and to work hard to fulfill."

14

Creativity: Your Story

Each of the women in this book, in one way or another, has paid enough attention to her own intuitive messages, thought processes, emotional responses, motivations, and abilities that she can say to herself and to others: "This is me. . . . This is what I believe. . . .This is what I like to do. . . . This is how I got here. . . . This is what I still have to learn." In the abstract, such statements may sound simple, but clear recognition of the self requires time, honesty, and openness to change. All the women interviewed for this book feel reverence for the mercurial nature of creativity and wanted to be portrayed as works in progress, not as people who have it "all together."

Everyone's creative story is evolving in a unique way. You might experience sudden insights that carry you in big bursts to a life of more beauty and meaning. Or you may claim your creativity slowly through small shifts in perception, slight changes in habit, or just a bit more clarity in seeing the self. The creative spirit doesn't always need a big push to start flying free; sometimes it's more like learning to drift with the prevailing winds in your life.

Through the stories of other women—those in this book, in your daily life, and in history—you can learn strategies for your own creative journey. How do you discover the best creative outlet for you? And then how do you gather the confidence and momentum to pursue your vision? The women in this book show how the answers differ from person to person. At the same time, the questions they've asked of themselves seem to run along parallel lines. Asking the right questions, as the old adage goes, can carry you halfway to the answer. For my co-authors and me, framing the correct questions was a creative challenge in itself.

You'll find the questions that emerged during the course of our interviews organized as subheadings throughout this chapter. Glance ahead if you'd like, but don't be fooled as I was. The questions seem straightforward enough, but as I began asking them of myself again, odd things started to occur. It's what happens when you're exploring the wordless sources of knowledge that Helen, the psychic, likes to call the "the watery dimensions." Normal rules of logic don't apply. I'd planned to present to you in this chapter a rational continuum of questions with examples of possible answers, but instead this chapter will unfold in a meandering way, with stories behind the stories. What happened to mess up my original tidy explanations? As you'll see later in this chapter, something that looked very much like an accident happened to make me drop any pretense of having answers for you. But now I am certain that, with a little guidance, you'll find your own.

As you read the rest of this chapter, you might like to have a pen and pencil, sketch pad, or tape recorder with you. Anything and everything that you express in response to the questions and ideas ahead could offer a new opening, or widen the access you already have, to your reservoir of creativity. Each of the sections that follow begins with a main question and goes on to ask for details. You might try writing down (or recording through your own creative outlet) your immediate response to every question posed. It's probably as close as you'll get to what's "right." Remember to leave room for your answers to change over time.

I think many women shy away from telling their own creative stories—even to themselves—because they consider such attention to the self somehow unseemly. It has helped me over the years to read books on creativity, talk with other women, and get support and validation that allowed me to embark in the direction of self-awareness that at one time in my life would have seemed self-indulgent. I recently heard someone say it would be good to invent the word "self-ist" to use as a replacement for "selfish," to honor the act of self-study. Rather than becoming self-absorbed, the result of self-reflection tends to be a healthy detachment from the ego, so that you're more inclined to connect with others in a meaningful way.

Exploring your creativity is a personal adventure that is no less than a birthright. You have plenty of creativity to explore. If you've ever received messages to the contrary, whoever sent them was wrong. As co-author Deborah advises:

> Declare yourself creative by fiat. It's not a question of permission but entitlement. You don't have to ask for permission. You simply do it.

There is power in knowing and believing that you are entitled to your creative self, as well as in commanding a place in your life for exploration. The more you know about yourself—and the more you are prepared to honestly be yourself with others—the more comfortable it will be to adopt a more creative lifestyle, carving out the time and space and gathering the resources you need for self-expression.

Tell your creative story in journal writings, pictures, poems, or sketches. Act or sing out your story, to yourself or others. Share your story with your children or other family members. Create something— a garden, a bakery, a nonprofit organization—that demonstrates your creative journeys. Many women frame their memories in a mental record organized around personal events such as career successes or job changes, marriages, births, deaths, or moves. What would happen if you began to document your creative-life story, tracking your relationship with your muse? Can you remember the beginnings, influences, halcyon moments, and struggles you've had with self-expression?

Telling your story can take any number of forms. Sarah, for example, grew up around storytellers. She loves telling stories about her childhood years, throwing in folk wisdom from her family and neighbors. When she talks about her creative development, the talk is spiced with anecdotes and pictures from her youth. Carole's paintings capture images and feelings from her life. Sometimes it's not until after she paints them that she can uncover the memories and experiences that led to the images. You can develop your own language for describing your own unique creative story.

How Does Your Intuition Speak to You?

How is the creative spirit revealed to you? "I don't know," is a profoundly acceptable response to this one, as it isn't an easy question. Creativity often involves visceral messages that come without language or reason. As much sensation as thought, it's something you may touch in a dream, glimpse between the maroon streaks of a sunset, imagine in the chords of a song, detect in the scent of jasmine-perfumed air, feel in the comfort of soft silk, or recognize in a painting that touches something locked inside. Each person has a unique creative sensibility, but that can so easily become buried beneath the stresses and responsibilities of adult life. Sometimes a re-awakening slowly occurs by one taking hold of a thread of something that's linked to something that remains pure inside each of us, a longing for expression, safe from the judgments or order imposed by the external world.

Recognizing that feeling is the beginning in claiming your creative self. As the women in this book have demonstrated, acting on it takes a bit of faith. Some recognize the source of inspiration as God, the collective unconscious, psychic awareness, the Goddess, magic, or some combination of these forces. How do you recognize what "speaks" to you of things you know without understanding *how* you know? And trust it, the way Donna did when she first got that instinctive flash bearing a complete mental picture of her garden? Students of the creative process often find symbols to honor the unknowable. That's why mystery novelist Sarah Andrew bows to the statue of Kali before she writes. Each person finds her own way of tapping into that wondrous whatever-it-is that brings a deep personal integrity to her work. For social activist Dyan, it's an abiding faith in

God, whom she credits with delivering her strength, ideas and, often by some last-minute miracle, the funding she needs to continue her work with youth.

Do you have a name for the source of your creativity? You may wish to define the source. Or not. Annie, the photographer, didn't feel the need to understand what or who presented her with imagery about her mother through which she came face-to-face with death and her own unresolved grief. It was enough for her to respect the mysterious force, believe it, and get on with the personal work she needed to do so that she would be more open in her life and in her work. Whether or not you can or wish to name the source, there is power in recognizing that unconscious forces may command your attention.

Everyone gets messages from their subconscious, but recognizing them requires attention. You can figure out the context that your intuition finds most welcoming. Try envisioning the settings where you find yourself in the routine course of your life. Where are you most likely to experience feelings of hope and wonder, feeling open to ideas that pop into your head? Lying on the beach? Hiking in the mountains? Snuggled under the covers of your bed? Alone in a certain corner of your house? In the middle of crowded rooms? Looking up at the stars at night? The materialization of those messages—the selection of a creative tool, the awareness of what to do with it—may happen elsewhere. But the wordless urge arises in a place and at a time when you are open to receive it. Birgitta's passion for baking was reawakened on a visit to her hometown in Sweden. Annie's openness to the creative spirit seems connected to the physical disciplines of yoga and sports. Vera's creative spirit comes to life on the dance floor, Donna's in the solitude of her garden. Pauline's creative moments can occur in quiet walks or in the middle of a laughing group of women in her improvisation class. All these women have grown attuned to recognizing "that moment" when something pure happens, even if it takes weeks or months to sort out what it means in any logical way.

The maddening part is that the muse doesn't always speak to us in language we understand. Finding the right time and place to "listen" to wordless messages involves belief in something that is essentially irrational. With my strong rational bent and journalist's skepticism, it's easier to accept the reality of such forces now that researchers are finding evidence of energy connections between people previously thought impossible. Helen is among those who never needed experts to offer her proof of psychic forces. For reasons that aren't entirely clear even to her, she can see things about her clients that they cannot see about themselves.

What Helen does know is that in order to tap into this energy, she must wrestle with her own ego every day, trying to get her conscious judgments out of the way so she can tap into some deep source of knowing, open herself to new thoughts and ideas. "I'm always working on myself, and it's a butt-kicker!" she declares. Carole, the painter, gives herself permission to be led by her unconscious when she paints, not attempting to analyze her symbols (as her college professor would've had her do) until long after they appear. How do you get past everything else to the place where intuition is pure, unobscured by shreds of ego, judgment, or opinion that may cloud it? Each person has a different way of doing that. And it doesn't need to make sense to anyone else.

For Linda, the inner self that informs her poetry and art work sometimes comes in dreams. If she hadn't attended to the dream where she was naked except for her shoes, she still might be spending her leisure time playing golf and swimming (not that there's anything wrong with those activities—she just had other things she needed to do). The dream prompted her to set her inner "crazy woman" free in words on paper and bold colors on canvas. Actor Pauline was haunted by "demons" clamoring for attention until, to quiet them, she made them into the characters of her play.

For me, messages from my intuition often come in the form of something that looks like an "accident." I "misplace" something that seemed important, but later it turns out to be unnecessary. I "forget" to do something that turns out to be ill-conceived. I "mistakenly" dial a phone number by memory, and instead of reaching the person I expected, I find I've called a friend I'd been wanting to talk with but hadn't made the time for until my subconscious did it for me. These flaky episodes at first frustrated me, but now I'm learning to greet them with a smile and to try to get the message.

Intuitive messages can be nettlesome until you embrace them. Dyan often awakes at night with ideas for her youth program, until she finds a way to materialize them. Linda found her dreams slightly disturbing until she found a way to act on them. And I was driven to distraction by my spaciness until I finally started paying attention to the ideas that were distracting me and acting on them.

Sometimes instead of bristling for attention, your intuition may assert itself as a sweet longing, a warm desire to do something that eclipses all else. Birgitta loved being in the kitchen and thought of her baking time as a refuge—the only activity she could count on to make her feel better during times of sadness and stress. Eventually she realized she could embrace that activity as a vocation. Sara felt pure bliss analyzing the harmonies in music so she could sing them with others and be part of those heavenly sounds. After Annie first discovered a camera, she couldn't stop herself from taking pictures; it was something she felt she had to do long before she realized it could become her life's work. Sherry Jean's "performance art" is a source of personal entertainment that helps her glide through the day, entertaining others along the way. Carole already had a successful art career as a papermaker, but she returned to the canvas as a beginner because painting was what expressed her soul.

What recurring episodes in your life seem like outtakes—events, thoughts, or dreams that don't seem to "fit in" with the rest of your life? Is there a thought, an image, a feeling, or just an amorphous sensation that tickles or distracts you at times when (your rational mind tells you) you should be focused on what you're "supposed to be doing"? Instead of lamenting, "What's wrong with me?" you might make a small mental shift and ask, "What's this telling me?"

Give whatever it is some room to expand and take shape. Any blank space will do. A blank piece of paper to be written upon. A blank canvas to be painted upon. Even simply clearing the mind, consciously sweeping away all ordinary thoughts, can allow the subconscious some room to speak to you. Ask yourself about that recurring feeling before you go to bed at night and see what your dreams tell you. Let your hand move freely across a blank page with permission to write or draw as it will. On an otherwise tedious drive, let yourself talk away into a tape recorder in a stream of consciousness, and promise yourself you'll consider anything that comes out as a potential creative seed.

Are You Willing to Be Surprised?

Each of the women in this book experienced certain catalysts for creativity and then developed techniques for acting on those experiences. Usually the work happened in stages. When my collaborators and I sat around Deborah's kitchen table one day thinking about our subjects' creative processes, we started talking about the "triggers and tricks" that each had. The trigger is that mysterious catalyst. The trick is how you deal with it.

Later in this chapter we'll look at some tricks for how some creative women get the skills and confidence to move forward. But that comes after recognizing the trigger—the intuitive message— which can be the most challenging aspect of the creative process because there are no rules or guidelines other than those of your own sensibilities. Often the trigger goes off unexpectedly. The results can be surprising, if not stunning. Sara hadn't been prepared to find herself absorbed in the harmonies of the 40s, needing to immerse herself in those harmonies; but she was open when it happened.

I have seen how blessedly irrational events intervene and alter the lives of so many women—including most in this book—and for years I've listened to stories about how the subconscious moves mysteriously to shape creativity. While it's still a challenge to honor those mysterious forces and not dismiss them, my own intuition has its own ways of surfacing. Hearing the stories of other women, and even telling my own stories from the past, has not been enough to predict the outcome of inspirational moments. With time I recognize patterns that may help me recognize the next one.

Creative inspiration might not look like anything you or I have seen before, but it may arrive in familiar ways. How do you know when something resonates as being "just right"? A valuable exercise is to reconstruct times in the past—in childhood or more recently—when you felt deeply self-expressive. How did you feel? What were the conditions? What helped you to relax your usual mind-set to allow in the new? For me, it's a matter of paying attention to where my mind is going when it's wandering. Most of my favorite stories began with a recurring thought that would distract me from other things unless I wrote it down.

Once you recognize your trigger mechanism, you can use it over and over again. Your triggers may come through dreams at night, daydreams at work, thoughts that linger in that nether time between sleep and waking, a mental picture that presents itself when you're all alone, and/or the ideas that fill your mind when you're in a relaxed state of meditation or exercise. Creative process involves an interplay between those unconscious signals and the conscious act of manifesting them. You get an idea, and then you can go just so far with it in the logical world before you need to tune in again to the wordless source of creative magic.

Slowly I'm beginning to see how the messages manifest themselves to me. If I am working too hard to control my writing by organizing it into some pre-established or routine form, something will happen to shake it up. At first, my subconscious tries to speak to me gently, with subtle signals indicating discomfort with the work—a sore body or grouchiness that means it's time to take a walk or take a hot bath. Logically, I know my work will be better if I shake out the tension, but my "work harder" voice drives me forward like a drill sergeant. That's when my subconscious starts to trip me up.

The first version of this chapter was drafted and just about ready to go when, all of a sudden, my computer crashed. The latest work was lost. Throughout the writing of this book, the process had paralleled the unpredictability of the subject, but this was too much.

Have you ever found yourself seemingly sabotaged by "circumstances"—something makes you late, forget an appointment, or maybe some family issue surfaces just when you're in the thick of a project. Your rational mind yells sarcastically, "Great, that's just what I need." Maybe your creative self is responding, "Actually, yes, that *is* great and it is just what you need. Now pay attention!" As it turned out, my losing my final chapter to cyberspace brought about just the message I needed to re-think my approach, tossing out the logical sequence of ideas and abandoning all hope that I could create some "perfect" synthesis of the ideas that came to me in the process of writing this book.

Do You Like Experiments?

From the subjects, authors, and literary sources for this book, there emerged a rich and wild stew of skill, opinion, insecurity, confidence, joy, pain, perseverance, flakiness, genius, and more than a few good ideas. I was trying to sort through all of that and create from that a recipe. The bomb on my computer screen appeared, I believe, because I was trying to "simplify" the ideas into a linear set of steps.

After rethinking that approach, I'm now compelled to acknowledge that the recipe is complex, ever changing, different for each of us, and likely to be messy. Yes, there's much to be learned from tasting the successful recipes of other women who are willing to share some of their ingredients and techniques for freeing their creativity. But it comes down to a willingness to throw in your own spice, take risks, try something new, and then continually alter your recipe. Feedback comes from the inner self, often in a language of its own. It's not a linear process at all. It's circuitous or—more accurately in my case—sometimes a little loopy.

Once you decide to follow a whim or a desire or a curiosity, you're conducting a personal experiment in which you can't know for sure what works until you try it. For women like Nancy who have a perfectionist streak, it can be frightening—though ultimately liberating—to plunge in without knowing what will happen. The better you know yourself, the better able you are to see what's working and to know when it's time to regroup. But along the way, expect the unexpected. This chapter certainly isn't what I expected, but the results feel more "right" than before.

Remember back to the intentional experiments you've done in the past: the formal ones, like making a potato power a lightbulb in science class, and the informal ones, like rearranging the furniture in your house. Do you enjoy the curious phase, where you don't know what will happen? Or does it make you anxious not being able to predict the outcome?

As Nancy learned during the talent show: Wading into a project where you can't anticipate the result—or even the process for getting there—forces you to jumpstart your creativity. Instead of anticipating, you can allow yourself to flounder alone in that blessed state of "not knowing," asking the questions that might lead in a direction more conducive to creativity than had you followed a clearer path.

What Is Your
Definition of Creativity?

As with any experiment, it helps to start with a hypothesis. A hypothesis, by definition, is neither right or wrong: It's a touchstone, something to refer to as you test your results along the way. You may have your own definition of creativity or you may borrow one, but, either way, it appears that the definition often changes over time. Having a definition provides a framework for viewing your experiences. A couple of women in this book changed their definitions during the course of the writing and interviewing. I ended up changing mine, too.

Sarah Andrews started out saying that, to her, creativity was the *"ability* to embrace ambiguity" and later amended that to say, "Creativity is the *willingness* to embrace ambiguity." One word, worlds of difference. As she reflected on her own development, she came to realize that a preexisting ability is not the factor in claiming creativity, but rather simply the desire to do so. Her new definition includes everyone, even if we don't see ourselves as "having it" yet. It's ours for the asking. Sarah's definition also helps illuminate Annie's statement that she didn't think she had a creative bone in her body until she started to photograph. Annie's definition of creativity changed through the work itself. You don't need a definition that will always apply, just one that gives you a place to start.

Deborah's definition of creativity allows for continual evolution. Rather than a strict definition, her fluid notion allows for change through problem solving as seen in her approach to building design.

> I usually start with some general idea about what I'm trying to do, which I phrase in a "how to" question. Then I get input from my clients, do some research, and then allow myself to get into the flow of the unknown, letting myself drift in that vast sea of inner knowledge, documenting my exploration in sketch form. Eventually something will crystallize. A large part of the most creative time is spent in a state of trusting.

As mentioned in the introduction, I started out with my glib definition that I saw somewhere in college: "Creativity is making order out of chaos." In the months of conversations and reflections during the research for and writing of this book, I've decided that my original definition implies too much hard work. And that has been my lesson: to relax my soldier-like tendency to make those words march forth on a mission to seek out information, round it up, and whip it into shape. Instead, I am learning to allow time for stumbling, slouching, playing, and taking the long way around, so I can take in what comes up along the way.

For me, writing will always be a venture through a scramble of ideas that need to be sorted out, but I've learned to trust that there is an internal order to the ideas, an integrity that comes from comfortable exchange between the external world and my internal self. I don't have to force order, I just have to keep looking until I find the patterns that are there. So, to give myself a break, I have changed my definition to, "Creativity is *finding* the order amid the chaos." And, warning: My definition may change tomorrow.

You may want to go back through the book and read the quotes that open each chapter; these quotes are each woman's summary of her sense of creativity. Some gave personal statement, some philosophical. All that matters is that your definition reflects how you feel today about your creative process, giving you a starting point for analyzing your experience in greater depth. You might even try out two or three phrases, and over the next few weeks see which one works best.

Having a journal or other method of recording your own creative story can serve as a symbol that you are embarking on your own journey. From women in this book and in your daily life, you're likely to find yourself catching and trading your own snippets of knowledge. Your definition of creativity may emerge bit by bit. One day, you may open a page of your journal and experience that blessed "aha," a flash of what it means for you to claim your creativity. Then you can revise your definition when the next flash of awareness takes you deeper or in another direction.

Creating Time

Somehow you found the time to read this book (or at least this particular sentence): no small feat amid the swirl of commitments, distractions, and information overload that define the existence of most women. Looking back through the stories in this book, I've decided that everyone can find the time to spend on the creative self, and that excuses are self-manufactured. Every story in this book shows a woman with responsibilities—to herself as well as her work, children, parents, and/or life partners.

My co-authors and I were impressed by the fact that Pauline takes at least two weeks before a play to get completely absorbed in her work. Her partner fully supports her need for creative space, and Pauline clears everything else out of the way. In order to make creative space for yourself, first you have to know what you need to be creative, and then you have to communicate your needs to those with whom you share your life. Doing these two things can help create the time and space you need to take your muse out for some exercise. In any event, it takes willfulness to remember that you have all the time there is, and that it's up to you to decide how to use it.

Sometimes we can carve out chunks of time, but often we settle for the moments: Meg getting up at dawn to sit on a futon with her laptop, Deborah staying up late into the night writing after an evening of lecturing, Susan writing down good lines she overhears on a napkin at a restaurant, me pulling out a chapter to edit between sets of my son's tennis games. Ideally, we'd all have hours a day for our creative activities, but until then, the minutes we find here and there keep us going. There's something about having the desire to take every spare moment for the creative work—again, motivated as if we had a clandestine lover—that may lead to a happy union of your creative self and the rest of your life.

How Can You Find Creative Community?

It doesn't matter if the creative act produces a cardamom bun fresh from the oven, a particular arrangement of flowers along a garden path, or a perfectly delivered one-liner, as long as the person behind it is somehow showing herself to you in an honest way. There's an adrenaline rush that comes from being in the company of actively creative women, a kinetic exchange that moves from one to the other, and perhaps that's because they bring themselves fully to the work at hand. If through her singing, baking, gardening, or writing, someone is showing part of her story to you, aren't you inclined to reveal some of yours?

The development of creative community comes about simply by revealing a bit of yourself to others. When people go into Donna's garden and find out that she is the creator of that magical place, they're often inspired to share their own creative dreams. When Linda held an art show and poetry reading, many of her friends felt more free to talk to her about their projects. When Sherry Jean does her performance waitressing, customers tend to be more open themselves, trading jokes and confidences. Vera's unmistakable good humor and sense of fun proved contagious with her women's group and school community, where gatherings inevitably lead to dancing, exotic cooking, and musical performances. Carole's Danger Rangers are women who play together with creative humor.

In what small ways are the people around you tipping their creative hands? As you catch glimpses of other's self-expression, what can you reveal of your own? At some point, as I found with my short story, the sharing isn't about "you" and "me," but about our mutual connection to something larger that seems to encompass all of us.

In Whom Do You Place Your Trust?

Even if you believe in the interconnectedness of creative people and that everyone has access to creativity, you can't trust everyone with your precious creations, words, and ideas. There are harsh critics, jealous judgments, and creative saboteurs. Remember Carole's thoughtless professor, the "established" poets who walked away from Linda and her fellow students' poetry reading, the fellow band member who received the credit due to Sara. Over and over again, we've seen how women have carefully constructed support systems so as not to trust their delicate expressions in the hands of someone who is clumsy or malicious.

I've found that baby steps are the best approach, revealing bits of my vulnerable creative self to people and gauging their responses. People who react with harshness or insensitivity may have a place elsewhere, but not as part of my creative life. Instead, I have what I like to call a creative "gang," a group of women who have worked and played and shared together enough over the years that we trust one another's best intent and care and, over time, we are learning how to communicate with one another in the way that feels most supportive. As Nancy found, women can be one another's "art slaves," supporting each other in our independent projects and in collaborative working situations, taking turns helping one another with visions.

Writing this book has revealed to me how much skill is involved in creative communication. My collaborators and I brought different perspectives and abilities to this book and learned to see how to blend those. There were moments of interpersonal stress, and in retrospect they make sense (though at the time they were among those creative "surprises" that aren't of the happy kind). What enabled us to not just survive but thrive as a team was a shared belief that each of us—and every woman—has something of value to offer. Learning to recognize and appreciate each other's offerings required that each of us stretch our ideas a little further and open our arms a little wider to embrace our differences, instead of feeling threatened by them.

How Did Your Childhood Shape Your Creative Self?

Dyan's understanding of herself made it possible for her to start empowering young people on the "fringe," reaching out to the kinds of kids she hung out with and worried about as a teen. Vera's joyful awareness of the importance of her cultural traditions enabled her to connect with children in ways beyond language—through dance, music, and song. Sara's reconstruction of the pressure she felt as a child to "blend in" helped dissolve the barriers that had prevented her from showcasing her musical talents, so that she could perform with confidence and teach children to do the same. Birgitta's embracing of the hearth from her girlhood enabled her to reach out to her family and ultimately to touch her community with the wholesomeness of lovingly baked bread. Sarah's memories of her father's storytelling have enlivened both her writing and her conversation, while keeping her beloved dad alive in her thoughts every day. Helen learned from her mother's depression how to alleviate her own.

By looking back into our childhoods, we find both the seeds of creativity and reminders of the toxins we must avoid. For Meg, remembering her singing and piano playing was incentive to bring more music into her life. In our conversations about making creative space, Meg also realized something difficult from her past that may still be a factor in her life. She shared a room with her sister, who couldn't stand for things to be messy, so Meg rarely had the chance to spread out with creative projects. If she had a painting project, a puzzle, or building supplies out for more than a day, her sister would come along and clean it up. To this day, Meg feels anxious during the brainstorming phases of her writing, the period of time where she is gathering information and sorting it in her "Rube Goldberg machine way." It all comes out in the end, but along the way there is that anxiety from her childhood that someone is going to sweep away the pieces before she's had time to put them together in her way.

Susan realized how much her midlife interest in public speaking and improvisational theater harkens back to her girlhood, when she and the neighborhood kids would write and produce plays for each other. She enjoyed performing and writing dialogue, but for years as a journalist she didn't get to indulge that part of herself. Recognizing the childhood link helps her claim the creativity—in front of an audience as much as behind a computer screen.

How Do You Persist?

This is the "tricks" part. Basically, a creative trick is whatever works to keep the creative wellspring flowing. No matter how much I do the unstructured creative work that contributes to a sense of "flow," I still need deadlines to reach any closure. My creativity needs a container, a format, and someone to say, "Okay, time to put the lid on it."

Susan functions best by biting off small, manageable chunks. She writes her columns in stages, just as she keeps herself from feeling overwhelmed by garden work by "weeding one section at a time," then enjoying a glass of iced tea and doing another section the next weekend. Breaking down a project into parts can also help you feel a sense of accomplishment along the way, which is especially helpful during a big or long project.

Having a scheduled concert gives Sara something to work for. Donna has weddings and community events, which require the garden to look "together." Many of the women in this book scramble before their exhibits or performances. It can be useful to have external pressures that make us "get it together," as long as in the process we allow enough time for exploring intuition.

I use the story of how I lost the original version of this chapter as a reminder of how necessary it is to keep the balance between creative flow and the pressure to do something with it. Just before the bomb appeared on my screen, I was talking to our editor, Angela Watrous, about how I might make the take-home messages from the stories in this book more clear to you, our reader. I confided to Angela *my* angst about how odd this process has felt at times. Meg, Susan, Deborah, and I learned much from our subjects and one another. Yet as delighted as we were to talk deeply with these women, we sometimes struggled with the interpretation of the stories, applying the women's truths to the body of knowledge about creative process—in addition to continually asking ourselves: What are we learning? At the same time, we grappled over how to find our collective "voice" for sharing our observations with you.

In this book, none of my old techniques has worked for reporting information, meeting deadlines, or maintaining distance. At the same time, never has the creative process appeared in such living color as through the lives of women who had found their own way and who demonstrate that you and I can do the same. Writing this final chapter took on the proportions of a Herculean task because of the complexity of ideas these incredible women left me with, as well as my effort to do the linear thing with an essentially nonverbal process.

When the bomb appeared, for some reason what first popped into my head was my fifteen-year-old son's term "da bomb," the parlance de jour for something really great. Then I dissolved into cries and grumbles and e-mailed Angela about the techno crisis. I ran a bath, but it was too hot to get into. So I went for a walk, waiting for the water to cool down. When I got back, I signed onto my e-mail, and there was a message from Angela:

> *I feel terrible for you. I'm so sorry that happened (though I like your attempts to look on the bright side). Please do not worry about getting chapter 14 to me. I won't be getting to it for a while, and in a way, as we continue to talk and hash things out, perhaps it's best that you work on it along the way.... I've had such things happen to me frequently, and I find it helps to moan aloud piteously for a while, then take a walk while muttering aloud, and finally return to the task at hand (or call it a day and take a bath). Here's to the Creativity Goddesses, whose knowledge and expertise far surpass our own on matters of technology.*

I could have cried. Of course Angela had no way of knowing that I'd run a bath and moaned piteously while running in the sunshine overlooking the Pacific Ocean, feeling as bleak and as small as the day was bright and the ocean expansive. But her message tapped into some shared reality.

I thought to myself about Angela, "Is she psychic?" There I was walking and planning a bath while she was writing me an empathetic note about enjoying those activities when she's hit a glitch. But upon reflection, it wasn't surprising at all. Angela was deeply involved in the evolution of this project, and those kinds of synchronistic episodes happen in close collaboration. I saw it again and again with my co-authors as we took turns reviewing the manuscript separately and then getting together with similar thoughts. Often we'd call or e-mail one another just at the moment when needed by the other. And during the interview process, when we'd talk to women separately or together, often some odd little event would occur to help us and our subjects clarify the themes—such as the day when Meg saw Nancy's statue under the piano, opening the door for our deeper understanding of how she has suffered for her perfectionism.

Again and again, inexplicable occurrences surfaced as themes in this book: Donna's bow to the mystical influences that seem to be at work in her garden; Dyan's faith paying off in funding that usually comes in just in the nick of time; Helen's ability to "see" into the lives of other people; Sarah's way of understanding geology by intuition. So with this chapter, originally designed as a kind of summary, the forces of creativity intervened to inform me: There's no way to draw firm conclusions. Perfection is not the goal. Be content with wonder. I went back to the very beginning of the book, to the hypothesis that inspired Meg, Susan, Deborah, Angela, and me to explore the magic of creativity in day-to-day life. It helped me remember to use what I've learned along the way, and then I could finish the book. Here it is again, no longer a hypothesis but an invitation:

> *Each of us possesses a creative self. Claiming that is a transformational act. When you begin to act on your creativity, what you find inside may be more valuable than what you produce for the external world. The ultimate creative act is to express what is most authentic and individual about you.*

References and Suggested Readings

Andrews, Sarah. 1994. *Tensleep.* New York: Signet.

———. 1995. *A Fall in Denver.* New York: Signet.

———. 1997. *Mother Nature.* New York: St. Martin's/Dead Letter.

———. 1998. *Only Flesh and Bones.* New York: St. Martin's Press.

Baer, Barbara L., and Maureen Anne Jennings, eds. 1998. *Saltwater/Sweetwater: Women Write from California's North Coast.* Forestville, Calif.: Floreant Press.

Barron, Frank, Alfonso Montuori, and Anthea Barron. 1997. *Creators on Creating.* New York: A Jeremy P. Tarcher/Putnam Book.

Bepko, Claudia, and Jo-Ann Krestan. 1990. *Too Good for Her Own Good.* New York: Harper and Row.

———. 1993. *Singing at the Top of Our Lungs.* New York: HarperCollins.

Brinnin, John Malcolm. 1959. *The Third Rose: Gertrude Stein and Her World*. Boston, Toronto: An Atlantic Monthly Press Book, Little Brown and Company.

Cameron, Julia. 1992. *The Artist's Way: A Spirituual Path to Higher Creativity*. New York: A Jeremy P. Tarcher/Putnam Book, G. P. Putnam's Sons.

Campbell, Don, 1997. *The Mozart Effect—Tapping the Power of Music to Heal the Body, Strengthen the Mind, and Unlock the Creative Spirit*. New York: Avon.

Clegg, Eileen, and Susan Swartz. 1998. *Goodbye Good Girl*. Oakland, Calif.: New Harbinger Publications.

DeMille, Agnes. 1991. *Martha: The Life and Work of Martha Graham*. New York: Random House.

Easwaren, Eknath. 1989. *The Compassionate Universe*. Petaluma, Calif.: Nilgiri Press.

Ealy, C. Diane. 1993. *The Woman's Book of Creativity*. Hillsborough, Ore.: Beyond Words Publishing, Inc.

Edwards, Betty. 1986. *Drawing on the Artist Within*. New York: Simon and Schuster.

Endicott, Katherine Grace. 1996. *Northern California Gardening*. San Francisco: Chronicle Books.

Firestone, Linda. 1997. *Awakening Minerva*. New York: Warner Books.

Fisher, M.F.K. 1976. *The Art of Eating: Five Gastronomical Works*. New York: Vintage Books.

Flinders, Carol Lee. 1993. *Enduring Grace: Living Portraits of Seven Women Mystics*. San Francisco: HarperSan Francisco.

———. 1998. *At the Root of This Longing*. San Francisco: HarperSan Francisco.

Goldberg, Natalie. 1986. *Writing Down the Bones*. Boston: Shambhala.

Goleman, Paul Kaufman, and Michael Rae. 1992. *The Creative Spirit*. New York: Dutton.

Hanh, Thich Nhat. 1976. *The Miracle of Mindfulness*. Boston: Beacon Press.

Harman, Willis, and Howard Rheingold. 1984. *Higher Creativity: Liberating the Unconscious for Breakthrough Insights*. Los Angeles: Jeremy P. Tarcher, Inc.

Heilbrun, Carolyn G. 1989. *Writing a Woman's Life*. New York: Ballantine.

Hirshfield, Jane, ed. 1994. *In Praise of the Sacred: Forty-Three Centuries of Spiritual Poetry by Women.* New York: Harper Collins.

Johnston, Andrea. 1997. *Girls Speak Out.* New York: Scholastic.

Keene, Julie, and Ione Jenson. 1997. *Emerging Women.* Carlsbad, Calif.: Hay House.

Lange, Dorothea. 1967. *The American Country Woman.* Los Angeles: War Ritchie Press.

Murphy, Joseph. 1988 c. 1963. *The Power of Your Subconscious Mind.* Englewood Cliffs, NJ: Prentice Hall.

Myss, Carolyn. 1996. *Anatomy of the Spirit—the Seven Stages of Power and Healing.* New York: Harmony.

———. 1997. *Why People Don't Heal And How They Can.* New York: Harmony.

Nelson, Victoria. 1993. *On Writer's Block.* Boston: Houghton Mifflin Co.

Nichols, Janet. 1992. *Women Music Makers: An Introduction to Women Composers.* New York: Walker & Co.

Rasberry, Salli, and Padi Selwyn. 1995. *Living Your Life Outloud.* New York: Pocket Books.

Robertson, Laurel, Carol Flinders, and Brian Ruppenthal. 1986. *The New Laurel's Kitchen.* Berkeley: Ten Speed Press.

Rogers, Lilith. 1995. *Raising Bread and Roses.* El Cajon, Calif.: Sunbelt Publications.

Rosner, Stanley, and Lawrence E. Abt, eds. 1970. *The Creative Experience.* New York: John Malcolm Brinnin Grossman Publishers.

Schaef, Anne Wilson. 1990. *Meditations for Women Who Do Too Much.* San Francisco: HarperSan Francisco.

Stasz, Clarice. 1995. *The Rockefeller Women.* New York: St. Martin's Press.

Steichen, Edward. 1983, c. 1955. *The Family of Man—The Greatest Photography Exhibit of All Time, 503 Pictures from 68 Countries.* New York: Museum of Modern Art, Simon and Schuster.

Walker, Christine. 1997. *A Painter's Garden.* New York: Warner Books.

Eileen M. Clegg has worked as a journalist since graduating from U.C. Berkeley with a B.A. in philosophy in 1976. Her challenge and her joy is absorbing scholarly research, drifting through abstraction, and then coming back down to earth and writing stories that show ideas in action. The co-author of *Becoming a Wise Parent for Your Grown Child* and *Goodbye Good Girl*, Eileen lives in Bodega Bay, California, with her husband—a scientist—and her teenage son.

During her seventeen years as a reporter, **Meg McConahey** has always found herself drawn to stories of creative achievement and endeavor. She has a degree in journalism from California Polytechnic University in San Luis Obispo and did her master's work in American literature at Sonoma State University. Meg's interview with renowned food writer M.F.K. Fisher appeared in "Conversations with MFK Fisher," published by the University of Mississippi Press. She live in Glen Ellen, California, with her husband—a psychotherapist—and her preteen son.

Susan Swartz is a newspaper columnist, feature writer, and public radio commentator who, after discovering improvisational acting in midlife, has decided there is no end to the surprising places you can find the creative self. She, however, cannot draw and plays no musical instrument. She has a B.A. degree in journalism from Ohio University. Co-author of *Goodbye Good Girl*, Susan lives in Sebastopol, California, with her journalist husband, and they are parents of three adult daughters.

Deborah L. S. Sweitzer is a licensed California architect and college instructor whose study and theories about creative process have led to innovations in building design and teaching techniques. She has published studies for the Science Council of Canada, articles in professional journals, and architectural texts. She is cofounder of a faculty union and serves on two statewide councils for the community college system. She has a Bachelor of Design from University of Florida and a Bachelor or Architecture from Carleton University, Canada. A jewelry maker, science fiction fan, and folkdancer, she lives in Sebastopol, California, on rural land shared with friends.

More New Harbinger Titles

GOODBYE GOOD GIRL
Good girls know all the rules—the rules that dictate what's becoming for a woman to be and do and what's unacceptable. The dozens of women whose stories are told in this book confirmed what Eileen Clegg and coauthor Susan Swartz learned from their own experience: it may be scary to challenge the rules, but the results can be astonishing, inspiring, and well worth the struggle
Item GGG $12.95

BECOMING A WISE PARENT FOR YOUR GROWN CHILD
Eileen Clegg and coauthor Betty Frain help parents assess problems and speak up or take action in ways that will strengthen their relationships with their adult children.   *Item WISE $12.95*

FACING 30
A diverse group of women who are either teetering on the brink of thirty or have made it past the big day talk about careers, relationships, the inevitable kid question, and dashed dreams.   *Item F30 $12.95*

HIGH ON STRESS
A variety of enlightening exercises help women rethink the role of stress in their lives, rework their physical and mental responses to it, and find ways to oost the potentially positive impact that stress can have on their well-being.
Item HOS $13.95

SEX SMART
"*Sex Smart* is *the* book on everything you probably didn't know about why you turned out the way you did sexually—and what to do about it."
—Arnold Lazarus, Ph.D.   *Item SESM $14.95*

A WOMAN'S GUIDE TO OVERCOMING SEXUAL FEAR AND PAIN
A series of exercises help women map the *terra incognita* of their own bodies and begin to overcome the fear or pain that inhibits or blocks their sexuality.
Item WGOS Paperback $14.95

Call toll-free 1-800-748-6273 to order. Have your Visa or Mastercard number ready. Or send a check for the titles you want to New Harbinger Publications, 5674 Shattuck Avenue, Oakland, CA 94609. Include $3.80 for the first book and 75¢ for each additional book to cover shipping and handling. (California residents please include appropriate sales tax.) Allow four to six weeks for delivery.

Prices subject to change without notice.

Some Other New Harbinger Self-Help Titles

High on Stress: A Woman's Guide to Optimizing the Stress in Her Life, $13.95
Infidelity: A Survival Guide, $13.95
Stop Walking on Eggshells, $14.95
Consumer's Guide to Psychiatric Drugs, $13.95
The Fibromyalgia Advocate: Getting the Support You Need to Cope with Fibromyalgia and Myofascial Pain, $18.95
Healing Fear: New Approaches to Overcoming Anxiety, $16.95
Working Anger: Preventing and Resolving Conflict on the Job, $12.95
Sex Smart: How Your Childhood Shaped Your Sexual Life and What to Do About It, $14.95
You Can Free Yourself From Alcohol & Drugs, $13.95
Amongst Ourselves: A Self-Help Guide to Living with Dissociative Identity Disorder, $14.95
Healthy Living with Diabetes, $13.95
Dr. Carl Robinson's Basic Baby Care, $10.95
Better Boundries: Owning and Treasuring Your Life, $13.95
Goodbye Good Girl, $12.95
Being, Belonging, Doing, $10.95
Thoughts & Feelings, Second Edition, $18.95
Depression: How It Happens, How It's Healed, $14.95
Trust After Trauma, $13.95
The Chemotherapy & Radiation Survival Guide, Second Edition, $14.95
Heart Therapy, $13.95
Surviving Childhood Cancer, $12.95
The Headache & Neck Pain Workbook, $14.95
Perimenopause, $13.95
The Self-Forgiveness Handbook, $12.95
A Woman's Guide to Overcoming Sexual Fear and Pain, $14.95
Mind Over Malignancy, $12.95
Treating Panic Disorder and Agoraphobia, $44.95
Scarred Soul, $13.95
The Angry Heart, $14.95
Don't Take It Personally, $12.95
Becoming a Wise Parent For Your Grown Child, $12.95
Clear Your Past, Change Your Future, $13.95
Preparing for Surgery, $17.95
The Power of Two, $12.95
It's Not OK Anymore, $13.95
The Daily Relaxer, $12.95
The Body Image Workbook, $17.95
Living with ADD, $17.95
Taking the Anxiety Out of Taking Tests, $12.95
Five Weeks to Healing Stress: The Wellness Option, $17.95
Why Children Misbehave and What to Do About It, $14.95
When Anger Hurts Your Kids, $12.95
The Addiction Workbook, $17.95
The Chronic Pain Control Workbook, Second Edition, $17.95
Fibromyalgia & Chronic Myofascial Pain Syndrome, $19.95
Flying Without Fear, $13.95
Kid Cooperation: How to Stop Yelling, Nagging & Pleading and Get Kids to Cooperate, $13.95
The Stop Smoking Workbook: Your Guide to Healthy Quitting, $17.95
Conquering Carpal Tunnel Syndrome and Other Repetitive Strain Injuries, $17.95
An End to Panic: Breakthrough Techniques for Overcoming Panic Disorder, Second Edition, $18.95
Letting Go of Anger: The 10 Most Common Anger Styles and What to Do About Them, $12.95
Messages: The Communication Skills Workbook, Second Edition, $13.95
Coping With Chronic Fatigue Syndrome: Nine Things You Can Do, $13.95
The Anxiety & Phobia Workbook, Second Edition, $18.95
The Relaxation & Stress Reduction Workbook, Fourth Edition, $17.95
Living Without Depression & Manic Depression: A Workbook for Maintaining Mood Stability, $17.95
Coping With Schizophrenia: A Guide For Families, $15.95
Visualization for Change, Second Edition, $15.95
Postpartum Survival Guide, $13.95
Angry All the Time: An Emergency Guide to Anger Control, $12.95
Couple Skills: Making Your Relationship Work, $13.95
Self-Esteem, Second Edition, $13.95
I Can't Get Over It, A Handbook for Trauma Survivors, Second Edition, $16.95
Dying of Embarrassment: Help for Social Anxiety and Social Phobia, $13.95
The Depression Workbook: Living With Depression and Manic Depression, $17.95
Men & Grief: A Guide for Men Surviving the Death of a Loved One, $14.95
When Once Is Not Enough: Help for Obsessive Compulsives, $13.95
Beyond Grief: A Guide for Recovering from the Death of a Loved One, $13.95
Hypnosis for Change: A Manual of Proven Techniques, Third Edition, $15.95
When Anger Hurts, $13.95